ALPINE WARRIORS

ALPINE WARRIORS

Bernadette McDonald

RMB

RMB | Rocky Mountain Books Ltd.
rmbooks.com
@rmbooks
facebook.com/rmbooks

Cataloguing data available from Library and Archives Canada

ISBN 978-1-77160-109-2 (bound)
ISBN 978-1-77160-110-8 (epub)
ISBN 978-1-77160-111-5 (pdf)

Printed and bound in Canada by Friesens

Distributed in Canada by Heritage Group Distribution and the U.S. by
Publishers Group West

RMB | Rocky Mountain Books is dedicated to the environment and
committed to reducing the destruction of old-growth forests. Our books
are produced with respect for the future and consideration for the past.

We acknowledge the financial support of the Government of Canada
through the Canada Book Fund and the Canada Council for the Arts, and
of the province of British Columbia through the British Columbia Arts
Council and the Book Publishing Tax Credit.

Nous reconnaissons l'aide financière du gouvernement du Canada par
l'entremise du Fonds du livre du Canada et le Conseil des arts du Canada,
et de la province de la Colombie-Britannique par le Conseil des arts de la
Colombie-Britannique et le Crédit d'impôt pour l'édition de livres.

CONTENTS

He who is in pursuit of a goal will remain
empty once he has attained it.
But he who has found the way
will always carry the goal within him.
—Nejc Zaplotnik, *Pot*[1]

Introduction

I PAWED THROUGH THE SLUSH from a late-summer snowstorm, searching for the cable attached to the narrow ridge leading to the top of Triglav, Slovenia's highest mountain. Stepping carefully, I made my way up toward Aljaž Tower, the small metal building that sits on the summit. A modest structure, it is a symbol to all Slovenians of their territorial sovereignty. In response to foreign oppression, the priest Jakob Aljaž actually *bought* the summit of Triglav in 1895 for one florin, as if to say, "We are the masters of our own lands." When I reached the summit, I could hardly believe my eyes. Dozens of people were gathered near the tower, laughing and talking, eating lunch and celebrating their ascent. Young students threw snowballs and clowned for their cameras. An elderly woman, flanked by her two mountain guides, wept quietly. A radiant smile lit the face of a man with neither arms nor legs.

I walked up to a group of young climbers. "Is this some kind of national holiday?" I asked.

"Not at all," a particularly athletic woman replied. "It's just the weekend."

"But why are there so many people up here?"

"Because it's the weekend and we have time," she repeated, smiling patiently. "We are Slovenians and this is Triglav. It is our duty to climb it. Every Slovenian must climb it at least once."

I gazed over at the crying woman, who was possibly relieved that she had reached the top or maybe fearful of the descent to come. Then I looked back at the man with no limbs, whose friends loved him enough to carry him up two thousand metres in less than ideal conditions. I tried to imagine how they felt on the top of their Triglav – the national symbol of Slovenia. And I wondered about the character of a nation that feels its citizens must climb its highest mountain to be truly Slovenian.

For the next few years I immersed myself in the rich, complex, contradictory and often divisive world of Slovenian climbers, who are among the finest alpinists in the world. Sometimes we talked over glasses of fine local wine; sometimes I climbed with them. These alpinists had made some of the world's most impressive climbs: Makalu South Face, Lhotse South Face, Everest West Ridge Direct, Dhaulagiri South Face, and many more. Edmund Hillary is a household name, but many great Slovenian climbers – and a few from neighbouring Croatia and Bosnia – are almost unknown, even though their remarkable achievements formed the backbone of Himalayan climbing for 25 years, during a golden era of alpinism from the mid-1970s onward. That explosive and exciting period of bold ascents was not an accident. The climbers of the time were blessed with legendary leadership, infused with dogged determination, supported by national training programs, and inspired by feelings of solidarity that propelled them up some of the most iconic climbs in history.

Although I don't speak their language and I live 13,000 kilometres away, I felt drawn to both the history and the heroism of this community of climbers. As I learned more about Slovenian alpinists climbing at the end of the Second World War and onward to more recent times, I found some common threads in their wildly different personalities. The first is a self-sufficiency and drive forged by the history of a country under almost constant political threat and deeply wounded by internal conflict. Slovenian climbers, like their Croatian and Serbian neighbours, were shaped by the chaos of two world wars, foreign occupation, dictatorship, religious intolerance and, ultimately, civil war.

The second common thread is their fierce ability to defend their nation, language, culture and, as alpinists, their reputations –

sometimes, even among themselves. In the post–Second World War years, when the standard of living was low, sports and the arts provided rare opportunities to prove individual excellence. Slovenian climbers competed for coveted positions on Yugoslavian expeditions, and they performed well – at times even better than their European rivals.

Third, every Slovenian climber I have met seems indelibly stamped by the nation's landscape, with its deeply shaded, forested valleys, impossibly clear rivers, cerulean blue lakes and endless supply of mountains – steep, shimmering, limestone towers rising up in every direction. Most climbers freely admit that their souls are defined by their beloved home mountains, which have always had a symbolic – almost mythical – importance in Slovenia.

Finally, another thread binds Slovenian climbers. It seems an unlikely one: a man and his book. Although the importance of this man and his writing took me some time to fully appreciate, I first became aware of him in 2006 while doing research for a biography of Tomaž Humar, one of Slovenia's most controversial climbers.

I remember the day well. Tomaž stood at his living-room window with a book in his hand. The late-afternoon light shone gold on its worn cover. He fondled it, his oversized hands turning it over and over. He handed it to me. The pages were thin and torn. Some were stained. Wine, I think.

"One of my prized possessions," he said. Then, he began to explain how this slender volume written by Slovenian alpinist Nejc Zaplotnik had taught him, inspired him and given him a reference point for his life as a climber. He told me that the book, *Pot,* had been written in 1981, just 13 years after Tomaž was born. Tomaž and Nejc never met, yet the author's words and his feelings and values had resonated for Tomaž in the most profound way.

"What does it mean?" I inquired.

"*Pot?* It means the Way or the Path."

"Can you explain a little more?" I asked.

"It's a way of living, like a philosophy. Nejc wrote about how he felt about the mountains and people and love, about making the most of his life. It's incredible, how he wrote. He was a poet, an artist, a climber, all wrapped in one. Here, take a listen: 'But now, in this moment, a harmony that we have almost forgotten has been reached:

nature, body and mind have become one. They mutually serve and complete each other.'"

I knew Tomaž well enough to be somewhat skeptical of his gushing. Tomaž was unusual, to say the least. He experimented with various forms of spirituality; was equally comfortable with Catholicism, Buddhism, and the third eye; and claimed he could even communicate directly with a mountain face. This volume was probably some kind of religious self-help handbook. Still, it seemed important to him, so I made a note of it and promised myself to look into it further.

A year later, I was with another Slovenian climber, Silvo Karo, seated on a limestone slab at the top of Anića Kuk in Paklenica, the Croatian climbing paradise. We had just climbed a 350-metre route that seemed a cakewalk to rock-master Silvo but was beyond my wildest dreams. My arms were pumped with blood, my feet were screaming inside my tight climbing shoes, and my brain was fuzzy from dehydration. But out of the fog, I realized that Silvo, while calmly coiling the rope and gazing out to the valley below, was also talking about some book. It was *Pot*. Again, *Pot*. I could sense how important it was to Silvo by the tone in his voice and the words he used to describe it. Words like "values" and "authentic" and "wise."

Interesting. Although both Slovenian and both climbers, it's hard to imagine two individuals less alike than Silvo Karo and Tomaž Humar. Silvo, the taciturn pragmatist, and Tomaž, the romantic dreamer. And yet they were both in awe of this book and its author.

I began searching for an English edition of *Pot*, to no avail. A translation did not exist.

Five years later, I was back in Slovenia, intent on writing a much broader story, which became this book: a history of the Balkans, of Yugoslavia's breakup, of the climbers of that region and their emergence onto the world stage of climbing.

My journey took me to the homes of many Slovenian alpinists, including Himalayan climber Viki Grošelj. We stood in front of his impressive library of mountain literature. Everyone was there: Herzog, Messner, Bonington, Bonatti and other names I was just getting to know – Slovenian climbing authors like Stane Belak, Franček Knez and the Croatian Stipe Božić.

Then I spied it: *Pot*. Oh, and a second copy. And another.

"How many editions of this book do you have?" I asked.

"I think I have them all," Viki replied. "And for this one, I wrote the Afterword." He tapped the spine of one of the books.

"Did you know Nejc Zaplotnik well?"

"Of course. I climbed with him on several expeditions. He was a friend. A close friend. I was there when he died. You know what happened, don't you?" he asked.

I did not, but I soon learned. Viki and Nejc were invited to join a Croatian expedition to Manaslu in Nepal in 1983. Viki was a few hundred feet above Nejc and two others when several towering ice seracs collapsed, sending tons of snow and ice down upon them. Viki heard the crack and looked down. He saw Nejc and the others stop and then run, but they had no chance. Viki and his partner sped down the slope and arrived at the site within 40 minutes. One of the three survived, one was never found, and Nejc was dead.

I waited while Viki struggled with his painful memories, then asked, "What did you write in your Afterword?"

He took the book off the shelf and flipped to the end. "I wrote a lot of things." He smiled after reading a few moments. "We had so many great times together. But this is how I began:

> Nejc Zaplotnik is without a doubt one of the most charismatic personalities of Slovenian alpinism. To earn this title it's not enough to tag a bunch of excellent ascents on Slovenian and foreign mountains. It's also not enough that three of those ascents were three difficult first-ascent routes on eight-thousanders, which, in 1979, made him the equal of the famous Messner. The most important fact is that Nejc really lived his life as sincerely as he described in *Pot*. This is why there is nothing to be taken away or added to this masterful text.[2]

Viki then explained how he first came to read the book. He and Nejc had been on the South Face of Lhotse together in 1981, and Viki had returned with a serious injury. It wasn't clear if he would ever walk properly again, and at the age of 29, he was awash in depression. Nejc burst in, laughing and excited, his face shining and his eyes bright. Dressed in a plaid shirt, his dishevelled curls peeking out from under a striped bandana, he bounded over and handed Viki a book – hot off the press, he said. The inscription brought tears to Viki's eyes. "To Viki: Although we came from different sides of the sky and we looked toward different horizons, we walked a large chunk of the way together and we munched crumbs from the same sack."

In the weeks that followed, Viki devoured the book, racing through it the first time, and then savouring it several more times, slowly and deliberately. "I read it from line to line, and then between the lines," he said, looking up. "He wrote it for himself, for me, for all of us who feel life, and who experience life alike."

Viki closed the book and put it back, next to all the other *Pot*s.

A few days later, I visited Andrej Štremfelj, one of the most accomplished Himalayan climbers alive. We sat at his kitchen table, steaming cups of strong Turkish coffee in front of us. As he reminisced about his unparalleled career as an alpinist, I asked what his most important climbs were. He hesitated, cupped his chin in his hands and stared across the table. His intense, blue-green eyes darted about the room as he mentally catalogued more than 40 years of ascents.

A few moments later Andrej announced, "I would have to divide my career into two parts in order to answer that."

"Yes," I said, "and they would be?"

"The first part would be up until Nejc's death, and the second part after. He was incredibly important to me. He was like an engine."

Andrej had many rich memories about Nejc that he wanted to share. Memories of time spent together in the mountains, in storms and on approach marches. Memories of summits. When I asked about *Pot*, Andrej explained that no one could have anticipated the impact of the book, and not only for climbers. That slim volume had become one of the best-loved books in the entire country, touching every Slovenian, as well as people living in other Balkan nations.

Obviously I needed to read this book. If I wanted to understand climbers from this part of the world, I would need to understand this man who, more than any other, had influenced their philosophy of climbing. I would need to hear his voice through the turn of a phrase. I would need to see life as he saw it. I would need to feel emotions as he expressed them. Because this man and his writing had influenced so many climbers whose stories I wanted to chronicle, I first had to get to know *Pot*.

Later that summer, I began working with Mimi Marinsek, a young translator from Ljubljana. Two or three times a week we would meet up in the cyber world of Skype, and she would read to me. Over the course of several months, Mimi translated many Slovenian and Serbo-Croatian books for me, but the one that resonated most profoundly was *Pot*. By the end of the very first page, I knew that it would be the key to unlocking the mystery of those Slovenian pioneers of the vertical world.

From *Pot*:

All this is my life. A path leads nowhere but on to the next path. And that one takes you to the next crossroads. Without end. This is freedom in the purest meaning of the word. I am sentenced to freedom. I am so free that, among the crowd of people who love me, as well as those who don't care for me, I continue to remain alone. Alone with my wishes, dreams, desires, and alone on my eternal path. This is not a story that I conceived in my imagination, sitting by a warm stove in the comfort of home. Rather, these words grew within me as I put my will and the limits of my human capabilities to the test by the sweat of my brow; and I tested them thoroughly. So thoroughly that I know I didn't reach them, not by far, and that others will soon surpass me. Therein lies the greatness of life.[3]

I remembered Tomaž's words about Nejc: a poet, an artist, a climber, all in one. It was true. I began to look forward to each Skype session with Mimi, each new chapter. I was caught up in his story and his way of telling it. Nejc's words honoured the poetry of the mountains and of alpinism. They searched for answers to the great human questions, and their simple wisdom was powerful. They became an unending poem, their tone sometimes clear and pure and confident, and at other times tentative, as if written in doubt and fear. They were the words of a climber who thought deeply. A deep thinker who climbed.

I was determined to search for the truth about this generation of climbers that emerged from the ruins of the Second World War, from the birth of Yugoslavia, then through its tragic and violent deconstruction. A group of people who endured hardship and poverty, who fought in despicable wars for which they were denounced, and who struggled to understand the changing ideological rhetoric that surrounded them. Throughout it all, they never lost their passion for climbing.

Although I never met Nejc Zaplotnik, he became my partner on this journey, and his words became my partner in this book.

ONE

Dare to Dream

T he ship glided across the mirror-like sea, baking in the
equatorial sun. A slight breeze cooled the climbers as they
scampered up ropes, ran laps around the decks and hung off
anything possible. The crew stood agape, marvelling at this horde of
"apes" – who were, in fact, Yugoslavian climbers en route to Karachi.
In the Socialist Federal Republic of Yugoslavia, the only way to get to
the Himalaya was as a member of a national expedition, and these
climbers had trained hard to win a spot on the team. They weren't
going to let two weeks at sea destroy their conditioning.

Yugoslavia's first venture into the Himalayan arena had been
planned for Manaslu in 1956. The plan was short-lived, due mainly
to cutbacks in government support. Four years later, in 1960, they set
their sights on 7816-metre Nanda Devi, one of India's most beautiful
mountains and its second highest. But placing foot on the "Bliss-
Giving Goddess" was also not to be. While the team, comprising
mainly Slovenian climbers, was steaming across the Indian Ocean,
they received a radio message from the Indian government revoking
their permit for Nanda Devi and offering its neighbour, Trisul,
instead. Of course, the climbers were disappointed, but not for long.
The first Yugoslavian expedition to the Himalaya was determined to
prove its worth, and Trisul would now be their testing ground.

Trisul's three summits form the southwest corner of the ring of
peaks enclosing the Nanda Devi Sanctuary. Trisul I, at 7120 metres
the highest of the trio, was first climbed from the north in 1907 by

an Englishman, Tom Longstaff. And now, 53 years after the first ascent, the Yugoslavians had arrived. But the modest team of seven Himalayan neophytes had no intention of following in Longstaff's footsteps. They would explore the mountain from the more difficult southern side and attempt a new route.

Still on the high seas, the climbers continued to train. Among them was a young man from Ljubljana, the capital of Slovenia, Yugoslavia's northernmost republic. Aleš Kunaver was born June 23, 1935, of educated stock. His Viennese mother was an accomplished pianist, and his father, Pavel, was a geography teacher and an astronomer, known in Slovenia as one of the best karst researchers of his time. But Pavel wasn't only an academic with his head in the clouds. He was a climber, credited as the first Slovenian alpinist to pound a piton into rock (although it later turned out to be a wooden clothespin rather than an iron piton).

Aleš was a good if unconventional student. His French homework was never done on time, yet he could speak the language fluently. He was also extremely inventive. If he needed a tool, he made it. If he needed a wind jacket, he sewed it. If he needed a piton, he forged it, for it was impossible to find sporting equipment – or almost anything – in Slovenian shops at this time. Even the very limited food supplies were still being allocated by ration cards.

Each summer Aleš accompanied his family to a hut in the Vrata Valley under the north wall of Triglav. It was a foregone conclusion that, at some point, he would climb it. His first foray onto the wall was as a lad of 13. Down below, Pavel monitored every move through binoculars as Aleš climbed up the steep wall with friends.

Nejc Zaplotnik understood Aleš's infatuation with the vertical world. As he wrote in *Pot*, "The start of my alpinism was very romantic. Mountains were my home where I felt safe and it was only here that I felt master of the situation. In the valley...I had to do things that people demanded and expected of me, but the mountains were as limitless as my dreams. My only limitation was my body."[4]

As Aleš's interest in climbing grew, he joined the Ljubljana section of the Slovenian Alpine Club. Also in the club was Dušica Zlobec, a 19-year-old student from Ljubljana. Her fierce intelligence was obvious in the direct gaze of her deep brown eyes. By the time they met, the handsome young Aleš with his finely chiselled face was already an instructor in and president of the club. It was New Year's Eve, 1954, and they were at the Tamar mountain hut. The club had a tradition of scrambling to the top of Jalovec to welcome in the New Year. They would head up from the hut around nine in the evening and remain on the summit for six or seven hours.

Dušica experienced several "firsts" on this New Year's Eve: first time in the mountains at night, first time climbing a mountain in winter and first time in love. The approach to the summit was up a couloir that left her shaking with fear. "When Aleš came, I felt so safe. I felt that he would protect me. He didn't say anything but walked behind me to make me feel safe." She later admitted that it was love at first sight. They married and eventually had three children together.

In those years following the Second World War, there were only a dozen or so climbers still active in all of Slovenia. Most of the others had joined the anti-Nazi resistance fighters – the Liberation Front or its armed division, the Partisans – and had either been imprisoned or killed. The International Climbing and Mountaineering Federation (UIAA) had classified climbing into a series of grades, with the VIth degree recognized as the most difficult at that time. Anyone in Slovenia who climbed at that level was famous. Aleš was one of them. The Slovenians' love affair with mountains also contributed to his fame. "I don't think there was a nation in the world that loved mountains like we did," Dušica recalled.

During those postwar years, climbers from all over Yugoslavia faced many obstacles just to travel to a foreign mountain. A cooling relationship between Yugoslavia and the USSR meant climbing in the Caucasus and Pamirs was out. The focus shifted to the Dolomites and the Alps, but climbers still required visas for European countries, and to obtain them they first needed to go to distant Belgrade, the Yugoslavian capital. Their second challenge was money. With no access to foreign currency, many Yugoslavian climbers experienced real hunger on those early trips to the Alps. Aleš was among them. But like Nejc, his commitment to the mountains was complete. From *Pot*:

> Mountains have given me what people in the cities lost long ago....For thousands of years people had to adjust to nature, from which they

drew strength and life. Now, however, they were suddenly expected to live a quiet, sedentary, mundane existence, day in and day out. We forget that, despite all the machines and buildings, we are still just a part of nature. Inside me, I carried the lives and deaths of millennia. But they didn't weigh me down. They gave me strength that even I wasn't able to fully exhaust. A fire burned inside me and I knew only two ways out: either keep stoking it or allow myself to be burned by it.[5]

Aleš's dreams extended beyond the Julian Alps. Beyond the French Alps. He wanted to go to the Himalaya, and in 1960 he got his chance.

◆ ◆ ◆

Everything about the Trisul expedition was new. The climbers had to make all their own equipment, find the materials, design their tents and clothing, and beg the factories for products and expertise. Nothing like this had ever happened in Yugoslavia; the climbers were decades behind their European neighbours in the world of expeditioning.

By the end of March their ship was in sight of Asia. Aleš, already showing signs of leadership, convinced the captain to let him command the ship for a bit. He took the helm, revelling in the sense of power he felt commanding eight thousand tons on the open sea. As the sun dipped below the horizon, the ocean became a glistening sheet of undulating gold. Aleš was keenly aware of the expectations for the team. Every day of that 10,000-kilometre sea voyage and the 2000-kilometre overland journey was filled with dreams of the Himalaya – and the pressure to succeed on an unclimbed route on Trisul's southern flanks.

By May 7, 1960, after a month of climbing and hauling countless loads of food and equipment up the mountain, the climbers established Camp II at 4700 metres. As they moved higher, through the icefall to a high col between the peaks, they tried to avoid the avalanches that thundered around them. They finally chose to climb at night when it was colder and safer. Aleš wrote in his journal: "A mountain is not only a game of four seasons, a game of light and darkness, a game of clouds, which sometimes encircle the mountain and create their own character...but also a personality with changing moods, sometimes not stable, sometimes welcoming. We believe in our duty; we have accepted its price, and we have dedicated to it all our powers. We fell in love with this mountain and slowly it is becoming our friend."[6]

As he absorbed the magic of the shimmering Himalayan peaks around him, Aleš began to form a deeper relationship with the landscape. He understood that success would not be the only measure of the value of this experience. "These huge cathedrals of rock and ice that are called mountains are able to return love for love."[7] He felt the intimacy that is formed when individuals face danger as a team.

Storms blew them off Trisul I, but they climbed both Trisul II and III, making first ascents of each. The narrow summit of Trisul III was particularly rewarding, for the sky was cloudless, with not a breath of wind. "What a present of nature," Aleš declared in his journal.

Their return to Ljubljana was triumphant. Aleš was stunned to see the streets crowded with thousands of people – so many that their bus was reduced to a crawl. He began to appreciate how many individuals had helped them succeed in the Himalaya. So many had contributed, some with just one small solution, one little piece of material, one bit of financing. All of the gifts added up to a pyramid on which only a few could stand – the summit few – but as he looked out at the welcoming crowd, he understood the importance of the base.

Reaching two mountain summits over six thousand metres was a good result for the first Yugoslavian Himalayan expedition. In fact, the European climbing fraternity was taken aback by this unknown Yugoslavian team, which seemed to have steamed in from nowhere – from the Balkans, for heaven's sake, an undeveloped region overrun, in the popular imagination, with gypsies and whirling dervishes. What next? The Yugoslavian climbers simply smiled, for they were eager and ready to make their mark on the Himalayan horizon.

◆ ◆ ◆

Aleš returned to Nepal in 1962, not to climb but to wander among those mountainous monoliths and scout for climbing possibilities. It was on this trip that his visionary side emerged, as well as the strength and drive he needed to become the "founder of Yugoslavian Himalayan climbing." It was also on this trip that Aleš first saw the South Face of Lhotse and began to dream of climbing it. This was eight years before any great Himalayan face was climbed; it wasn't until 1970 that a British team climbed the South Face of Annapurna, and the British had been exploring the Himalaya since well before the turn of the century. Thinking about climbing the South Face of Lhotse in 1962 was like dreaming of going to Mars. But Aleš was serious, and the mountain came to dominate his life.

Not only Lhotse captured his imagination that year. His eyes were drawn to the most difficult features of other Himalayan giants – massive faces and tortuous ridges – many of which would form the backbone of Yugoslavia's expedition efforts in the coming years and catapult them into the forefront of climbing in the great ranges.

TWO

Triglav in Winter

Yugoslavia was not only an unlikely incubator of alpinists; the country itself grew out of an unusual combination of nations, languages and religions. Yugoslavia, which literally means "south Slavs," first became a state in 1918 when what had been the Kingdom of Serbs, Croatians and Slovenians was named Royal Yugoslavia. Initially formed as a united response against its Austrian, Hungarian and Turkish oppressors, the country had a brief existence. Germany invaded in 1941 and dismembered it, taking the best part for itself and handing the rest to Italy and Hungary. Chaos ruled for the next four years as Yugoslavians fought against their Fascist invaders, and then among themselves in a civil war that pitted neighbour against neighbour and brother against brother.

Communist-supported Partisans kept the idea of a Yugoslav state alive as they prowled the forests and mountains, killing both Fascists and suspected collaborators. Leader of the Communist Party and ally of the Partisans, Josip Broz Tito emerged victorious at the end of the war, and Yugoslavia was intact once again. Now called the Federative People's Republic of Yugoslavia, it was controlled by Stalin until 1948, when the relationship cooled between Yugoslavia and the USSR. To reflect the loosening Soviet grip, the nation's name changed once again in 1963 to the Socialist Federal Republic of Yugoslavia.

But Yugoslavia was still a complicated reality, consisting of six republics – Slovenia, Croatia, Serbia, Bosnia and Herzegovina, Montenegro and Macedonia – and two autonomous provinces –

Kosovo and Vojvodina. It included three major religions – Catholicism, Eastern Orthodox Christianity and Islam – and its peoples spoke half a dozen languages. The geography varied from desert to craggy coastline, from high plains to deep forests and soaring peaks. By far the most mountainous region was Slovenia, the most northerly republic. So it's not surprising that the majority of Yugoslavia's best climbers came from Slovenia. The topography, combined with the hard-working, pious, matter-of-fact Slovenian temperament, honed and perfected under German/Austrian domination, created the perfect climbing machines.

As Yugoslavia entered the Himalayan arena, proud of its survival of the Second World War and eager for success in the realm of expeditioning, Belgrade looked north for talent. North to those climbers trained in the Julian Alps – Slovenian climbers. As it turned out, Belgrade's instincts were correct.

◆ ◆ ◆

Triglav – the three-headed mountain that symbolizes Slovenia – is surrounded by mystery and myths that carry messages of the magnificent yet vulnerable nature of mountains and the mortality of man. One legend has it that on its rugged flanks once lived a kind-hearted giantess who, before she was turned by a curse into stone, guided hunters through the fog and mist. Another legend tells of a majestic white chamois named Zlatorog who ruled the highest ledges of the mountain, flashing his golden horns in the evening light. Despite dire warnings, a smitten, young hunter from the Trenta Valley killed Zlatorog and sold his soul to the devil, all for the love of a girl. However, the magically resurrected Zlatorog blinded the hunter with the glint of his horns, and the hunter plunged to his death, eventually floating down the turquoise waters of the Soča River to the valley below.

Triglav is part of the Slovenian psyche. Not only its mythology, but its physical mass, which, as I discovered, every Slovenian feels obliged to ascend. First climbed in 1778 by a group of three, eight years before the first ascent of Mont Blanc, its narrow and exposed summit ridge was widened and secured with an iron cable in 1895 to help Slovenians fulfill their sacred duty.

The highest peak in the Julian Alps, at 2864 metres, and the undisputed centrepiece of Triglav National Park, Triglav is also maddeningly near the Austrian border. It is so close that Austrian and German climbers routinely claimed impressive new routes on Triglav's magnificent north wall, which looms four kilometres wide and one kilometre high above the Vrata Valley. They not only climbed them, they *named* them. The German Route, the Bavarian Route – these names became major irritants for Slovenian climbers. So many foreign climbers came immediately after the First World War that Slovenian alpinists found themselves in a defensive position, scrambling to stay ahead of the foreign hordes. Even as early as 1908, native climbers felt compelled to form the *Dren* Society, whose main purpose was to climb Slovenian mountains before the Germans did.

The first man to climb the north wall of Triglav was, thankfully, a Slovenian – Ivan Berginc, a logger, hunter and mountain guide from the Soča Valley. He climbed it in secrecy in 1890, because at that time the chamois living in the Julian Alps belonged to the Kaiser in Vienna: Ivan could have been jailed on suspicion of poaching. The story of his daring ascent was spoken of only in whispers in the Trenta Valley. And like the mythical hunter who shot Zlatorog and was washed down the Soča River, Ivan was later found dead in the same river, one of many casualties of the fierce battles fought on the border between Italy and Slovenia during the First World War.

Among the most impressive routes on the north side of Triglav is Čopov Steber (Čop's Pillar), first climbed in 1945 by 52-year-old Joža Čop and 44-year-old Pavla Jesih, one of the finest female climbers in all of Europe at the time. Famous for opening long and difficult new routes, she almost lost her life in 1933 while climbing with Joža Lipovec, a man who loved to knit as well as climb. He was known to take his needles and wool along on his climbs and knit while resting. Perhaps it helped him relax. After the accident Pavla stopped serious climbing and started up a chain of cinemas. But 12 years later she returned to the mountains to try the famous Čop's Pillar.

On the third day of the climb, Pavla became too exhausted to continue. Joža Čop finished the route, ran back for help and returned to the face. Because of dense fog, it wasn't until the fifth day that the rescue party reached her. She insisted on completing the climb under her own steam, earning herself credit for the first ascent alongside Joža. But for political reasons it was only Joža Čop's name that graced the route. Joža was a working man, employed in a local steelworks factory, a man so committed to climbing that his prenuptial agreement allegedly stipulated that his wife could not prevent him from climbing – even with women. Pavla was a wealthy city girl and, as such, out of favour in postwar Yugoslavia. Her affluence was a problem for the Socialist masters, and they had no intention of honouring her with the landmark route. (It's a problem few female alpinists have had to face – too much money.)

But Čop's Pillar had yet to be climbed in winter. Slovenian climbers threw themselves at the snow-covered route, determined to beat any foreigners intent on scooping one of the biggest prizes still remaining in the Eastern Alps. The winter of 1966 was particularly irksome, with East German climbers claiming a new route on Triglav and Czech climbers poised to climb the Čop's Pillar route. A race developed as Slovenian and Czech teams headed up the north wall simultaneously. Bad conditions forced both parties back.

Two years passed and the pillar still waited. On January 20, 1968, the weather forecast looked promising. For days, a north wind had blown at more than 180 kilometres per hour and had swept the wall bare of snow. Conditions were ideal. On January 23 three of Slovenia's best climbers, Tone Sazonov, Aleš Kunaver and Stane Belak, known by all as Šrauf, departed for the Vrata Valley.

◆ ◆ ◆

Born in Ljubljana on November 13, 1940, Šrauf spent the first few years of his life behind barbed wire, a direct result of the arrival of the Second World War in Yugoslavia. When German bombs rained down on Belgrade on April 6, 1941, Yugoslavian citizens knew that their lives had fundamentally changed. Eight hundred planes flew low over the capital, destroying the palace, the university, churches, schools and hospitals. Twenty-four thousand corpses in four days. When the German army, assisted by the Italians, marched across Yugoslavia, the age-old Germanic hatred of everything Slavic could be felt throughout the country. In Croatia the Germans installed the criminal classes to lord over local citizens, quickly replicating the Nazi model of death camps and torture. Serbian men and boys were sent to concentration camps in Romania or were simply executed. Macedonian Serbians were evicted from their properties and sent wandering, homeless.

Slovenia was the first Yugoslavian nation to fall and within months was wiped off the European map. Germany expected former Slovenians to join the Nazi Party, although they were selective about whom they would accept. Those with Germanic heritage were given full membership, questionable citizens were allowed probationary membership, and many were outright rejected and deported, primarily to Serbia. But Slovenians proved resilient. They had endured foreign occupation many times in the past and had adopted a strategy of national survival that emphasized accommodation of their foreign masters rather than outright resistance.

When Germany divided Slovenia into three parts in 1941, Italy was awarded the northwestern portion, which included the capital city, Ljubljana. At first a benevolent occupier, Italy ignored the buildup of Partisan resistance at its peril. By the time it took notice, the movement had grown to a formidable size, and support from the Allies only added to its momentum. Italy responded by digging trenches and erecting fences around Ljubljana, making it the largest concentration camp in Europe. The strategy succeeded in discouraging the Partisan stronghold inside the city, but the surrounding forests provided the cover the Partisans needed to keep up their pressure on the Italians. Civilians inside the capital did their best to help them, and the Alpine Association of Slovenia headquarters in Ljubljana became a gathering place for supporters of the illegal Liberation Front.

Living conditions behind the fence were difficult. Food and money were scarce, and freedom of movement was a distant memory. Citizens sold everything they owned to survive – even the floors in their houses for firewood. Šrauf's family was luckier than some because they owned a small plot of land on which they grew vegetables. Šrauf became the man of the house at the age of 8 when his father was killed by a bus while riding his bike. Although Šrauf was a good student with natural intelligence, his singular passion was sport. He began climbing at the age of 18.

Four years before their winter climb on Triglav, Šrauf popped into the local climbing school to meet some friends. There, at the door, was 17-year-old Jožica Trček. Compact and fit, the dark-haired beauty with the dazzling smile was also a climbing instructor. For Šrauf, there was much to attract him. Female climbers were rare at the time, and Jožica was good. She had already solo climbed a number of the classic north wall routes on Triglav and had climbed the Čop route in summer when she was just 15. She was amused by Šrauf's rough way of talking and the fact that he was often surrounded by an adoring flock of girls. His powerful, athletic body and brooding good looks were mesmerizing.

They were both smitten and the romance flourished. Jožica repaired Šrauf's equipment. Šrauf brought Jožica alpine flowers. "Our dating consisted of climbing together. That's it," she recalled. After one year of knowing each other, they married in 1965. Jožica joked that she married him simply in order to have a belayer. They started a family and their second daughter was born in 1968, three weeks before Šrauf headed up onto the north wall of Triglav.

◆ ◆ ◆

After wading through deep snow on Triglav for four hours, Aleš, Tone and Šrauf arrived at the Aljaž lodge, where they spent the night. By late afternoon of the next day, they had lugged all their food and equipment to the base of the ominous yet tantalizing wall that loomed above them. They began climbing the next morning at five, but the weather had changed without their noticing. The sky was now a dull, leaden grey, and the wind battered them with powerful gusts. As the snowstorm moved into the valley, the wall became blanketed in white. They secured their equipment at their high point and fled.

By the end of January, the sky cleared, the temperatures rose and the three hopeful climbers returned to the Vrata Valley. Šrauf voiced their determination: "The conditions are excellent and the only way is up. Nothing can hold us back."[8] They took three packs weighing almost 70 kilograms in total and an 80-metre rope for a climb they thought would take four or five days. They began the adventure: up an icy gully, across a ramp, up an avalanche couloir, and over a steep, overhanging step, the last obstacle before the first bivouac spot they had established on their previous attempt.

So far, so good. Their confidence soared. They were making good time and had no intention of stopping at the bivouac, so they launched up onto the vertical part of the wall. Šrauf removed his crampons, arranged his rack of homemade pitons and prepared to tackle a steep chimney that was frustratingly bereft of visible handholds. With bare hands stinging from the cold, he cleared off the snow and scratched his way up. When he reached a relatively level stance, he stopped in order to construct a belay station and bring up the others. But he was unable to pound even one piton into the rock, so with a certain nervousness, since he wasn't secured to the wall, he called down.

"Aleš, come up. But be careful – the belay isn't good."

"Okay, we'll pay attention," Aleš replied.

The next pitch was even steeper. The hours slipped by. The lengthening shadows rose higher up the wall, but the tops of the peaks shimmered in a golden sunset glow. By the time all three reached the bivouac site, Šrauf was shaking with exhaustion.

Day two dawned clear. Tone took over the lead on the next, occasionally overhanging stretch of rock. They reached the highest point of their previous attempt and surpassed it. Triglav seemed to be smiling at them. An icy ramp led to a troublesome gully blanketed in soft snow; it would be difficult to belay and treacherous to cross. Progress slowed. Although it seemed they had just started, it was already late afternoon. They heard shouts from the valley below, where scouts were watching them. The climbers yodelled back in reply – their agreed-upon signal that things were all right.

But they weren't. Behind schedule now, they hacked out a spot in the thin, glistening film of verglas ice. Tucked away under an overhang, they were absorbed by the wall, completely hidden from view. A sly wind moved in from the west and cirrus clouds appeared, a climber's nightmare, since they usually herald bad weather. Still, the wall needed to be climbed; after two more, 50-metre pitches, the trio reached the beginning of their main objective: Čop's Pillar. Tone had stashed some cans of beans and a bottle of gas at this point the previous summer, so the climbers stopped for a bit, ate and rested, while they surveyed what lay ahead of them – and below. A sinister mist crept up from the valley, and they knew that the fine weather would soon end. They had one more good day, at the most.

Šrauf led up the gaping chimney feature that split the pillar, belaying his partners pitch by pitch. He could see the storm building, and it became obvious that they would soon be engulfed by snow. But he knew of a large cave at the top of the pillar that would provide protection from the avalanches that were sure to come. Unfortunately, between them and the cave loomed a large rock step. They were tantalizingly near the top of the pillar when night fell. Stuck on an exposed and ice-encrusted ledge, they had to descend 20 metres in order to build a bivouac. Again, they could hear voices calling up from the valley, and they glimpsed one dim, lonely light. They yodelled back down into the darkness. Everything okay.

They discussed the situation over dinner that night. A sombre group now, their earlier confidence was dissipating as quickly as the fog rose up from the valley to obscure them. The cave had become their most immediate goal. It would provide a safe haven in which to wait out the storm.

The morning of the fourth day revealed what they had dreaded: all the peaks rearing up from the Vrata Valley were wreathed in fog and cloud. Even the uppermost part of the Triglav wall was veiled. The air quivered with tension – the kind of pressure felt before a violent storm. The ice-covered pillar required great care, yet they were tempted to rush. Nine hundred metres above the Vrata Valley, they were still a long way from the cave.

Šrauf removed his crampons, as he was now faced with a vertical wall that demanded all of his attention and technique. Tiny handholds were covered with snow or, worse, a thin film of ice. Not enough ice for crampons, but too much for boots. He struggled to hang on, shaking from the effort and worry. The heavy snowfall created a complete shroud of silence on the north wall of Triglav.

Aleš and Tone followed Šrauf, hauling the packs behind them. Suddenly the cave was within reach. Šrauf kicked steps in hard snow and hacked handholds with his ice axe. With white fingers he hammered three pitons into the crumbly rock and then he called down to his partners to ascend. Almost sick with relief to be inside the cave, he watched as the first snow sloughs began slithering down the mountain. It had taken them six hours to climb a mere 60 metres, but it no longer mattered. They were safe.

It snowed all night and all the next day. On the fifth day of their climb – the day they had hoped might be the last one – they remained snowbound in the cave.

The sixth day dawned, and it continued to snow. Their safe haven had become a prison, and they were running out of food. With each passing day, the size and intensity of the avalanches increased. At some point they would need to leave. Go out on the wall again. The mere thought was terrifying. They knew they were completely on their own, for rescue was not an option. When Šrauf left the cave around 9 am that day, he stepped into a world of chaos. He tried to climb a difficult rock section, but avalanches pounded him from above. The usual arsenal of equipment – pitons and carabiners – was of secondary importance, as now his most important tool was a little broom he used to sweep off the holds. One metre at a time he crawled up toward an overhang. The fog began to lift. Glancing down, he realized that he could see the entire thousand metres to the valley below. He watched as avalanches thundered below him into the gaping abyss. Then he crawled up onto the overhang and rested on a narrow ledge, waiting for his companions to join him. Every moment of this climb was training for the great alpinist he would one day become.

Shouts rang up from the valley. Yodels ricocheted back down. Still okay.

When Aleš arrived at the ledge, Šrauf headed up again, climbing bare-handed now, the handholds being too small for gloves. He climbed precisely but as quickly as possible, since every minute counted. He focused on finding a safe haven from the avalanches that threatened to sweep them off the wall. When he reached a cave, he yelled to Tone and Aleš; the storm had strengthened, however, and his calls disappeared into the swirl of fog and snow. Finally, tugs on the rope and other pre-arranged signals told them they were meant to climb, but it took another hour for the two to reach the cave. Heavily laden with the enormous packs, they slumped down, relieved yet surprisingly still in high spirits.

Climbing had become a game of waiting and racing: waiting for the snow slides to slither past, then racing upward to gain some headway before the next one appeared. Fifteen metres above his last piton, Šrauf was almost carried off by a snow slough. Completely separated from his companions and covered in snow, he clung to the rock while struggling to pound in a piton to secure himself. He continued upward. Then the rope became stuck in an unseen crack. He pulled and wiggled it, finally loosening it enough to wade up a gully choked with chest-deep snow. Convinced that the entire snowpack would slide off the slope, carrying him along, he managed to nail in a piton and call for the others to come up. Nothing happened. Twenty minutes later they finally heard and understood what was expected of them. As twilight approached, the three were together again, strategizing their escape from the wall and preparing their last meal: three cubes of soup stock, three pieces of chocolate and a small package of sugar.

Day seven dawned. More snow. The muffled sound of avalanches surrounded them. Aleš burrowed through the deep snow to find some old, rusty pitons, remnants from the first ascent 23 years before. Centimetres at a time, he moved up, finally reaching the spot where Joža Čop had begun his diagonal traverse off the wall. Aleš later recalled the moment: "We climb upward in this white inferno and there is nothing we can say to each other. Our faces are fixed in a sort of grimace. We are trying to keep our spirits up."[9]

The frozen grimaces were justified, because the next stretch of climbing was extremely dangerous – a tiny ledge, undoubtedly one of the most exposed places in the Slovenian Alps, where the wall drops 1100 metres straight down below your feet in a single sweep. Thankfully, the snow and fog obscured their view so they couldn't actually see the abyss. But they knew it was there. Šrauf focused on each minuscule problem, avoiding any thoughts of the larger issue: getting off the wall in one piece. Only three rope lengths from relative safety, they could taste the end.

In front of them reared a vertical crack, difficult enough in summer but now almost impossible. Just 12 metres from the top, Šrauf ran out of strength.

"Aleš, I'm going to fall. Hold me."

"Don't do anything stupid, Šrauf. You can't afford to." So much for sympathy.

Šrauf rallied, composed himself, found a hold and made the moves. He jammed his knee into a notch in the wall and spied an old piton. Life was good again.

They had reached the ledge where in summer it was a simple matter of packing up the ropes and racing upward to the top of the wall. But this wasn't summer. And the situation was anything but simple. The wind howled, and a sizeable snow slab broke off as Tone and Aleš lumbered up through the waist-deep snow, burdened with their heavy packs. As night approached, they reached a small crest in the wall – completely unrealistic for a winter bivouac. Šrauf rappelled down a gully stuffed with snow, sinking up to his neck. Perfectly aware that this massive snow load could be triggered by their body weight, they nevertheless stamped out a bivouac platform. Suddenly a tremor shook the slope, and a huge avalanche slid by them and disappeared into the depths. Miraculously, it missed them. They dug as fast as possible, trying to create a cave into which they could crawl. The night stretched on as they took cover in their hole, which was silent as a tomb. Would they get through the night? Would tomorrow finally be the day?

At Aleš's home, the tension was high. Dušica consoled their two daughters, trying to explain why Daddy wasn't home, how the nasty snowstorm had delayed him, how it would soon be over and he would be with them again. But they weren't buying it. They were tired of Dušica's bedtime stories. They wanted to snuggle up with their dad and hear his tales: fairies creating the lake at Bled, Vikings discovering America and Pinocchio in the whale's stomach. Dušica was helpless when faced with their tears, as well as her own fears. Nobody had survived this long in winter on Triglav's north wall.

The mood was even more stressful at the Belak home. Jožica was alone with their two daughters, the youngest only three weeks old. Everyone knew about the snowstorm raging in the mountains. It being long before cellphones, there was no communication with the climbers, and they were seriously overdue.

On their eighth morning on the wall, they excavated a tunnel out of the snow hole with their ice axes. Although it seemed impossible, the weather was even worse than before. Snow filled the air, the wind roared like a freight train, and avalanches slid by them from the Kugy Ledge above. Still, when they reached the top of the wall, they were breathless with joy. They yelled and pounded each other, then they came to their senses: they still had to get down. They abandoned their packs, as it was impossible to make any headway in the deep drifts with the extra weight. They tried to walk forward but their legs wouldn't move. They were buried up to their chests in what felt like quicksand sucking them ever deeper. They began to crawl in a kind of swimming motion, aiming for one exposed rock after another.

Crawling and rolling down the slope, Aleš yelled, "I can see footsteps."

"You're hallucinating!" screamed Tone. But then he saw them, too. As the three of them lurched about in a haphazard manner, the slope was suddenly full of people screaming at them in happiness and relief. It was the crew from the Vrata Valley – the same people who had been monitoring their ascent, plus many, many more. Šrauf recalled the scene: "The moment when we realized that the people down there were worried about us was unforgettable. To imagine that you are going to sleep in a dry place, to eat bread again."[10]

It was the end of a grand adventure. Čop's Pillar remained Slovenian, even in winter.

Theirs was a fantastic ascent that captured the nation's attention, in part because mountaineering was one of the most popular sports in Slovenia. But the story that resonated most was the rescue effort: even though no rescue had been officially called for, over 70 people had left the warmth of their homes and their families, ventured out into a howling blizzard and voluntarily put themselves in danger and discomfort in order to help the climbers.

A few days later, the trio paid a visit to Joža Čop. When he learned that his precious pillar remained in Slovenian hands, even in winter, a contented smile lit his deeply lined face. "Well done, boys."

◆ ◆ ◆

Slovenia's pride in the climbers' accomplishment was, at least in part, a reaction to the not-so-recent war that had shattered the country. It was a complicated and conflicted pride that grew out of a heartbreaking period of history, rife with contradictions: tragedy and victory, grief and denial. Čop's Pillar in winter provided a small beacon of dignity and honour in a time of national anguish.

In the last days of the Second World War, the Partisans had the Axis armies on the run, scuttling as fast as they could back to Austria. British troops waited on the other side of the Austrian border, confused about what to do with these tens of thousands of soldiers streaming in. Not only soldiers. Among them were Slovenian citizens – some of them collaborators with the Germans and Italians, and others who were pacifists but who feared for their lives. Many had fought with the Partisans up until 1943, when they realized that they were actually fighting for Communism. Their families didn't support Communism, so they called their sons and brothers home. Now those unfortunate boys were considered enemies of both the Partisans *and* Tito. As it became clear that the Partisans were going to be victors in a very short period of time, both the pacifists and collaborators grew justifiably afraid. When the British troops stationed in Austria herded the Slovenians onto trains and sent them straight back to Slovenia, they landed in Tito's unforgiving arms.

Tito, who was born Josip Broz in Kumrovec, a village on the border between Croatia and Slovenia, was a Soviet-trained soldier who took the *nom de guerre* of Tito and nurtured a Himalayan-sized ambition to rule Yugoslavia. A vain and greedy man, he changed clothes several times a day and amassed a ridiculous amount of stuff: 32 private residences – including hunting lodges, islands and palaces – two sea-going yachts, two river yachts, a private train, and more. His vision for Yugoslavia left room for neither nationalism nor tolerance for ethnic diversity. You were either with Tito or you were against him. He counted as his enemies Germans, Italians, Croatian fascists (Ustaše), Slovenian collaborators and Serbian monarchists (Četniks). Eventually he would also include Stalin in that bunch.

But the fact that he was a strong supporter of the Partisans, those brave men and women who had effectively liberated Yugoslavia from the invaders, made Tito a postwar hero. When he ordered the Partisans to slaughter any soldier or collaborator rolling back in from Austria after the war, they did as they were told.

His gun-barrel approach to rule continued for several years after the war ended, and the atmosphere throughout Yugoslavia was one of fear and trepidation. "Brotherhood and Unity" was his official doctrine, but it would have been more accurate if he had operated under the slogan of "Power and Control," for power was much more important to him than reconciliation. His was a one-man, single-party state. He systematically and brutally carried out purges of

Serbs, Croatians, Slovenians, Macedonians and Albanians – anyone who showed the least sign of separatism. More than ten thousand of his imagined enemies were sent to his island concentration camp on Goli Otok, where they were tortured and starved, and an estimated four thousand were killed. The camp was closed in 1988 and was completely deserted by 1989.

As Tito's iron grip softened – around the same time his relationship with Stalin cooled – Yugoslavians, including climbers, were allowed passports to travel and work abroad. Many chose to work for their old enemies, Germany and Austria. In the southern states, the human exodus was primarily to Turkey, particularly from the Muslim community. Even within Yugoslavia, citizens were on the move, abandoning the poorest areas such as Kosovo and Macedonia for the more highly developed and prosperous states of Slovenia and Croatia. Others moved south, filling the gaps left in Kosovo and Bosnia by the fleeing Muslims.

The irony of this morbid history is that the Partisans, who had valiantly fought in the name of all Yugoslavians against the occupying Fascist forces and collaborators, eventually morphed into something else entirely – Tito's army. Under his forceful guidance, they turned on their fellow citizens: hounded them, murdered them and expelled them from the country, all in the name of Brotherhood and Unity. Wartime, civil war and postwar casualties number at least one million, and 90 per cent of them were Yugoslavians killed by other Yugoslavians.

When the messiest work was done, a veil was drawn and silence reigned. The revisionist line was that Yugoslavia was "healing from the war"; Socialism was the salve, and Tito the benevolent leader. On the surface, life did improve, but citizens were generally reluctant to undertake the painful process of self-examination relative to the wartime atrocities. This turned out to be a critical missing step in the reconciliation process. In the end, the healing was only superficial, and the scars were still fresh. It wouldn't take long before the bleeding began anew.

THREE

A Lesson in Patience

The Alpine Association of Slovenia is no modest enterprise: it oversees nine thousand kilometres of trail, 176 huts, 25 professional mountaineering and mountain-safety training programs, 284 alpine clubs and almost 60,000 members. All this in a country of just two million people. One of the oldest alpine associations in Europe, it was founded on the last day of February in 1893 to promote and preserve Slovenian national identity in the mountain areas in the wake of aggressive hut-building by the German Alpine Club. But it soon began developing Slovenia's distinctive mountaineering strength and became the most active association of its kind in Yugoslavia.

The club set up a training program for aspiring alpinists that consisted of a series of courses, and then formalized three levels of qualified alpinists: regional, national and international. The association also organized international expeditions, sending out notices of upcoming climbs to interested members. The core of the team would usually consist of five or six experienced climbers who had already been tried and tested on the most difficult routes. A chart would then be prepared with all the relevant criteria by which the remaining applicants' climbing experiences could be evaluated: difficulty level, winter or summer, and altitudes reached. From 60 applicants, the top 30 would undergo a series of physical tests to determine the final team. But even though the process appeared highly structured, choosing the right climbers was difficult.

Mountaineering is not strictly competitive, with clear winners and losers, and trying to predict the team dynamics between individual climbers from various clubs left those in power with room to manoeuvre. As a result, clubs and climbers vied for attention.

Despite being less affluent than other European countries, Slovenia produced, through this system, some of the strongest and most skilled alpinists of the 1970s and 1980s. Following the 1960 Trisul climb, two more expeditions headed east to the Himalaya. A team of seven travelled to 7903-metre-high Kangbachen in 1965, and Aleš led a successful team to Annapurnas II and IV in 1969. But the real action was still to come.

◆ ◆ ◆

Makalu, fifth-highest mountain in the world at 8485 metres, is just 19 kilometres southeast of Mount Everest and has a dramatic pyramidal shape. After a couple of attempts in 1954 by American and New Zealand teams, it was climbed in 1955 by French climbers Lionel Terray and Jean Couzy. Their line of ascent was up the North Face to the East Ridge. Fifteen years later, a Japanese team climbed the Southeast Ridge, and one year after that, in 1971, the French returned to climb the West Pillar. But nobody had even considered the forbiddingly steep South Face.

The 1970s were a time of transition in the great ranges, when the most ambitious Himalayan climbers turned their eyes from the more obvious (and easier) lines – the ridges and buttresses – to the massive faces that were constantly swept by rock and icefall. British climbers initiated the charge, under the guidance of Chris Bonington. In 1970 he led a team up the South Face of Annapurna, and two years later he was eyeing Everest's Southwest Face.

At the time, the Slovenian newcomers were still feeling their way, but that didn't stop them from thinking on a grand scale, thanks in large part to Aleš Kunaver. He was the one who refused to allow the past to limit his dreams for the future. He was the one who believed in the skills of Slovenian climbers, honed on the steep walls of the Julian Alps in both summer and winter. When wandering the valleys of Nepal, scouting for climbs, his eyes didn't linger on the easier lines or the routes already climbed. Instead, he fixed his gaze on the great unclimbed walls. Those, he believed, were where Slovenia's Himalayan future lay. His passion was shared by Nejc, who wrote in *Pot*:

> Nothing but mountains as far as the eye can see. Bold rocky pinnacles, glaciers, great ice-covered slopes of the highest mountains of the world. The groaning of ice beneath me, snowstorms, cold polar nights, the dying murmur of a glacial stream slowly turned into ice by the cold, and wind that is trying to tear you off the ground and toss you into the abyss. Your friends' exhausted faces and their glowing eyes, frozen beards, frostbitten fingers, the crackling of the fire, a softly hummed song, tiny articulations in the rock showing you the way, a feeling of weightlessness, roads, trails, airports, children, home, work, nights without sleep, mud up to the knees, rain, leeches, fear, courage, hard training day after day, partying, a crazy race, the slow, quiet tread of a lone traveller, success, happiness, sadness, disappointment, death, drudgery without rest, lazing around, a warm home, love, danger, adventure…all this is my life.[11]

And so, in September 1972, Aleš was at Makalu's South Face with a team of 14 of Slovenia's best. Among them were Stane Belak (Šrauf) and a young, sharp-eyed climber, Danilo Cedilnik. A mountain guide and rescue specialist, Danilo was also a painter and author, bringing a sensitivity to the team as he observed and recorded the goings-on from an artist's perspective.

Joining the group was 22-year-old Marjan Manfreda, hailing from the heart of the Julian Alps. Lean and hard, dark-haired and swarthy, with a fierce intensity in his eyes, Marjan was born in 1950 in the tiny hillside village of Bohinjska Bela, the second of three children. His father worked in a steel plant down in the Sava River valley, commuting each day on the local train that clattered past the family's front door. Originally from Opicina, a border area just inside Italy, his father was actually conscripted into the Italian army – the enemy – during the Second World War. He was captured by the Americans in Sardinia in 1943 and served his prison time in the kitchen.

Marjan was a natural climber, often bouldering among the cliffs near his village after school. His first climbing experience didn't bode well, however. Spying a carabiner left behind by some soldiers high on a cliff above his home, he climbed up, pulled on it and promptly fell to the ground below. He regained consciousness later that night but suffered from a broken collarbone and a concussion. With his signature wry sense of humour, he later credited this day as having been the most important in his climbing career: "If I had gotten myself killed, I would have been obliged to stop climbing."[12]

At the age of 16, Marjan joined a group of friends in Paklenica, the rock-climbing mecca on the Croatian coast where fluted, razor-sharp limestone walls rise up from the Velika Paklenica canyon. There, he attempted the difficult Klin route on the Anića Kuk wall, and failed. He and his partner returned for an easier line, but when the latter took a nasty fall while leading, it was left to Marjan to finish the route. This was his turning point. Climbing first on the rope, discovering the holds, feeling that surge of adrenalin, at 16 years, he knew he would be a climber.

A year later he was testing himself in the Tatras Mountains along the Czech–Polish border, and in 1968 he was invited on an official trip to the Caucasus, where he climbed Kazbek, his first five-thousand-metre peak. The following year he walked a few steps from his house to catch the local train to Ljubljana, boarded another train to Martigny, Switzerland, and then took the narrow-gauge railway up to Chamonix, the centre of climbing in the French Alps. The journey took two days. He stayed one month, camping illegally next to the cemetery. When he was evicted, he moved over to the garbage dump. It was all about the climbing: Les Droites, the Brenva Spur and more classic lines on impeccable granite.

During his army stint, which lasted 18 months, he was lucky to score mountain duty, instructing and climbing in Montenegro and the Julian Alps. In January 1971 he returned to his village to work on the railway, his head swimming with unrealistic dreams of climbing full-time. Then in 1972 Aleš invited him to join the team going to Makalu. Marjan couldn't believe his good fortune.

♦ ♦ ♦

The team of ten climbers, three scientists and one journalist arrived at the base of Makalu in early September. Together with dozens of barefoot porters, they set up base camp and began preparing for the climb. But which route? They gathered in the cook tent after dinner to discuss their options. Aleš spoke first. "Boys, we have two possibilities. We can focus on the summit by the easiest route or we can try the South Face." He knew his climbers, and he knew what they had climbed. He felt they were capable of solving the technical difficulties on the face, but nobody knew what cumulative effect the cold, wind, altitude and exhaustion would have on them. Would fatigue cloud their judgment on the wall? Would the sheer magnitude of the project defeat them? The scale of the unknown was both tempting and intimidating.

Aleš would not make this decision alone. He reminded them that the Slovenian ascents of Trisul, Kangbachen and the Annapurnas had been on less difficult routes. This face would present something quite different: a massive Himalayan wall, starting at the altitude of 6200 metres and rearing up more than two thousand metres. They all knew that the British had triumphed on the South Face of Annapurna and now had their sights set on Everest's Southwest Face. But succeeding on Makalu's South Face would also be something truly great.

As the evening wore on, like a meandering river that begins to straighten its course, their discussion zeroed in on the decision at hand. Aleš asked each climber's opinion and encouraged them to be honest. One by one they responded. "If a person could be sure that we wouldn't get stuck somewhere below the summit, then I'd vote for the face...The face is a more beautiful goal...I like the face better...I vote for the face." [13]

Although pleased with the response, Aleš felt obliged to warn them of what might lie ahead. "You have to know that the Japanese expedition in 1970 took 65 days to climb the Southeast Ridge. They had 16 climbers and 25 Sherpas, and still, it was not enough time." [14] They agreed that a reconnaissance was the best strategy: one team up the ridge and a second team on the unclimbed face. They would reconvene at the end of the day and decide on their route.

That day ended. They met, and they decided. It would be the South Face.

By the middle of October they had secured two thousand metres of fixed lines, nailed countless pitons into the rock and ice, and set up their high camps. The climbing was difficult, but setting up the camps was even harder, for the face was so steep they had to hack out small, exposed terraces in the rock and snow for each site. The winds some-times reached 190 kilometres per hour, battering the vulnerable camps. Heavy snow buried their tents, and they even managed to burn one down. They learned a new language – the language of the face. A curt shout, a wave of the hand. It was all the climbers needed to warn one another of a hurtling stone or piece of ice or an incoming avalanche.

Finally the last camp was pitched at eight thousand metres. Above it, the ropes were fixed to the end of the difficult climbing. After 50 days on the South Face, they were ready for the final push. Šrauf reflected on their efforts: "What does it all mean? Pointless risk-taking is what many would say...And what about our mountain? It's a goal beautiful enough to make up for everything that I have experienced and have yet to experience on this mountain."[15] Climbing this face would become the formative experience against which Šrauf's entire future would be measured.

The face became shrouded in snow flurries. On October 19 Marjan descended to Camp I, his fingers black with frostbite. He was one of the star climbers on this trip, pushing the route upward through steep, dangerous ground, but two fingers froze in the process. This, his first experience with frostbite, was minor in comparison to what he would endure in the future. Meanwhile, Šrauf carried a load of food to Camp IV. The weather forecast predicted 160-kilometre winds and −38°C for the upper part of the mountain. Teams of climbers were poised at various camps on the face, but there was a critical gap in this human chain, placing the summit team at risk. Aleš intended to fill that gap.

He filled his pack with equipment, including a camera and rolls of film, and left base camp early. He reached Camp I, stopped for a short rest and stuffed a few more provisions into his already-overloaded pack. He stopped at Camp II and saw without asking that the climbers were emaciated, tired and dejected. The next morning he continued up, marvelling at the unrelenting steepness. Not a single spot on which to sit and rest, only snowfields, rock and ice. "In the mountains, magnificence is diametrically opposed to comfort," he later recalled.[16] Darkness crept up from the shadowy valley, the remaining rays of sunlight reserved for those chosen to climb up toward the sun.

Meanwhile, those chosen ones – Matija Maležič and Janez Ažman (Janko) – were now in Camp V, poised for the first summit attempt. They struggled to keep the tent upright against the force of the shrieking wind. Uncomfortable, tired and dehydrated, they concentrated on the only thing they could alleviate – their thirst. They melted snow by the hour and drank countless cups of tea, well aware that only two functioning rope teams remained on the face, two days' climbing distance apart. It was now late October, and the first signs of the coming winter were visible: fishtail-shaped clouds above Makalu, mist seeping up from the valleys, followed by a bubbling mass of blue-black clouds. They understood the signs but chose to ignore them, since they were the highest ones on the mountain and were so close to their goal.

While they were at Camp V, Aleš reached Camp IV. He had planned, together with Danilo Cedilnik, to bring more equipment and three bottles of oxygen up to Camp V. But Danilo's face was swollen with edema, and he was racked with violent coughs. Next morning they crept out of the tent to see the sun suspended like a brilliant gem on an invisible chain. "During such moments a person forgets he is just a part of a machine working toward a single common goal," Aleš thought. "For one moment you become a climber, climbing upward, enjoying the freedom of motion, the void beneath your feet, the sun and the wind."[17] It was clear that Danilo was too weak to make it to Camp V, but he agreed to climb as high as he could and then wait for Aleš's return.

When Aleš arrived at Camp V, he yelled out. "Janko. Matija. Are you there? Hello?" There was only silence. Good sign. They must be climbing higher up. As he scanned the vast horizon, he felt twinges of regret. How nice it would be to stay up here, to realize his own personal dreams, to forget about being a leader and just climb – bold and strong – maybe to the summit. But he reined in his thoughts, unloaded his pack, wrote a quick note and slid down the fixed ropes to Danilo. It was all he could do. Now it was up to the boys.

In the eyes of his team, Aleš's actions represented something akin to a miracle. All those weeks of organizing, cajoling, strategizing, encouraging, humping loads and fixing lines. Then, after more than 50 days, when he knew there was a break in the chain of climbing teams, when energy levels were so low that the expedition was in danger of collapsing, he summoned the will to load up his pack, leave base camp, and climb, climb and climb some more. All the way to Camp V. Always with the sure knowledge that the summit would not be his. All for his team. That was leadership.

Janko and Matija had left Camp V the same morning and headed up. The wind knocked them over, threatening to tear them off the face. They came first to a snowfield, about one hundred metres long, and then to a chimney. They fixed ropes to the edge of a ledge that provided an exit from the face, somewhere between 8100 and 8200 metres. Almost at the summit ridge, they turned back, confident that they had reconnoitred the area and would continue the next day with oxygen. While returning to camp, they saw someone leaving: it was Aleš who had brought them the precious oxygen. Everything and everyone was in its proper place.

But the impending storm had waited long enough. Snow began to fall heavily, and with an ominous sense of worse to come. There was no need for discussion. Janko and Matija packed up, preparing to abandon their high camp. Heavy snow would mean avalanches, and it was still a long way down to safety. The climb was over.

The great Maha Kali, the divine mistress of Makalu, was already tearing the ropes from her frozen flanks: three kilometres of rope was too much for the freedom-loving goddess. She swept the face with blizzards and avalanches, cleansing the rocks of any human trace. Two by two, the climbers retreated off the mountain, loaded down like mules. Makalu disappeared behind a curtain of white. The climbers could sense its presence, but they could not see it. There was no chance to even say goodbye.

As the storm raged on, a single file of barefoot porters snaked off into the murk, staggering through snowdrifts on what had been a trail just two months before. Several became snow-blind, and others abandoned their heavy loads. It continued to snow. A few porters developed frostbite, yet still they marched on. After six days they saw a patch of green – the valley below. When they bade the climbers goodbye, one of the porters threw out a challenge: "Come again! Makalu will still be here!"

The South Face. It had been an ambitious goal, and the climbers had spent more than 60 days on the wall. Difficult climbing. Complicated route finding. Terrible weather. Camps that were repeatedly destroyed by storms, wind and avalanches. Fixed lines that were ripped out by falling ice. Still, they had come within 50 metres of the ridge, where there was easier ground. They had climbed without oxygen above eight thousand metres. Not without sacrifice, though, for Marjan's frostbite was severe. But nobody died on Makalu's South Face in 1972.

The climbers returned home feeling confused and baffled by the face. Was the goddess of Makalu punishing them? Or did they simply need a lesson in patience? As Nejc Zaplotnik wrote in *Pot*:

> I have been taught many things by people halfway around the world who struggle for a handful of rice and a miserable, half-collapsed roof over their heads…They taught me how to wait for love and how to love waiting, which is more beautiful than the act itself. They taught me how to find joy in the little things that at first sight appear so perfectly ordinary, rather than hunger for the great events at the very limits of my existence. I learned that I can achieve even that which seems infinitely far away, the unattainable, if only I am willing to be as infinitely patient and to submit myself to an equally unattainable yearning.[18]

While the team struggled with their defeat on Makalu's South Face, a new crop of Slovenian climbers was preparing for the next challenge. They had no delusions about punishing goddesses. They were too busy getting fit and racing around the Julian Alps, climbing as much as they possibly could. Among them was Nejc Zaplotnik. And although he showed great promise as an alpinist, nobody could have imagined then the profound influence he would have on future generations of climbers.

Nejc was born on April 15, 1952, in the small village of Rupa, where he, his parents and two siblings all shared a cramped two-room apartment. A vibrant red church tower dominated the village, whose dramatic backdrop was the shining mountains of the Karavankan and Kamnik Alps. On the other side of the valley, far to the west, loomed the sharp ridges of the Julian Alps, Slovenia's highest mountains.

Nejc had been a sickly child, suffering from the autoimmune disorders celiac disease and rheumatoid arthritis. "They had already put a cross over me," he recalled of his parents' and doctor's pessimism about his chances for survival.[19] He could eat very little; his body ached, and he caught every disease that drifted through the valley. He was so small that people hardly noticed him. Although he was thin as a reed, his swollen, bloated stomach was "white, like a dead fish turned onto its back."[20]

Once, while bedridden in the hospital with scarlet fever, he was fed oranges and bananas, the only foods his delicate system could handle. The other sick children stared with envy at these expensive delicacies, but Nejc longed for their aromatic, crusty Portuguese rolls. Finally, fed up with his monkey food, he opened a black market: for every roll he would trade two bananas, or one banana and an orange.

His mother was a cleaning lady who instilled in Nejc the sense of pride that comes from humble work done well. His father was a tailor. Nejc remembered him sewing and mending, his spectacles perched on the edge of his nose. He would push the thread down, then pull it back up through the worn rags of clothing, hour after hour, late into the night. While sewing, he would tell stories and the kids would crowd around him. "Quiet, slow, monotonous, just like the needle...his words opened the world of witches, heroes, rich and poor people to us children," Nejc recalled.[21]

He may not have looked like much, but puny Nejc had another life – almost a secret life. Each summer he spent a month at his cousin's farm at the base of Grintovec, the highest mountain in the Kamnik Alps. Here was his spiritual home, where nature ignited in him a sense of awe. The hard work on the farm, hunting chamois in the forest, riding horses and scrambling on the rocks – living in a natural environment simply made him feel good, not sickly at all. The harder he worked and played, the better he felt. He herded animals, scythed hay, plowed fields, harvested grain and hauled lumber. "I learned that if you want nature to accept you, you have to work hard and be alive," he later wrote.[22]

There, at his cousin's farm in the shadow of Grintovec, he had his first encounter with mountaineers. While raking the golden, sweet-scented pasture hay, he and his cousins eyed the red-faced climbers with their heavy packs, lugging themselves up into the hills. When the climbers paused and speculated with the elders about the weather, the kids sidled up for the chocolates and sweets that were sure to come. His aunt gave the mountaineers bowls of sour milk, and *mosht* (young wine) for their flasks. And off they went to those unbelievable heights. What courage, Nejc thought.

When Nejc was 9, his cousins took him up Grintovec. The overwhelming exposure excited him. He stepped to the edge of the void, grabbed onto a rock outcrop and yodelled as high and loudly as he could until his cousin Peter explained that in the mountains it is better to "receive sounds than give them."[23]

He next took up skiing, starting with skis his neighbour had constructed out of two boards with leather-strap bindings. Nejc added rubber boots to complete the package. Unfortunately the boards weren't curved, so arriving at the bottom of the hill was a somewhat abrupt experience. He learned to jump out of his rubber boots at the precise moment the skis slammed to a stop. He tried ski jumping next, but soon gave it up. "I was very decisive and safe in the air but the landing on hard Mother Earth was never successful."[24]

All of this was great fun for Nejc, but school was not. He spent as little time there as possible, for freedom was sacred to him. Freedom was working in the fields, shepherding the sheep, wandering around in the canyons – this was Nejc's world. Everything else was an evil necessity. Despite his distaste for school, he devoured books. His father eventually unscrewed the light bulb in Nejc's bedroom to encourage the boy to get some sleep. But Nejc learned that a good flashlight under his blanket worked just as well, allowing him the freedom to read through the night. The subject of the book didn't matter: fairy tales, adventure stories, serious literature. Books opened his eyes and stimulated his already active imagination. He was hungry for foreign places and wild experiences. For a young lad, Nejc understood himself quite well: "As long as I could read, smell the plowed earth, manure and hay, could run around the pastures and forests, I was happy."[25]

Then came puberty, the difficult and beautiful age when you don't know what you want to be and everything seems possible. That's when Nejc's problems started. First at school and then with his father, who recoiled from both Nejc's independent nature and his values. Life at home became chaotic. "No one understood that, within me, there was an energy boiling that the devil himself was afraid of," Nejc later wrote. "I was looking for my own path of freedom and independence."[26] This search would consume him throughout his life, and he would write about it with great eloquence.

The first time Nejc went to Triglav, he swore to his father that he would only walk. No climbing, he promised. But he and his closest friend and fellow altar boy, Tone Perčič, did just that on Triglav and Krisakpod and Razor and Prisijoke, the soaring grey limestone peaks of the Julian Alps. They became addicted to precipices and exposure.

Nejc's love of books deepened at the same time. Whenever he discovered a new author, he would read everything he could get his hands on, including the author's letters and essays. He devoured Hermann Buhl and Maurice Herzog, whose climbing accounts fired his ambition and simultaneously offered a balm for his turbulent soul. Their stories ultimately led him to a gathering at the local section of the mountaineering club. There, he and Tone stood scrunched in a corner, listening to the experienced climbers telling their tales.

As the lure of the mountains strengthened, so did his ability to describe his experiences. As he wrote in *Pot*:

I go from one rock face to the next, most often with Tone, but occasionally alone. At night I don't turn on the headlamp. It's beautiful to just feel your way along the path and give yourself up to your senses, to a force of some kind that guides you through the darkness. The first storm is arriving at the wall. Friends are anxious, hurrying, getting all tangled up in their pitons and jumbles of ropes, while I sit and drink in the splendour of nature. Fat droplets of rain caress my hot face. Close by, thunder rolls and lightning flashes merge into a blinding curtain. My hair is crackling and standing on end. Everything is so magnificent it's a bit of a shame when the thunderstorm disappears toward the east. Every now and then I sit awhile in the hut, as quiet singing echoes through mysterious evenings, full of restlessness before an ascent. Folk song always transports me into the past, to the mysterious life of my ancestors, people who loved their land, people who had no choice but to work hard for their very existence, risking even their lives to survive.[27]

Nejc and Tone soon began heading off on their own, even in winter. Stol, Storžič and Grintovec. All respectable summits. They fashioned pitons that they then had to learn how to use. They discovered discarded ice axes and restored them. They trained and became fit. And when Nejc fell in love for the first time, it was on top of Grintovec. "She grabbed my axe and I helped her to the top. We fell in love so hard it was intense."[28] Any remaining interest in school vanished.

Instead, Nejc enrolled in a climbing school and learned the various knots and belaying techniques, how to place protection in the rock and how to free climb, without using the aid of the rope. Even more important, while herding sheep on Grintovec, he learned how to move quickly and surely on descents, a skill that not only saved his life on numerous occasions, but also saved him from frostbite. On weekends he and Tone climbed in the Julian Alps, rain or shine, fog or snow. They often got lost, barely catching the last midnight train back home. Mondays found them dozing in class, mistakenly chastised by their teachers for weekend partying. Nejc's life became an obsessive cycle of constant motion: pedalling his bike to the mountains in the early mornings, then working in the forests, pedalling back to Kranj in the afternoon, playing tennis until evening, reading until midnight – and repeating as necessary.

But the forests held a hidden danger. Ticks. Nejc was bitten by one and became infected with meningitis. It was while he was climbing that the disease hit. Stiff, weak, shivering and struck by a crippling headache, he struggled not to fall. Finally, back in the valley, he was hospitalized and treated for the debilitating illness. Two months of complete rest, his doctor ordered. Impossible! He ignored the advice, and years later he regretted what he had forced his parents to endure. "It must have been difficult to have a son like this. But Mother...was a person of dreams and desires, like me...I didn't consider whether meningitis could come back or not. All I knew was that I had to return to the mountains. Otherwise I would get an even worse, more difficult and incurable disease – the rotting of the soul."[29]

He and Tone hitchhiked to Tamar, a serrated limestone beauty in the Julian Alps. They slept out in the damp, chilly nights without tents, sleeping bags or mats. They climbed to the pyramidal summit of Jalovec and up Spicek's spiny ridge in dense fog, and then they continued on to other peaks, traversing their narrow, rocky summits and wandering through meadows carpeted by pure white edelweiss. In the middle of a torrential rainstorm, they broke into a hunter's cabin for a dry, peaceful night, then they carried on to more peaks, exploring every metre, sometimes flummoxed by sections too difficult for them, retreating, retrenching, all the while gaining valuable experience.

A friendly shepherd invited them into his hut and fed them polenta made from thick sheep's milk. They stuffed their undernourished stomachs and slept like the dead on a bed of leaves covered with sheepskins. As fall advanced, the valleys became smothered in a blanket of fog, but the boys were high on the ridges, basking in the precious autumn sun and the reflected glow of golden larches, beech leaves and white limestone walls. The climbing seasons were never long enough for Nejc.

> The season is coming to an end but inside I am bursting with the energy of youth. Sometimes I feel I could smash up the local joint "Brioni" were it not for the fact that I'm going climbing tomorrow... Hitchhiking again. On this occasion I run into problems with a German homosexual. Handsome guy, there's no denying it...Too bad I'm not his sort. He probably thinks that we Yugoslavians are cheap southern goods, but he made a mistake. I can't wait to get to Mojestrana.[30]

Surviving his youth was something of a miracle, as he didn't recognize danger in the mountains; all he saw was beauty. He cavorted on exposed alpine terrain like a young calf, banging into things, slipping and sliding, learning the hard way. But whenever he returned to the valley, his body carried a lightness of spirit.

When Nejc was finally accepted into the Alpine Association of Slovenia as an alpinist, he was faced with the usual barbaric hazing process that accompanies such an achievement. His new colleagues beat him and forced him to drink copious quantities of alcohol. He later wrote that it was "the first time in my life I felt the charm of alcoholic vapours, which, after that, I gave a few years' special attention to."[31]

Life was full. Perhaps too full. He tried – unsuccessfully – to live at what musicians call *tempo giusto*, or the right speed. But trouble arrived in the love department. His girlfriend, whom he had met in the mountains, was now annoyed that the mountains demanded so much of his time. Like countless alpinists before and after him, he had to choose: mountains or love. He couldn't understand how anyone could claim to love him and yet want to pull him away from the mountains. They were his life. That would be like loving a corpse, not a complete human being. "To love me is difficult," he admitted, but his path was clear. The mountains were calling him, and not just for weekend pleasure. They were waiting for him to commit.

> On a hidden clearing veiled by heavy curtains of slim fir trees,
> I halt, gather brushwood and build a fire
> To warm my cold soul.
> It turned cold because of the race that life forced upon me.
> Dry wood crackles and throws tongues of flames
> Toward the black sky.
> Around the fire, strange figures from the ancient past begin to dance
> And the muffled footsteps of gypsies
> Passing through my heart remind me
> Of a fairy tale that is soon to become reality.
> The swaying of women's hips
> Did not warm me back then,
> For Plato was my father.
> But he went and left me
> With these yearning flames a fairy tale come true.
> A fairy tale so beautiful I became afraid of tomorrow!
> I was called by a sighing, gentle woman's voice,
> Calling so clearly I had to respond.
> And even today
> The fairy tale still lives on below the white sugar cone,
> Although the fire was extinguished by force
> And the flames of longing were forced to devour themselves![32]

Despite the long, lonely months that followed the painful breakup, his decision was final. "Whoever is willing to accept me for who I am, only this person truly loves me. I will not change for anybody."[33] Eighteen months later he met Mojca – still a teenager – with her thick mane of hair and wide-open smile. Within a short period of time they married and started a family, and Nejc landed a full-time job in a bank. There, he pushed a mountain of paper and withered in its shadow. His life appeared calm, but beneath the surface were the familiar irreconcilable emotions. His was the struggle of all conflicted alpinists: work, family, responsibility and, always, the siren call of the mountains. He was terrified of losing that special feeling of lightness and peace the mountains gave him.

> Day after day I sit at the window in a smoky office. Darkness falls quietly on the bustling city streets, only the mountains still glow scarlet. Their blinding light falls directly onto my miserable window. Women's chatter, rattling away like a coffee grinder, washes over me amidst the clacking of adding machines and the rustling of paper. My co-workers are beautifully adjusted to me, so perfectly that they never even notice me. How I would like to share with them at least some of the yearnings and hopes and blue horizons within me...How poor must these people be, sitting there wreathed in cigarette smoke, discussing their salaries, new clothes and cars. Right now...while the mountains are glowing in the setting sun.[34]

Like many other Slovenian climbers, Nejc's hopes and dreams went far beyond his miserable office window, beyond the Julian Alps, all the way to the Himalaya, to Makalu, where a great adventure awaited those who were prepared.

FOUR

Friends Like These

As daylight faded and the bitter cold of night crept in, Stane Belak (Šrauf) and Marjan Manfreda took shelter in their tent at Camp V. It was October 5, 1975, and the pair was at eight thousand metres, high on the South Face of Makalu, thirsty as camels in the desert. Šrauf melted snow on the stove and Marjan tinkered with the oxygen bottles. Four bottles, each weighing six kilograms, had been lugged up with enormous effort to this highest camp. Each canister was fitted with two pressure-reducing valves, a regulating rubber bladder, masks and tubes – a complicated system that was critical to their attempt on the mountain. Lost in daydreams while staring at the hissing stove, Šrauf was stunned when Marjan announced, "This canister is empty!"[35] He fumbled with the other bottles, examining the gauges. They emitted a slight hissing sound, as if the oxygen was leaking. He could not pinpoint the problem. Was it the bottle? The valve? Frustrated, he lashed out: "I can hardly believe…this is really happening. Is this the end? Will we be forced to turn back here, just below the summit? Not because we have exhausted our strength, but because of a technical glitch? No, that would be too cruel!"[36] Šrauf and Marjan twisted and wiggled and adjusted the valves, but they could not stop the leakage. They were left with three bottles and just one functioning valve. Too much oxygen for one climber, but not enough for two.

Suddenly the summit seemed remote. Šrauf grabbed the radio and begged base camp to respond to his urgent, raspy message. But the only sounds were the wind and the static. With the radio stuck to Šrauf's ear, they made it through the long night. Toward morning, the wind died down as they waited in gloomy silence for the first thin light. Šrauf radioed base camp at the predetermined time and told Aleš the bad news. Aleš's reply was clear and unequivocal: "One of you should go to the summit with full equipment; the other should follow with backup for as long as he can."[37]

Now they were faced with the most difficult decision of the entire expedition—maybe of their lives. After a short discussion, Marjan offered to relinquish his chance at the summit. He would climb with Šrauf for as long as he could without using supplemental oxygen and would carry the extra canisters for Šrauf's use further up the mountain. Šrauf was crushed by Marjan's generosity. But he stifled his emotions. He realized that there was now no question of his turning back. He simply had to reach the summit. For the team. For Marjan.

◆ ◆ ◆

A year after having returned from Makalu in 1972, the team's perspective of their failure to reach the top had changed. Aleš was philosophical about their effort: "There wasn't just one summit, there were several…The face was interspersed with our own personal summits…We gave our best to the steepness, the wind, the snow and time, and together we achieved a major undertaking which surprised the connoisseurs in the alpinist circles."[38]

More than surprised them. Two expeditions had ventured out onto the South Face after their 1972 attempt: Reinhold Messner, as a member of a high-powered Austrian team; and an American-German team. Neither reached the 1972 high point. The teams even expressed some doubts about the Slovenian claims, but when some of their equipment was found just below the exit gully, the naysayers were silenced.

Now, three years later, the Slovenians were back. The South Face, which had been completely obscured by snow and fog in those last days of retreat in 1972, came back into view, just as grand and complex and alluring as before. Aleš had assembled a 21-person team, including several veterans from 1972 – those who had already proven themselves on the face, among them Marjan Manfreda, Šrauf and Danilo Cedilnik. But there were others for whom this was their first

Himalayan climb. Aleš didn't see himself merely as an expedition leader. He was developing a climbing program in Slovenia that mentored ambitious and talented young climbers. Each one had made a number of impressive ascents back home and had kept careful score of his achievements. From the moment they joined the Makalu 1975 expedition, however, every bit of knowledge and strength and experience became joint property, collective capital for the purpose of the common goal: the South Face of Makalu.

◆ ◆ ◆

One of the youngsters Aleš chose to join the 1975 Makalu team was 23-year-old Viki Grošelj, a future Himalayan powerhouse. Fair-haired and blue-eyed, Viki was born in 1952 in a house located just a hundred metres from his current home in Gunclje, now a suburb of Ljubljana. It was a small village in 1952, perhaps one hundred people and as many cows and horses.

His parents were profoundly affected by the Second World War. His father, Rock, was expected to join the Partisans near the start of the war, since the area outside Ljubljana was a Partisan stronghold. Rock wasn't a German sympathizer, but he wasn't keen on the Partisans, either. He preferred to wait and see what the war would bring. In the meantime, his girlfriend and future wife, Maria, was captured and taken prisoner to a farm in Germany where she did housework, looked after the children and fed the livestock – unpaid, of course.

When Rock learned that she had been captured, he went to Germany to look for her. Upon finding her, he remained and worked as a carpenter nearby. Within two years he was forced to participate in the local defence – on the German side – building barricades against a coming British division. The Americans arrived first and captured the Germans, including Rock. He was sent to England to join the overseas Yugoslavian army and returned to Slovenia after the war, clad in a British uniform. Rock wasn't the only Slovenian who briefly took part on the German side. The father of another Slovenian climber, Tomo Česen, was forced to fight in the German army on the Russian front. He was eventually injured and finally escaped, but it took two weeks of hitchhiking, hiding in forests and hopping trains to get home. So many complicated and unnatural allegiances.

The years immediately following the war were treacherously dangerous in Slovenia. You could be accused of being either a German sympathizer or a Partisan-hater. Viki's wife's grandfather was killed simply because his neighbour concocted a story that had him sympathizing with the Germans. The facts were quite different. He was a butcher. When the Partisans came through his village, he gave them meat. When the Germans came through, he did the same. There was no choice. But when Tito gave the order to kill all collaborators, he was one of them.

Rock had better luck. Back from the war, he and Maria married and started a family. Rock worked as a carpenter, and Maria gardened. For years their garden sustained them. That and the forest, where wild blueberries grew. Rock and Maria's family picked blueberries each morning and sold them at the local market, a bad memory for Viki. "I hate blueberries till this day because I had to pick them all the time. Every single morning. Very traumatic...I hated it. I just wanted to play."

Viki was not a prize student. In fact, he repeated Grade 6 for the simple reason that he was distracted. "I was so much in love with a girl in school that I couldn't even eat or sleep."

The family vacationed each year in the bucolic alpine meadows of Vila Paklanina, perched high above the Kamnik Valley. There, in a traditional wooden house nestled in undulating pastures, the family assumed a shepherd's life, wandering along the cow paths, eating creamy, fresh cheese and breathing the crisp alpine air. Viki enjoyed those rustic holidays, but something else grabbed his attention even more when he returned to the valley: people climbing rocks. With ropes. What's going on? he wondered. When he learned it was a climbing school, he approached his schoolteacher. Could he do it, too? The teacher agreed, but on one condition. He would need written permission from his parents. Easiest thing in the world. Viki went home, wrote out the permission slip and signed it. No point in bothering his parents.

He began climbing school after repeating Grade 6. Apart from the physical fun of clambering about on rock, the serious aspect of climbing interested him, too. Although the course was run by the Alpine Association of Slovenia, Viki later scoffed at the level of expertise. "They knew how to make a secure station, how to belay, how to put on crampons, but that was all. After that, we taught ourselves. Nobody knew anything about training." Šrauf was the captain of their club and was clearly number one, deciding where they would go and with whom they would climb. He motivated the youngsters to try bigger and higher and harder climbs, encouraging them to have ambitious goals.

Viki's mandatory service with the Yugoslav National Army was a dream assignment. The army asked him where he wanted to go. "To the mountains," he answered. For some reason, they listened, and for 16 months Viki enjoyed the best mountain holiday he could imagine in Bovič, a mountain paradise in the Julian Alps. He climbed and skied and became fit. His only official job was to assemble and install signs indicating the Yugoslav-Italian boundary. In 1972, while Viki was in Bovič, training to become an alpinist, Slovenia's finest climbers were on Makalu making their first attempt.

Viki's journey from novice climber to full-fledged alpinist took nine years. After his first serious climbs in Slovenia, he went with his club to Chamonix in France. Fourteen days of bad weather set them back a bit, but the camping experience alone left an indelible mark on him. Like so many poor, visiting climbers, the Slovenian group camped illegally behind the cemetery. The local gendarmerie would show up every second day, explain that camping was not allowed and then leave. Eventually, the gendarmerie gave in. They brought large garbage bags and politely asked if the visiting climbers could package up any refuse and take it down the street to the bins provided.

All the training in the Julian and French Alps paid off; when Viki was just 23 years old, Aleš invited him to join the team that would make a second attempt on Makalu in 1975. Viki had listened for hours to the 1972 climbers and felt he knew every inch of the wall. He acknowledged the visionary attempt of the first team, and he also understood the expectations of the 1975 expedition. "It was impossible for us not to climb it. We went with such self-confidence and commitment." Viki knew he was lucky to be invited and to be climbing with those who had been there before. He knew that his role was to support the senior climbers, not to reach the summit. Above all, he wanted Aleš to know, at the end of the expedition, that he had chosen well. This was not meant to be Viki's last Himalayan climb: he wanted a lifetime of climbs. Makalu would give him the chance to prove himself.

◆ ◆ ◆

The team reached base camp on September 5 and set up Camp I two days later. By the middle of September, Camp III was in place, and the climbers began fixing lines up to Camp IV. Over the next two weeks, however, storms and avalanches ripped out their fixed lines and destroyed Camps III and IV. Everyone retreated to base. It was like some kind of demented dance: one step forward, two steps back. But by the beginning of October, they had rebuilt both camps and were fixing lines again.

After climbing up and fixing rope above Camp V, the first summit team, Šrauf and Marjan, returned to find their little tent in ruins. When they had scrambled up the chimney above camp earlier that day, they had dislodged a huge amount of snow that had cascaded down on the tent, melted in the afternoon sun and subsequently frozen in the falling temperatures of early evening. The tent had disappeared under a solid lump of ice. After a day of incredible effort, climbing and fixing ropes at about eight thousand metres, they now had to dig out their tent. The wind roared down the slopes, lacerating their faces with bits of ice while they dug like madmen, tearing the shovel from each other's hands, so anxious were they to crawl inside and escape the elements. Only after two hours of digging could they repitch the tent. It was then, when they were finally sheltered and safe, that Šrauf and Marjan discovered the malfunctioning oxygen bottles. What more could go wrong?

On the morning of October 6, the two crawled out of their tent and started up, Šrauf with oxygen, Marjan without. The day stretched before them, sunny and clear, but their situation was serious, and they knew it. Everyone on the mountain was well aware that any thought of rescuing the pair above eight thousand metres on the south wall was delusional; it was simply too high. Any injury would be fatal. Above Camp V, there was no way to get help. Šrauf and Marjan only had each other.

They climbed up to a narrow avalanche slope, pure white, eerily pristine. At the top was a steep exit ramp. The moment was solemn and anxious. They would have to cross this deadly slope, above which tall slabs of granite protruded like an uneven row of teeth, etched against the black sky. The splendid view signalled to Šrauf that a magnificent climb was drawing to a close. But there was little time for reminiscing, because a huge, cantilevered snow cornice, almost a serac, was suspended among those granite slabs. He scurried across the avalanche path, stopping on the other side to calm his heart, which pounded with fear. Marjan watched silently from the other side, waiting for his turn to cross.

As Šrauf neared the top of the exit ramp, adrenalin pulsed through his body. He raced up the last few metres like a young mountain goat, pushing through the deep, powdery snow with a surge of power and confidence. Now that the endless work on this dangerous face was almost over, he anticipated a gentle snow slope to the summit. He stared down, gaping at the spot one hundred metres lower where the face disappeared into a funnel of nothingness, a deadly void. But where was Marjan? Šrauf flopped down and waited. He turned off his oxygen flow and immediately felt dizzy. When he looked up he was shocked to see that the snow-covered summit dome was still a long way off. Could it be an illusion? His thoughts drifted to Everest, now so visible, almost like a companion. Then he thought of the South Face they had just climbed. So many people had said it was impossible. Not fit for human beings. But here they were. Slovenian climbers had taken on this impossible mission and succeeded. The summit must surely be possible now.

As he waited for Marjan, his mind continued to wander. "It's funny how every moment seems like ancient history. At the altitude of 8200 metres, one becomes different. Or maybe this is because of a burning desire to progress further up the mountain until we reach that point where endless ridges converge and which, in a way…can mean more than your life." [39] He looked down and noticed a red helmet. It was resting. At this altitude, on the edge of survival, he felt a deep connection to Marjan: "How is he feeling? I myself am not feeling too great. My friend lacks something that allows me to think at all. Oxygen, this life-enabling substance, played a trick on us at the most crucial moment. Now my friend is doing his utmost to finish this ascent, which represents at the same time a once-in-a-lifetime athletic achievement, an inconceivable emotional burden and, last but not least, an act of national importance…My friend is lurching toward me. His face is full of suffering…What moments are these."[40]

Šrauf rested his head in the soft snow and whispered, "Marjan, it's ours! It's ours!"[41]

Meanwhile, step by step, Marjan climbed up the interminable snowfield toward Šrauf, gasping for oxygen, fully aware that his pack was weighed down by just that: bottled oxygen. The snowfield ended at the bottom of a steep, rocky chimney, the most difficult point on the entire face. He and Šrauf had fixed ropes up this section the day before, so he clipped in and hauled himself up. The effort left Marjan dangling from the rope like an empty sack, gulping for air. He began to lag, stopping to rest more often. Waves of fatigue washed over him. His lungs craved relief from the painful effort. But his heart insisted that he carry on, at least up to the ridge. From there he would be able to see Everest. It was this anticipated view that kept him going up to the rim. When he reached the top of those last steep metres he flopped down on the ridge.

There was Šrauf, waiting for him. As Marjan stared up at Makalu's narrow, snow-covered ridge arcing above them to the summit dome, he was overcome and wept with frustration. The summit that he yearned for was there, directly in front of him. But for the man *carrying* oxygen – not *using* it – it might as well have been on the moon.

Marjan said simply, "Šrauf, I want to come to the top."[42]

His words lay heavily on his companion's heart.

◆ ◆ ◆

As Marjan and Šrauf struggled above, Aleš was busy coordinating from below, calling each camp, checking on equipment.

Aleš: Calling IV. How's your oxygen?

Den (Danilo Cedilnik): Five out of eight canisters are okay. The pressure gauge reads 180 to 200. We've been considering that only two climbers should continue and that they should take four canisters with them.

Aleš: I suggest you all go to Camp V. You can make fast progress up

the ropes…I have one more suggestion: all four of you should climb
to the edge of the rock face, that way we'll have two men on the
rim and two on the summit.

Den: Good. We'll come to an agreement. This is an acceptable
suggestion.

Aleš: The next radio contact will be at 2:00 pm. Give this some
thought. Conditions are changing. In the Himalayas, ascents to
the rim of the rock face will count as much as they do in Europe.
Reaching the summit as well won't be a must any longer. This is why
any information on who reaches the rim of the face is of great
interest to us.[43]

Of all the climbers on Makalu's South Face, Aleš understood the
European standards of alpine climbing best. He knew, even back in
1972, that climbing Makalu by its normal route was not enough for
Yugoslavia to break into the rarefied air of the European alpine scene.
Only the South Face would do. He had seen the reaction – some of it
disbelief – when his team had climbed so high in 1972. Of course, this
year they would reach the summit, but he wanted to get as many
climbers to the top of the face as possible. This was important. He was
also aware that the British team, led by Chris Bonington, was over on
the Southwest Face of Everest. He could even hear their faint British
voices on the radio. Their story was similar to that of the Yugoslavians:
first attempt in 1972, back for another try in 1975. History was being
made on two great Himalayan faces at the same moment.

At 11:00 am the radio crackled from base camp. They could see
Šrauf reach the rim of the face and Marjan arrive not long after. Šrauf
heard the chatter, stood up, took off his pack and waved. The radio
came alive again. Whooping and hollering, base yelled, "Marjan, show
you're better than the Parisian!"[44] Šrauf looked at Marjan, who stared
back in stunned silence. They both understood. Four years before,
a French expedition had stood on this same spot after climbing
Makalu's West Pillar. One of the climbers, Jean-Paul Paris, had
reached 8300 metres without the use of bottled oxygen. These simple
words were a challenge for Marjan: to better the Frenchman's altitude
record. Maybe even go for the top!

Aleš came back on the radio. "Šrauf, we were going crazy here when you reached the ridge. Now you still have seven hours you can use to get to the summit. Tell the man from Bohinj [Marjan] that he can't let the Frenchman get the better of him. Call whenever you want to. We'll stay on the line at all times. It would be incredible if Marjan summited without oxygen. Help him, support him, encourage him!"[45]

The two rose from their snowy reprieve and turned to face the ridge soaring above them. The day was still. So quiet. Only soft whispers from the oxygen mask accompanied Šrauf's footsteps. The snow was deep, sometimes almost up to his waist. He wanted to make the ascent easy for Marjan, so he slowed the pace. Even so, Marjan couldn't keep up. Little by little, he fell behind. Aleš called again, urging Šrauf to wait for Marjan, to help him, to drag him if necessary.

Even in his hypoxic haze, Marjan now realized that the ridge seemed less steep. He could take as many as 40 steps at a time without resting. He caught up with Šrauf at the junction of the French and Japanese ridges. Slumped over his ice axe, he became aware that Šrauf was talking on the radio to base camp. Somehow, that connection brought a feeling of warmth; he had company up in this harsh environment, so high above the valley. But there was still a long way to go. How easy it would be to sit down. Stop thinking. Sleep. Then another voice spoke: Don't give up.

When he raised his head he was alone on the ridge. A deep, snowy trail led upward. Marjan straightened his back. He lurched to his feet, his exhaustion falling away just enough for him to stand. He lifted one leg and then the other. The broken trail made it easier. But now he needed several breaths between each step. This would take forever. His goal shifted from the summit to a point just a few metres ahead. When he reached that point, he reset his goal again. In this way he crawled up the ridge of Makalu, the fifth-highest mountain on Earth.

Šrauf stopped, leaned over his axe and watched Marjan toiling up the slope at a funereal pace. Oxygen, what a precious commodity. If you don't have enough oxygen, you are confused and weak. Reflexes are slow. Judgment is impaired. A mistake – even a small slip – would be fatal for Marjan in his state. As he came closer, Šrauf cheered him on, giving him courage. Marjan said nothing, simply took off his pack, gave the full oxygen canister to Šrauf and planted the empty one in the snow. Now his pack would be lighter. Šrauf switched on the new bottle.

Before them reared a steep rock step, the last puzzle on the route. Once again, the depth of their partnership revealed itself, for who was there to belay Šrauf if not Marjan? Who would carry the full oxygen bottle as backup for Šrauf if not Marjan? Šrauf looked at him: "Maybe he is aware of my feelings…the elder, rope-team member. I am ten years older. Or maybe he is aware of his own hidden strength…It's very beautiful to approach the summit with a friend like this. My friend's gasps for air are slowly calming down."[46] They orbited around each other, offering their strength, composure and support. Their love.

As Šrauf began climbing, the rock crumbled in his hands. Finally he was able to pound a piton into a small crack. With the tip of his ice axe he probed above for possible holds on the scaly, frost-covered granite. The frost seemed to help, making the holds slightly more reliable. His complete absorption and focus calmed him as, hold by frosty hold, he advanced upward.

Marjan leaned against a rock and belayed Šrauf. The sun caressed him, and there was a gentle breeze. The rope slid through his hands a few centimetres at a time. Without even looking, Marjan could sense the difficulties. When Šrauf reached the edge of the rock step, he secured the rope and continued toward the summit. Years later, Marjan remembered these moments. "I said to him, 'Go on, I will wait here for you. Only one person needs to reach the summit.' I sat down and waited." He continued: "It got cold. *I* got cold! Finally I was freezing. I could have gone down, but instead, I went up." Bone tired, he clipped into the rope and forced himself to ascend the fixed line up the wall. Forty metres later, the route to the summit opened before him. The tension eased and a horrible exhaustion overwhelmed him. He collapsed into the snow, gasping in the thin air.

Šrauf continued on above the rock step, then suddenly stopped. He couldn't breathe. His vision clouded and his lungs raged as he fell into the snow while trying to rip off his mask. There must be a problem with it. His frantic eyes rested on the regulator. It read zero. The bottle was empty. The veins in his temples grew close to bursting, and the signature crease in his massive forehead deepened into a crevasse. Šrauf cursed. Technology had failed him. His body had failed him. God had failed him. But then he watched himself rise up from the snow and begin to walk. Through an eerie haze, the summit neared. Time is malleable, and at this moment it seemed agonizingly slow. His body was no longer being guided by reason. He was now like a robot, programmed to reach a certain point on Earth.

He kept the empty bottle with him, intent on taking the wretched thing to the top as proof. Angry now, and even more determined, he attacked the last slope. Like Marjan below him, he concentrated on a position a few metres in front of him, plunged his axe into the snow, lifted one leg, and then the other. A stranger to himself, he watched his own body, a machine-like creature, advance up the slope toward a rock just below the summit. Or perhaps it wasn't a rock but some kind of cruel hallucination. He straightened his body and lunged for it. Yes, it was a real rock. His head pounded and the atmosphere shimmered with tiny white crystals. But it was clear enough for him to see that he was on the summit. The first Yugoslavian eight-thousand-metre summit: 4:00 pm, October 6, 1975.

Šrauf's memories of these moments are precise: "I forget all resolution to act with dignity on the summit; forget all fear and disappointments of the giant rock face, across which we fixed four kilometres of rope; forget the heat and the rains of the trek through the foothills; I forget the days of feverish preparations for this great moment. I lie on the summit and grab at the crystals of snow around me. I want to be absolutely sure! I'm really on the summit! On the very tip of the mountain consecrated to the great goddess Kali!"[47]

He swivelled around and looked back down the ridge. Could that be a human figure? He watched someone moving up from behind the sunlit curve. It was not a hallucination. His friend and partner had climbed across the rock pinnacle and was advancing toward him. Šrauf screamed with joy. To reach this summit with no oxygen! Could it be possible?

Marjan stopped and looked up. "I watch Šrauf as the dream of his life is coming true. He is shouting and whooping on the summit, he is ecstatic. I force myself to get up and go on. I slowly follow in Šrauf's footsteps. By now the mind, which thinks of nothing else but the summit that has to be reached, is the sole one left in command. The body has given up long ago. Every few metres I sit in the snow and gasp for air. Šrauf is calling me. A few more steps."[48]

Marjan reached the summit 45 minutes after Šrauf. They hugged. For Marjan there was no exhilaration, joy or feeling of triumph. He was simply relieved that he no longer had to climb upward. Šrauf turned on his radio and started screaming, "Summit! Summit! Summit!" Base camp responded:

Aleš: Bravooo! Where is Marjan?

Šrauf: [incomprehensible]

Aleš: I don't understand you. If Marjan is with you, just say yes.

Šrauf: YES!

Aleš: Take some photos of the Tibetan side, Šrauf, and then descend immediately! Immediately! Descend immediately! Slowly, carefully, pay attention! Don't lose anything! [Aside: Ye gods!][49]

Aleš stayed on the radio, encouraging Šrauf to pay close attention to Marjan. Base camp erupted into a mad chaos of joy, climbers yelling and running about, slapping each other on the back, punching each other and laughing. The radio crackled up and down the mountain, every camp eager to get in on the action. Aleš fired off some rockets to give a sense of direction to the two climbers, who were now starting to lose the late-afternoon light on their delicate descent.

He then sent a string of instructions to the other camps. "Hello, II! We won't stop with the ascents; we're going on as long as the weather holds. You will follow them at one-day intervals, so that IV will always be available to the teams coming from the summit. The crossover must be at III."[50]

◆ ◆ ◆

The sun was beginning to sink. Šrauf and Marjan gazed at the remarkable panorama and then turned into robots again, this time focused on descent. Marjan's crampons were damaged from earlier in the expedition, so he had jury-rigged them with a sling. But he had pulled on that sling so tightly that it blocked the circulation in his foot. As a result, his foot was slowly becoming a block of ice, although he didn't yet realize just how solid.

Šrauf and Marjan reached base camp two days later. "An amazing feat!" Aleš pronounced. "Summiting without oxygen! You'll see, boys, it will take a month or two before the full significance of this will be really understood...Let's toast. First to you two! To this incredible ascent! It will open so many doors to us, it will be difficult to close them all!"[51]

Beautiful words from Aleš, and prophetic. The Makalu South Face climb set the stage for twenty years of inspired performances by Slovenian alpinists. The doors had indeed been opened, but at a high price for 25-year-old Marjan. After arriving in base camp he felt pain in his foot. When he removed his socks his toes were black. With a sickening feeling, he knew he would lose them. But they still had 12 long days in camp. And then the walk out, on frostbitten feet.

Forty years later, when I spoke with him as we sat on his front porch, Marjan looked down at what was left of his foot and remembered the ordeal. "Yes it was painful, but I was young." Then he shrugged, looked up, and added, "Still, pain is pain."

♦ ♦ ♦

After Šrauf and Marjan summited the mountain, the story of the first ascent of Makalu's South Face was not over. Three more teams were ready. On October 8, four more climbers set out. Cedilnik was hit on the left knee by falling ice and Roman Robas had difficulty breathing, so they returned. But Nejc Zaplotnik and Janko Ažman reached the top that day, followed by Ivč Kotnik and Viki Grošelj on October 10 in strong wind and snow.

Then another drama began. On October 11, Janez Dovžan and Zoran Bešlin started for the top. Janez summited and returned safely, but Zoran collapsed only a few metres from the summit. He was forced to spend the night out at 8400 metres with no bivouac equipment while Janez waited for him in Camp V at eight thousand metres. The next morning an exhausted Janez headed back uphill, looking for Zoran. Although he made it almost to the rim of the face for the second time, he found no trace of his partner. Once more he returned to Camp V, where he knew he would need to stop and rest before heading down.

From top: Aleš Kunaver, whose legacy of leadership, vision and teamwork in the story of Slovenian mountaineering is unparalleled. *ALEŠ KUNAVER COLLECTION*

The Trisul expedition returns to Ljubljana in triumph. *ALEŠ KUNAVER COLLECTION*

Yugoslavian climbers train on board their ship en route to Karachi. *ALEŠ KUNAVER COLLECTION*

Top: Joža Čop's membership card in the Club Skala, a breakaway group that was focused on purity of climbing style. *ALEŠ KUNAVER COLLECTION*

Centre, left: Pavla Jesih, one of the top female climbers in Europe in the 1930s. Together with Joža Čop, she made the first ascent of Čop's Pillar in 1945. *WIKIMEDIA COMMONS*

Centre, right: Josip Broz Tito, leader of Yugoslavia from 1945 until his death in 1980. *WIKIMEDIA COMMONS*

Bottom: Croatian women bringing salt to Slovenian Partisan fighters. *WIKIMEDIA COMMONS*

Top: The team that tackled Triglav's Čop's Pillar in winter: Aleš Kunaver, Stane Belak (Šrauf) and Tone Sazonov. *ALEŠ KUNAVER COLLECTION*

Below: Steep ground on Čop's Pillar on the north wall of Triglav. First winter ascent by Aleš Kunaver, Stane Belak (Šrauf) and Tone Sazonov. *ALEŠ KUNAVER COLLECTION*

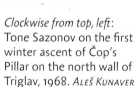

Clockwise from top, left: Tone Sazonov on the first winter ascent of Čop's Pillar on the north wall of Triglav, 1968. *ALEŠ KUNAVER COLLECTION*

Painting by artist and alpinist Danilo Cedilnik. *DANILO CEDILNIK COLLECTION*

Viki Grošelj on one of his first climbing excursions at Turnc. He was 13 at the time. *DANILO CEDILNIK COLLECTION*

Nejc Zaplotnik as a young man. *Left*: with his brother (at right) and sister. *NEJC ZAPLOTNIK COLLECTION*

Nejc Zaplotnik training with his son. *NEJC ZAPLOTNIK COLLECTION*

Nejc Zaplotnik (on the right) as a young man, just learning to climb. Note the sit harness. ANDREJ ŠTREMFELJ COLLECTION

Top: Climbing on the South Face of Makalu at 7500 metres. *Viki Grošelj collection*

Centre, left: Stane Belak (Šrauf) with edelweiss, the flower with which he courted his future wife, Jožica. *Stane Belak collection*

Centre, right: Stane Belak (Šrauf) at Makalu in 1975. He and Marjan Manfreda went on to make the first ascent of the South Face. *Aleš Kunaver collection*

Left: Marjan Manfreda at Makalu in 1975. *Aleš Kunaver collection*

Steep ground on Makalu's South Face. *ALEŠ KUNAVER COLLECTION*

Top: Stane Belak's (Šrauf's) empty oxygen bottle at the top of Makalu, October 6, 1975. *ALEŠ KUNAVER COLLECTION*

Below: Marjan Manfreda slowly ascends the summit ridge of Makalu toward Stane Belak (Šrauf) after having made the first ascent of the South Face without supplemental oxygen. *ALEŠ KUNAVER COLLECTION*

Nejc Zaplotnik on the summit of Makalu in 1975, having just climbed the South Face. *NEJC ZAPLOTNIK COLLECTION*

The South Face of Makalu with high points of various attempts, including the successful 1975 ascent. *Aleš Kunaver collection*

Above: Nejc Zaplotnik at Makalu in 1975, writing as always. *Aleš Kunaver COLLECTION*

Right: Aleš Kunaver fired off rockets from base camp to give a sense of direction to Stane Belak (Šrauf) and Marjan Manfreda, who were descending from the summit of Makalu in the dark. *Aleš Kunaver COLLECTION*

Left: Janez Dovžan lowering Zoran Bešlin from Camp V at 8000 metres on one of the most heroic self-rescues in Himalayan climbing history. After a four-day battle with exhaustion and extreme frostbite, the two reached help and safety. *Janez Dovžan collection*

Below: Zoran and Janez safely back in base camp at 4900m. Zoran lost his toes in the process but both men survived Makalu. *Janez Dovžan collection*

Eighteen-year-old Andrej Štremfelj in the process of becoming an alpinist. *ANDREJ ŠTREMFELJ COLLECTION*

Left: A young Andrej Štremfelj, whose climbing mentor, Nejc Zaplotnik, invited him to Gasherbrum I in 1977. It was their first major summit together. *STIPE BOŽIĆ COLLECTION*

Below: Andrej Štremfelj climbing with Nejc Zaplotnik in the Julian Alps in 1973. It was the beginning of an amazing alpine partnership. *ANDREJ ŠTREMFELJ COLLECTION*

Bottom: Andrej Štremfelj on the summit of Gasherbrum I in 1977 after having climbed it with Nejc Zaplotnik. *ANDREJ ŠTREMFELJ COLLECTION*

Above: Nejc Zaplotnik on Gasherbrum I in 1977. *Andrej Štremfelj collection*

Left: Mojca Zaplotnik with her three sons, 1981. *Nejc Zaplotnik collection*

Late in the afternoon he heard faint cries for help. Zoran had survived and was descending alone on horribly frostbitten feet. For the third time, Janez left his tent and headed up. When he reached Zoran, he half-carried him to the tent and all the way down the mountain over the next couple of days. The last two climbers on the face, they were completely on their own. Their performance was an incredible example of the will to live and the strength of the brotherhood of the rope. Both men survived Makalu, but Zoran's frostbite resulted in partial amputation of his feet. Many consider this self-rescue one of the greatest stories of Slovenian alpinism.

Seven climbers reached the summit that year, and nobody died. Aleš credited much of the success to the feisty group of 20-year-olds who had joined the veterans. And although he knew this ascent would open the doors to Yugoslavia's future in the Himalaya, his personal feelings were somewhat different. "I'd like nothing so much as to shut the door behind me, because things couldn't get any better than this."[52]

But Aleš was unable to shut that door: the mountains kept drawing him back, as they did for Nejc:

> You are slowly overcome by the eternal restlessness of high mountains, by the natural current of life that we have almost forgotten...when you sense that you were given birth by Mother Earth, that you are just a part of desolate valleys, green meadows, broken glaciers, that you are part of the rushing river and the black, silver-strewn sky. This is when you become aware that these lonely paths keep drawing you back to the highest peaks, where the sky and Earth meet amidst the howling wind.[53]

FIVE

The First Casualty

Somewhere toward the east, after days and weeks of driving along hot, dry, dusty desert roads, lies the land where the earth touches the sky. Somewhere there is a land where black glaciers carve deep valleys amidst vertical granite towers. Somewhere in the heartland of Baltistan are dusty goat trails that turn to knee-deep mud during the rain. And then the little grey villages turn verdant and steep, muddy slopes are torn apart by heavy, falling rocks. Somewhere in the heartland of Baltistan there are tiny villages where women hide in their stone huts when they see strangers coming. Somewhere there are villages where huge shepherd dogs meet you with threatening growls. And then you say in greeting, As-salamu alaykum. You cross your hands on your chest and bow respectfully. Calls to evening prayer echo among white peaks and rocky ravines. Allah Akbar – God is Great – drowned by the roar of the surging glacial river.

Untamed yaks, from which you are best to keep a respectful distance, graze in the high-altitude meadows. Tiny flames from porters' fires throw wild shadows across the wreckage of moraines. And when the chapati is done, the Hunza sing a song that melds with the moaning glacier long into the night. And you lie there among sparse bunches of yellow, sharp-bladed grass; your open heart drinks in the eternal paths of the stars; you count the falling stars while the wind slowly covers you with fine-grained sand that grits between your teeth and sticks to your forehead.

—Nejc Zaplotnik, *Pot*[54]

Higigh, wild country, where people live close to the earth and where the earth touches the sky: Nejc Zaplotnik had been dreaming about such a place ever since he began climbing. They were a small group, just nine people. Minimal equipment, no supplemental oxygen and no high-altitude porters. A new route on one of the highest peaks in the world. Nejc had proven himself beyond question on Makalu's South Face in 1975 and repeatedly in the Julian Alps. When Janez Lončar proposed a climb in Pakistan's Karakoram region in 1977, the answer was an immediate yes. Nejc then approached Andrej Štremfelj, an even younger climber from the Kranj climbing club: "Do you feel like going to the Karakoram?" Andrej's eyes shone with anticipation. Again, yes.

◆ ◆ ◆

Andrej Štremfelj did not come from a mountaineering family. His parents were much too busy eking out a living in the factories of Kranj, a picturesque city situated on a rocky prominence between the Sava and Kokra rivers. A junction of important trading routes between northern Europe and the Adriatic Sea, the city was, and still is, a manufacturing centre: clothing and furniture and huge rubber-tire factories. Andrej's mother, Paula, began working in a textile factory at the age of 14, directly after primary school. His father, Franc, worked in a furniture-making factory. They married in their early 20s and moved into the house where Paula was born, in the village of Orejak, now a suburb of Kranj. The same house where later Andrej and his brother Marko were born. The same house where Andrej remains, with his wife, Marija, and their children. And very likely the same house that will some day be occupied by their grandchildren.

The modest dwelling was enlarged several times over the years and now stands two storeys high, surrounded by a vegetable garden and beehives, both still tended by Franc. The entire family was sustained by that garden of potatoes and cabbage and tomatoes, and nearby farmers provided them with milk and cheese. "We didn't feel poor," Andrej recalled. "We felt normal." His memories were echoed by Tomo Česen, another Kranj climber, who added that life was "quite okay" in those days. He added, "We couldn't get what we can get now, but this was not a problem. I mean, what is the problem if you don't have ten different kinds of yogurt? Especially not a problem if you don't know that there *are* ten different kinds!"

Andrej was born on December 17, 1956. He was a contented child. He would walk three kilometres across open fields to school and, at the end of each day, would run home and disappear into the nearby forest, searching for mushrooms and chasing anything that moved. "I didn't study much because I was smart enough," he said laughing.

When Andrej was just 13 and his brother Marko 15, they began an eight-day trek across the mountains of Slovenia. Starting in Maribor in the eastern part of the country, they climbed the high ridges, crossed countless passes and scrambled up precarious *via ferratas* (iron- and cable-equipped high-alpine pathways) to the airy summits. Eight days of adventure in the highest mountains of Slovenia. "We felt confident," Andrej said. And although he was not yet doing any technical climbing, Andrej was becoming fit, as well as knowledgeable about mountain weather and topography.

Real climbing began when he was 15. He joined the Alpine Association of Slovenia and was soon scrambling, rock climbing, winter climbing and ski touring. His first true alpine experience was in January of 1972 when he joined a mass ascent of Stol, a two-thousander in the Karavank Range near Kranj. He subsequently recorded every single climb in a mountaineering journal. Each member of the Alpine Association had to prove ten ascents a year in order to be a registered alpinist, and Andrej's book was proof of his climbs. Initially, Andrej climbed with his brother and other older alpinists in the club. He was a quick study, and he was ambitious. Within two years he had already climbed a long, difficult route on Triglav's North Face. He received his alpinist papers at the tender age of 18. Now as a full-fledged alpinist, he could lead less-qualified climbers in the mountains, something that was strictly regulated in Slovenia, a country small enough that transgressions were easily spotted and reported to the Alpine Association authorities. "Even if you didn't tell, after four or five days everybody knew what you had done," Andrej recalled.

He joined Alpine Association trips to the Tatras, the Dolomites, the Alps and the Caucasus. And then came Nejc's call, inviting him to Gasherbrum I, to join the first Slovenian expedition to the Karakoram. Nejc recognized Andrej's natural talent, drive, and ambition. "Our first relationship was as teacher-student," Andrej explained. "Later we became partners." Andrej saw him simply, through a climber's eyes. "Nejc was just very interested in climbing. So was I. Better to say I was like him. We were both totally obsessed."

The two climbed together as much as they could, held back only by Nejc's responsibilities to his young family. Even though Nejc was committed to climbing, Andrej understood that his decisions were influenced by three little creatures who depended on him – his boys. But his responsibilities didn't prevent him from living hard. As Andrej recalled, Nejc liked to party. He liked to drink, and he loved to sing, usually at the same time. "He was also, once a month, quite drunk, let's say," laughed Andrej. Other climbers confirmed that it was not unusual for Nejc to go on a spree for several days at a time. Many saw a different side of Nejc: complicated, frighteningly intelligent, sometimes difficult, moody and utterly fascinating. Not to mention a very good alpinist. Perfect for Gasherbrum I.

◆ ◆ ◆

Gasherbrum I, also known as Hidden Peak, is the highest of six peaks in a horseshoe formation that encircle South Gasherbrum Glacier in Pakistan's Karakoram Range. At 8080 metres, it attracted the attention of British explorers as early as 1892. But the mountain turned back all comers until 1958, when Nick Clinch led an American team to the summit. Later, because of border disputes between India and Pakistan, the area was closed to climbers. In 1975, however, Italian climber Reinhold Messner and Peter Habeler from Austria established another step in the evolution of Himalayan climbing: an alpine-style ascent of Gasherbrum I without supplemental oxygen. Two years later, the Slovenians arrived for the first time in the Karakoram, hoping to summit via a new route.

The team included climbers from various clubs and, from the outset, seemed to lack leadership. Three times they applied for a permit from the Pakistani government. On the third try, they succeeded. Now they had just two months to raise money for the trip. They managed, but their modest budget was barely sufficient to buy food and equipment. Early one dark and drizzly Sunday morning in May, the climbers gathered to say goodbye to their families and begin the long journey. With one truck and a borrowed van, they lumbered along for 11 days through Bulgaria, Turkey, Iran, Afghanistan and Pakistan – seven thousand kilometres, a transition from West to East, from the familiar to the exotic.

They camped by roadsides, trying to sleep amidst the roar of nighttime truck traffic. They learned how to manage border authorities. They endured blistering heat. They marvelled at their driver's almost circus-worthy skills. They were eaten alive by mosquitoes near the Caspian Sea and mesmerized by the mysterious black tents and long lines of nomads striding along the Afghan roads. And they were constantly thirsty from the heat and the dust.

They faced more delays in Pakistan while waiting for their climbing permits. For 17 days, they were guests of a group of Slovenian workers in Tarbela, where the largest earth-filled dam in the world was being constructed on the Indus River. Each day Nejc and Drago Bregar would drive one hundred kilometres to Rawalpindi to knock on doors and cajole the various bureaucrats: customs officers, the department of tourism, the police, the insurance company and the airlines. By the beginning of June, they had what they needed and flew to Skardu, capital of Baltistan. Now their approach march could begin.

But first they needed help. Several hundred porters gathered in the centre of Skardu, forming a line down the middle of the narrow, stone-paved street; sunbeams threaded through the dense, wind-driven dust. The climbers' liaison officer suggested they choose porters by their appearance of strength. Nejc was shocked. Was this some kind of cattle fair, where people were selected for their legs and teeth? He rejected the idea and insisted on simply taking the first hundred, who subsequently marched off, heading for Bola, 20 miles away. Nejc and the other climbers travelled the same distance by tractor. They trundled along next to the Indus River, the drivers wrapped in shawls and ski goggles for protection from the dust, the climbers perched in the back on top of their precious cargo. Completely white with dust, the men bounced along, clinging to the tractors.

The approach march began the next morning, each porter loaded down with his cargo allotment. Nejc watched them jostling for position and noticed one named Karim. "I never saw a man sweat so much in my life. Sweat was not only running down his face, it was literally spurting off his forehead."[55] Karim pushed his way to the front of the line, eager to get on the trail. With his broad face, his shorn head and a neck as thick as a bull, he raised his hand and offered a cheery grin that screamed "Pick me!" His wide, willing shoulders were rewarded with a 40-kilogram barrel of ghee (clarified butter) that he lugged up the hills, wheezing like a yak. Even though he carried the heaviest load, he was always the first to finish the day's march.

Nejc liked Karim and would sit with him each evening, smoking and munching on chapatis. They never exchanged a word, for they had none in common. Besides, Nejc suspected that Karim might be a bit simple. "But we were friends," he said. "I couldn't walk behind him because he raised so much dust with his huge feet that you couldn't breathe. Not to mention the strong odour of sweat and ghee that he emitted. Karim never washed."[56] Karim understood that he had earned a privileged spot in Nejc's heart. He didn't have to fight and jostle for extra treats. One day it might be a larger ration of flour. Another, a bit of sugar. Or some specially flavoured tea.

Gulam Mohammed, with his big heart and his dark Mongolian eyes, became an even better friend of the team. Born in the desolate, brown hills of Tibet, Gulam had spent his youth in Skardu. He was a tiny, energetic man with a balding forehead and a salt-and-pepper mustache and beard. Gulam was almost too small to do a proper job of portering, but his language skills more than made up for that. He knew Balti, Urdu and English. And he knew how to bake. Soon he was promoted to expedition cook. He created chapati variations they had never dreamed of: potato chapatis, apricot chapatis and dal chapatis. His goat-liver stew, prepared with Pakistani spices, was the best the climbers had ever eaten. Gulam's palace was the kitchen tent; the door was always open and the tea was always on.

Talk of children drew Gulam and Nejc together. Gulam's wife had died young, and his expedition earnings were for his three children's schooling. Nejc felt that on this expedition full of bachelors, only he and Gulam understood the powerful pull of family – the desire to return home. But for now, they had each other for companionship and support.

Drago Bregar and Nejc knew each other only slightly before the expedition, and both were fine alpinists. Drago, born just a few months after Nejc, was the most experienced ice climber on the team and took the expedition to Gasherbrum very seriously. He and Nejc walked together on the approach march, hunkering down under too-small umbrellas during the frequent deluges and lurching side by side along the steep, muddy trails. Together, they clasped the fragile suspension bridges stretched like threads above the foaming rivers. The porters were terrified of the bridges, so Drago and Nejc coaxed, dragged and bullied them across, one screaming porter at a time. The peace-loving Nejc even resorted to violence. "I hit a man for the first time. I hope it will also be the last time!"[57] One of the porters was so afraid of a bridge that Nejc hoisted his load and then grabbed him by the nape of the neck and began pushing him across. In the middle of the bridge the porter broke free and ran back. Nejc deposited the cargo on the opposite bank and came back for the terrified man. Once again he escaped, crying and cursing and offering himself to Allah. When they approached the crucial midpoint of the bridge for the third time, Nejc gave him a swift kick in the ass, and off he ran, this time to the other side.

They also had the goats to contend with. Nejc tried carrying one on his shoulders, pressing all four legs to his chest with one hand and hanging onto the bridge with the other. All went well until the goat spied the brown river rushing below. Petrified, it gave a fierce struggle, almost toppling them both into the river. Drago tried another approach. He tied the animal's two front legs together, then hoisted it onto his pack and secured all four legs across his chest. This curious two-headed creature somehow managed to scurry across the bridge, the goat bleating wildly and Drago hanging on tightly.

◆ ◆ ◆

After nine days of walking, a slender rock pyramid appeared, glowing in the evening sun. Gasherbrum I greeted them like a temptress with its icy pillar, its long Southwest Ridge and its three-thousand-metre high South Face. After careful examination of the mountain's various features, they decided to try the unclimbed Southwest Ridge. Their route to Camp I would cross a badly shattered shelf on the Gasherbrum Glacier, which presented a dangerous array of tilting seracs, gaping crevasses and suspicious snow bridges. It didn't take long for Nejc to fall into a crevasse; although he was saved by the rope, he suffered a concussion.

"You will need at least one week of rest at base camp," the doctor ordered.

"Absolutely," Nejc agreed.

After one day of rest, he was back in Camp I.

◆ ◆ ◆

At base camp all the porters except Karim were sent back. The climbers thought he might be able to carry cargo to Camp I, so they outfitted him with shoes, gloves and a pillow. But all the equipment in the world couldn't save Karim from his fears. His nightly prayers to Allah saved him from this mountain, but not without some pain. His head ached so badly he bound it in rope, even as he buried his Aspirin tablets in the snow. He spewed vomit among the seracs, and finally, the climbers had to admit that Karim wasn't cut out for altitude.

Drago and Nejc worked together on the mountain, breaking trail in the waist-deep snow, humping loads of food and equipment, fixing lines and setting up camps. They were a well-balanced team and hardly needed to talk. The sun shone on their efforts – too much most days, for they sweated almost as much as Karim. Their partnership deepened into friendship as they slaved on the mountain, collapsing together at the end of each long day. Both young and ambitious, they saw this climb as a dress rehearsal. Their sights were on Everest, plans for which they knew were on the horizon. If they performed well on GI, they would be chosen for the expedition.

But they soon discovered they had much more in common than climbing. On rest days they would sit in front of their tents, repairing equipment and cooking, talking and dreaming. "Together we dreamed of white rock walls back home, of our friends, of our families, of the difficult ascents and pleasant evenings in the mountain huts," Nejc recalled. "I could never climb with a man who is seen only as an alpinist but not a genuine friend at the same time."[58]

And while they dreamed and talked and ate and rested, their eyes were drawn upward to the jagged scene that surrounded them: the mighty walls of the Gasherbrums and the sharp needle of Muztagh Tower. The only sounds were the cawing crows flitting about camp scavenging for scraps, and the constant hissing of the stove. Sometimes a serac would collapse in the distance, sending a thundering shudder through the camp. At night, as the cold seeped in, they would burrow into their sleeping bags and dream of tomorrow.

But then, in an instant, the partnership configuration changed. Personal ambitions became secondary to the collective goal. High on the mountain, Janez Lončar became sick, and a rescue operation was needed for the next morning. Two climbers would help Janez down and two more would carry on to Camp II. It was 20-year-old Andrej Štremfelj – not Drago – who was chosen to climb up to Camp II with Nejc. It was clear from the start that the two going up to Camp II would be the first pair to try for the summit. Everyone understood that.

As Nejc watched the sun set his last evening in base camp, he daydreamed about the summit he was so sure to touch. He thought about his experience on Makalu. And he thought about friendship:

Pictures from Makalu flash before my eyes. The wall, soaring into the sky, the heavy packs, the miles of fixed ropes, the snowstorms, friends' suffering. And then suddenly, Janko and I stand on the summit and shake each other's hands. And Šrauf, who crowned decades of hard work with such success, and Manfreda, happily soaking his frost-bitten foot in the water, and Viki's tears at our return to base, and Ivč, who entertained us with his funny country accent until we were rolling with laughter, and Misko, who wanted to raze the mountain to the ground when he was afraid for his friends' safety in Camp IV, and the exhausted Zoran, who stayed alive by sheer willpower, and Janez's help, and Aleš, crying with joy at our success, the tears of a 40-year-old man who is used to everything but tears. In those moments I missed all of you. I felt somehow melancholy because you were not with me. How far behind me is Makalu! Two years in the past and hundreds of kilometres away from me, and yet so near! I am growing increasingly aware that friendship is worth much more than success. Friends have remained and everything else is history.[59]

Nejc barely slept that night, apprehensive about Andrej's inexperience, excited about the possibility of his young friend climbing an eight-thousander, intimidated by the amount of hard work in front of them and terrified at the 1200 metres between them and the summit.

Gasherbrum I was Andrej's first experience at extreme altitude. And it hurt. "I remember the first time we came to 5600 metres, I was so sick. I was just looking at Nejc eating some meat and I was vomiting." The ever-practical Andrej seemed to come to terms with altitude sickness on Gasherbrum I, however, since he was never bothered much with it on subsequent expeditions.

Two days later Andrej and Nejc were in their tent at Camp III. A pale grey hue began to suffuse the tent, giving them hope that the long night was ending. A sharp wind snapped the nylon walls and penetrated every small crack. They stuck their heads out of the doorway to a world of ice: petrified, frozen and dead. There was nothing welcoming or tender about the scene, only the imperative that a steep and unforgiving mountain needed to be climbed. They heated pots of milk laced with honey and forced themselves to drink the nourishing liquid. Slowly, so as not to knock over the stove, they packed up: extra clothing, cameras and flags. No ropes. There would be safety in speed.

No sooner had they left the tent than the first black clouds rolled in from the west, low and heavy, swallowing their view. Next came a thick, murky fog, and then snowflakes began to dance around their heads. The wind increased in velocity, hammering them to the ground. Everything merged into a grey nothingness; there was no distinction between sky and mountain.

Climbing by braille, they reached the beginning of the ridge, where the snow and ice became interspersed with rocks. Nejc's right hand lost all feeling, and his feet felt like two blocks of wood. Every few metres he would stop on a small ledge, rest his head on his axe and gasp for breath. With one foot on the ledge, he would wiggle the other one up and down in the hope that the blood would circulate as far as his unfeeling toes. Andrej kept up, always one step behind Nejc. Like two soldiers serving the same master, they repeated this sequence. Step up, rest the head, wiggle the toes, and step up again.

Amid the tedium and exhaustion, Nejc's thoughts drifted again to Makalu: "He [Andrej] is probably experiencing the same thing I did when Janko and I marched up the ridge toward the summit of Makalu. I wouldn't have overtaken him, not even by one step, not for anything in the world. I stood still below the summit and watched his last steps, watched as the dream of his life became reality. At that moment I was overcome by an unearthly happiness." [60]

But this was Gasherbrum, not Makalu, and the sharp, icy needles lashed his cheeks. As the world around him roared and howled and twisted, Nejc struggled to cope with the madness. His mind wandered again, this time dangerously far: "Back home it's 6:00 am and the children are just going to kindergarten. My thoughts always drift homeward when I am in the mountains, but when I am at home they are drawn to the mountains. Work, children and mountains: these are the utmost I can experience in my life." [61]

A rude gust of wind brought him back to Gasherbrum's steep summit pyramid. The ridge rose in front of him, to that point where all ridges merge and where all of his desires and efforts would converge: the summit. But even as he tried to focus on those few metres in front of him, his mind wandered again. He was transported down, down to the valleys below, poverty-stricken valleys where people lived in miserable hovels, wrapped in mud-caked rags. He was sitting around their fires, baking chapatis, watching their children playing in the dust: laughing, crying and fighting, like children everywhere. As he contemplated their extreme poverty, he became angry, thinking of all the fat, bored people back home who invented problems where none existed. He grappled with the question of fairness: what had they done to deserve such poverty while others had so much? He vowed that he would never again complain about his modest salary or the high cost of living. As the echoes of the foaming glacial rivers below faded from his imagination, he refocused on a rock rib that rose straight up into the murk.

He and Andrej were driven by the knowledge that they were near their goal, and by noon they had climbed the rocky rib and were standing on a small notch in the ridge. All that remained was a gentle snow slope. That, and the wind and the fog. They removed the flags from their packs, tied them to their ice axes and took the few remaining steps to the summit.

Although they had climbed in expedition style with fixed lines and pre-set camps, it had taken them only 16 days to climb Gasherbrum I. This was just one day more than Messner and Habeler had managed, climbing alpine-style without fixed lines or camps, two years before. Slapping each other on the back and sharing a few tears, the two celebrated their first summit together. The wind swirled around them, shoving them off balance, sometimes almost toppling them off the ridge. The clouds ripped apart for a moment, revealing a strange yellow ball suspended in the sky. Then they closed in again. After taking a few photographs with their backs bent to the wind, they began the worrisome descent.

Now that they were facing into the wind, their faces and goggles became encrusted with ice. They could see nothing, and their tracks were already buried by the newly fallen snow. As the adrenalin of ascent retreated from their bodies, a strange kind of apathy set in. Their slithering descent among the small spindrift avalanches seemed almost easy, until reality jolted them awake and they slammed in their axes to brake. Slipping and falling down the snow-laden slope, they sometimes became separated in the fog. Whenever he heard Andrej's panicky screams of "Nejc, wait, wait!" Nejc would slump in the snow, relieved to rest.

The complexity of the terrain, the confusing fog and the relentless wind created a real crisis for the pair as they felt their way down a series of gullies, searching for the couloir that would lead them to their bivouac tent. They fought a constant battle between speed and precision and against a pervading fear of becoming lost on the great wall of Gasherbrum I. They finally spied a few familiar-looking rocks and then, there was the tent – a tiny blue refuge. They collapsed inside, tore at their ice-encrusted hair and rubbed their faces and fingers to restore some feeling. Even though raging with thirst, neither had the will to start the stove.

Suddenly they heard cursing. Somebody was ripping at the tent, trying to get in. Almost like a vision, Drago appeared. He had climbed alone from Camp III, fixing one hundred metres of rope along the way and carrying a desperately heavy pack. He burst in, full of congratulations and energy, enough to prepare countless mugs of tea and explain his plan: he would wait for the rope team from Camp III and climb to the summit with them. If that wasn't possible, he would descend with Nejc and Andrej the following day. The mood in the tent was a strange mix: complete contentment and exhaustion contrasted by a taut desire that can only be released by extreme effort. Drago wanted the summit too.

The morning dawned sad and grey, and the wind howled even more fiercely than before. "Drago, descend to the valley with us, and if the weather improves we can all try together again," Nejc said.

"No, I'll wait for a day or two. The weather will surely improve. I have food."

How often does this conversation take place in the big mountains? After days and even weeks of hard work and suffering, all for one goal – the summit – there comes a moment when one climber is on his way down, another on his way up. How difficult it is to convince your teammate to relinquish his goal when you are descending from that very goal. It was clear to everyone that the mountain was closing its doors, but ambition and desire are stronger than reason. Drago's mind was made up.

Andrej and Nejc could wait no longer. Another day at that altitude could be fatal. They crawled out into the fog, hoisted the heavy packs onto their bent backs and started down, searching for the fixed lines. Every moment was filled with thoughts of Drago, alone in the tent, waiting for a break in the weather, hungry for an eight-thousander. For six hours they slithered down the steep gullies and near-vertical chimneys choked with icy rocks, before finally wading through the deep snow into Camp III. They stopped, drank some hot soup with their friends and headed out into the storm again. Descent – continuous descent. Andrej wanted to stop at Camp II, but Nejc drove him onward. It was nearly dark when they arrived at Camp I, where they dived into the tent and collapsed into their bags.

The ordeal was still not over, however. The heavy snow and warm weather had created a deadly trap between Camp I and base camp. The glacier was almost unrecognizable, and crevasses were lurking, unseen but deadly. Snow bridges had collapsed, and newly formed bridges were deceptively weak. They floundered across this labyrinth, sinking in snow up to their thighs, nerves frayed by the fear of crevasses. Five hours later they reached base camp and the warmth of the kitchen, where they were shocked to learn that the team from Camp III was also descending, their fear of the growing avalanche danger propelling them downward.

But what about Drago?

The Camp III climbers reported that they had spoken with him on the radio the previous evening but morning had brought only silence. They had waited a bit to see if they could spot him descending toward them but then decided to go down themselves. Nobody knew whether Drago was descending or had chosen to make a bid for the summit.

"Drago, report back! Drago, report back!" they howled into the radio. But the only reply was static.

After two days the climbers began heading back up the mountain to search for Drago. But it was hopeless; they were too exhausted. They retreated to the kitchen tent, silent and morose. The radio remained on, yet everyone knew there would be no message from Drago. Gulam gave them tea and reassured them that all was not lost. All those endless evenings, they sat sombre and broken, ripped apart with sadness.

It snowed for the next six days. Six days to sit, completely powerless, counting the snowflakes. "No ascent is worth wasting a life," Nejc wrote in his journal. "I know it now as I am sitting in a warm tent with a bitter lump in my throat. But up on the mountain I would have done exactly as Drago did. To give up a goal is much more difficult than to reach it."[62]

The climbers talked about what awaited them back home. Difficult questions. When? How? Where? And the toughest one: why? They knew that very few would grasp the meaning of what had gone on up there. Most would not understand that, despite the wind and snow and altitude that had eroded their strength and enveloped them in an icy shell, their eyes could still radiate the terrible will to live. Somehow they would need to explain and defend their actions on Gasherbrum I, the first foreign mountain to claim a Yugoslavian alpinist. The tragedy overshadowed the success.

After a week the porters arrived. Nejc watched Gasherbrum slowly disappear under a blanket of fresh snow. His second eight-thousander, and Drago's grave. For the first time in his life, he realized how insignificant the difference was between success and failure. Finally it was time to turn his back on Gasherbrum – and Drago – but first he reached into his pack and pulled out the little elephant that had been his good luck talisman, and he left it behind. It was all he could offer his friend.

As Gasherbrum's slim pyramid receded from view, the group of tormented climbers turned toward home.

In the midst of this desolate yet beautiful landscape, a small group of foreigners, infidels in dirty trousers grown ragged from the long journey, in shirts white with dried sweat, march on. Their hair is glued together in stiff locks from sweat and the desert sand. Their faces are gaunt and their cheeks are hollow from their efforts and poor food. Their skin is burnt from the high-altitude sun and wind. Their lips are swollen and cracked from the lashing needles of snowstorms. Their bodies are thin and bony, bent double beneath the heavy packs. Are these the same people who sought the sun but looked to the ground and saw only its pale reflection in muddy puddles? Only their eyes glow with the fullness of life tested by the most difficult trials. Only their eyes bear witness that they found the sun itself...This is how an expedition returns to life.

Surrounded by the foreigners' hairy faces, the Hunza, their backs bent double, move with short, quick steps. On their backs, wrapped in canvas rags, their heavy loads sway from side to side. When the evening cold halts the sliding of the moraines and the glacial streams, the Hunza stop, light small fires and toast thin chapatis on glowing slabs of rock. Then the Hunza take off their clothes, lie down on their rags and press their naked bodies against each other to keep warm. They cover themselves with a tarp, and their endless half-whispered conversations, murmured songs and prayers fill the camp. This is how, shivering, the Hunza make it through the night, whereas the foreigners burrow into their sleeping bags, talking quietly about the country they are about to leave and the country they are returning to, about the people they love and the people they never knew before but who became their friends during their long shared journey. Slowly the voices die down and the moaning of the glacier is interrupted only by the occasional cough and quiet sniffling...

This is how we returned from the Karakoram. To think of all we'd been through. Long kilometres of sun-baked roads stretching from one horizon to the other as straight as a ruler; endless narrow trails where the dust fills your eyes and mouth and the hot sun dries fat beads of sweat on your forehead; little villages with their stone huts...the shattered, icy snake of the Baltoro, one of the longest glaciers in the world; the slender granite pinnacles, unearthly in their boldness; searching for a path through the confusion of seracs and crevasses; back-breaking toil on the mountain; the wild joy upon reaching the summit, only to be followed immediately by the horrible disappointment at the death of a friend. Now we are leaving this land where we spent the most magnificent days of the rest of our lives. We are older. Many days of suffering, joy, happiness and sadness have made us older. And what lies before us? Our homeland!...Then we will be back in the land where there are people who love us, in the country with the most beautiful mountains in the world.[63]

SIX

Everest West Ridge

I am back in Kathmandu, cycling along dusty, rubbish-strewn streets, surrounded by a surging crowd, by merchants' cries, car horns and taxi drivers' shouts, droning lamas, shuffling shamans; surrounded by shit-caked, four-legged, slowly ruminating saints; surrounded by wasted, drugged-up hippies lounging about, by the prim, heavy tread of rich, self-absorbed tourists who look down their noses at Eastern slowness and dirt and can hardly wait to get back home to their spotless mansions. And above all this pandemonium, the gods walk – and with the help of good and evil demons, watch over this crazy planet so that, in spite of all the confusion, things happen as they should.

—Nejc Zaplotnik, *Pot*[64]

Sherpas have been a part of foreign expeditions for as long as climbers have been coming to the Himalaya. From the beginning, Sherpas performed well, due to their phenomenal strength and natural acclimatization. But when teams began attempting more difficult routes, their climbing skills were not always sufficient. More died in the mountains each year. During Aleš's expedition to Annapurna II in 1969, he was shocked to note that several Sherpas didn't know how to attach their crampons or use their ice axes. Their natural abilities and strengths no longer matched the skill levels needed for the kind of terrain Aleš knew was the future of Himalayan climbing. He became obsessed with the idea of righting this wrong.

In 1979 he set up a mountaineering school for Nepalese Sherpas in the Manang district, in the upper valley of the Marsyangdi River. One-month-long courses covered everything from bivouacking tips to diet in the mountains, from altitude sickness to technical skills, from first aid to personal hygiene. The students learned knots, self-arrest, front-pointing and dozens of other techniques that would get them up – and down – the more difficult routes on which they were now expected to perform. By 2008, 683 participants had passed through 23 courses. But in 1979 the school was just getting started, and it occupied all of Aleš's time. As a result, in a cruel twist of fate, he felt he had to hand off the Everest West Ridge expedition, his dream since 1962, to another man to lead. That man was Tone Škarja.

◆ ◆ ◆

Born in 1937, Tone Škarja came from a family that was fundamentally shaped by war. The Germans captured his grandmother and uncles during the Second World War and shipped them off to Germany. One of Tone's Partisan fighter uncles was killed in 1942. His cousin, another Partisan fighter, was killed at the age of 19. At the other end of the political spectrum, Communist authorities punished his aunts for speaking out against the regime. It was a confusing, dangerous time in which to grow up.

Choices, especially those made during war, when the outcomes were shrouded in mist, were seldom easy. During the Second World War, nowhere throughout occupied Europe was the decision to resist or collaborate more difficult than in Yugoslavia. As soldiers infiltrated the towns and villages, citizens were faced with terrible uncertainties. They had no idea how long the war would last. They didn't know who would win. And there was a real possibility that their identity, as a nation and as a culture, was history. One option was to join the growing movement of Partisan fighters who refused to be bullied by the Nazis. They roamed the hills, killing Italian and German soldiers. Another was to support the Partisans, sending them food and clothing, giving them shelter when they needed it. Either way, if they were caught by the Nazis, they would be killed. Alternatively, citizens could co-operate with the invaders, providing them with information about Partisan movements. If they were caught doing this by the Partisans, however, they would also be killed. Finally, they could simply sit tight and wait to see who would emerge the victor.

Tone's first memory of that fearful time was when German fighter pilots attacked the local radio station. His family hid and watched as the planes circled then dropped their terrible bombs. He learned from his parents that the Germans were their greatest enemy and that the black-uniformed Gestapo soldiers, who tortured and killed Slovenians, were the most dangerous of all. Yet his school classes were taught in German, the only language allowed. To add to the confusion, Tone also attended a clandestine Catholic school, where he was taught in Slovenian by nuns. Although most in Tone's community supported the Partisans, there were Nazi collaborators among them, many of whom were killed when the war ended.

The confusion intensified after the war when people realized that having supported the Partisans in the past now meant endorsing Communism, an ideology not universally embraced. Politics divided the country. It divided communities. And it divided families. During the war, Tone's family had been united against the Germans, but after the war, their differing beliefs tore them apart. Family gatherings often ended in passionate and angry political arguments. Tone was ashamed of his family's intolerance and of his inability to change things. When three of his schoolmates were killed by land mines left over from the war, he struggled to understand whether cheering for Tito also meant cheering for Stalin.

In 1962 the tall, lanky Tone married Jožica Trobevšek, a keen mountain enthusiast from a mountaineering family, and a new and welcome chapter in his life opened up. One year later the Alpine Association of Slovenia created a commission for foreign expeditions. Led by Pavle Šegula, the commission helped climbing become recognized as an official sport, which meant more financial support for climbers who travelled abroad on expeditions. This made it easier for climbers to juggle their domestic obligations with their alpine aspirations. Tone's first Himalayan expedition was to Kangbachen in 1965. Although the team didn't summit, Tone felt he had performed well, so he was crushed when Aleš Kunaver didn't choose him for the 1969 expedition to Annapurna II.

Tone led the 1974 return expedition to Kangbachen, which was successful to a point. Just one month before leaving, they learned that a Polish team had made the first ascent of the peak, bringing into question the need to go at all. Tone was particularly dejected because he felt that the Poles had scooped their route, except for the last hundred metres. In his opinion, it was the Yugoslavians' own fault for not finishing the job when they were there in 1965. They had missed their moment. Although his 1974 expedition had placed ten climbers on the summit, Tone and his team were not satisfied. There was an air of competition among the climbers. Strangely, the fact that so many reached the top seemed to diminish the success of each individual. Tone felt bad about his inability to motivate the climbers to act and think like a team. He attributed this to his own failure to lead. As he wrote in his journal: "I felt the real burden of leadership and I don't feel good as a leader...I want to climb. I want fellowship. I don't want anyone at any time to look up to me...I am not born for this sort of thing." [65]

Aleš must have thought differently, because when he stepped back from the Everest 1979 trip to set up the Manang mountaineering school, he chose Tone to lead the trip. And it was Tone who led the small group that sweated its way up the trail toward Namche Bazaar on the 1978 reconnaissance expedition.

The scouting team included Nejc Zaplotnik, Stane Belak (Šrauf), Štefan Marenče and Roman Robas. With them was a young kitchen boy, whom Nejc nicknamed "the little vampire." The boy's gigantic teeth protruded out over his lower lip at a wild and wacky angle, and no matter how hard he tried to hide them, the little vampire could not.

The climbers were tasked with finding a new, exciting and challenging route for the following year. As they plodded up the trail toward Everest, Nejc felt like a fragile old man, as he was depleted by diarrhea, a gift from some lettuce he had eaten in Kathmandu. His legs wobbled and his head swirled. Completely dehydrated, he recalled the experience in some detail: "I felt like my sphincters were tearing apart and my brain was draining through my ass." [66]

He arrived in base camp five kilograms lighter than when he had started. But the very next day the team climbed more than six hundred metres to the Lho La – the lowest point on the West Ridge – Nejc bringing up the rear. The effort did him in, so his lot for the next couple of days was resting at base camp. Plenty of time for him to watch and be amused by the little vampire. "The little vampire wipes his eternally snotty nose with his hand, scratches his buttock and then peels the cooked potato with the same hand and offers it to Šrauf. This is when an atomic bomb explodes in base camp on the Khumbu Glacier. The little vampire has only his immense good fortune and protection of the gods to thank for his survival." [67]

Šrauf was on a mission to teach all of Nepal about personal hygiene. He was trying to introduce the concept of handkerchiefs and towels to wipe the noses of all those future Snow Tigers, who, up to now, were happy to run barefoot and half-naked around the patches of snow and frozen mud in their villages. His teammates laughed, convinced that it would take centuries to effect such a change; but if anybody could do it, Šrauf could. Excluding the little vampire, of course. "After a thousand years he will still scratch himself, pick his lice, scratch his head and swallow his snot," Nejc declared. [68]

The reconnaissance team learned what they needed to know: the West Ridge Direct route just might be possible; it would be relatively safe from avalanches, but a cable car would be required to haul their heavy loads up to the Lho La. They returned to Yugoslavia, reported in to the Alpine Association and offered some advice for any climber wanting to join the coming expedition: "Train! Train! This is going to be bloody difficult!" [69] Tone withdrew as leader for the trip, calculating that the chances for failure were greater than the possibilities for success. Aleš eventually convinced him to change his mind and stick with the original objective, saying, "Guys, the West Ridge of Everest is unclimbed. If we climbed the South Face of Makalu, we cannot do the normal route on Everest." Despite Aleš's enthusiasm, everyone knew it would be hard – if not, somebody would have climbed it already.

That wasn't from lack of trying. By the time the Americans arrived at Everest in 1963, the mountain had been explored on two of its three main ridges: only the West Ridge remained. Most of the American team was focused on simply getting up the thing, by whatever route was easiest. But an adventuresome duo, Tom Hornbein and Willi Unsoeld, were keen to try the West Ridge – just the two of them. Their plan was to climb the ridge, meet their friends at the top and descend the other side. When they reached the greatest difficulties on the ridge, it became blindingly obvious that this was not a problem for a party of two. The practical pair traversed left to a couloir that led straight up to the summit. Later called the Hornbein Couloir, their route became a classic on the mountain.

But as iconic as the Hornbein route was, the complete West Ridge remained. And now that the reconnaissance team had taken a look, the Yugoslavians were determined to climb it. For the rest of the year, a group of hopeful and ambitious young climbers set about training. They lifted weights, ran laps and climbed and climbed and climbed. Meanwhile, the Belgrade-based Alpine Association sent out a notice of the impending expedition. Interested climbers responded with a formal expression of interest. Although most climbers were from mountainous Slovenia, Everest was the seventh Yugoslavian national expedition, and the association decreed that at least five members come from other parts of the country. There were between 80 and 100 applicants. After the first elimination round, 40 remained. The second elimination round determined the final 25 climbers. Twenty-two-year-old Andrej Štremfelj and his 24-year-old brother Marko were among them. From the beginning, Andrej expected to be a support climber.

The team of 25 included many of the old hands who had cut their teeth on Makalu, but there were also a few newcomers, including four climbers from Bosnia and Croatia. "Serbia didn't have any good climbers at the time," Tone said. Rising to the top of the elimination rounds was Croatian climber Stipe Božić. He first became known to Slovenian climbers during his military stint, which he served in the Julian Alps. There, the dark-haired, olive-skinned and classically handsome Stipe met – and impressed – many Slovenian climbers, including Viki Grošelj. He had trained on rock in Split and climbed with Stanko Gilić in Paklenica on the Croatian coast. It was Stanko who instilled a set of values in Stipe that combined a love for climbing and a need to communicate, at first through writing and later as a filmmaker.

Still young and innocent, Stipe couldn't have been happier. Nejc understood that feeling of freedom and youthful state of grace, and he described it in *Pot*: "I was free. As free as a man is in those years. He is not aware of his own freedom; he doesn't have to fight for it. All he feels is that he is alive. He hasn't achieved anything big yet, so he has no enemies; he is open-minded, so has lots of friends. He is not yet aware that people, even when they are the closest, are as distant from each other as the stars, and is therefore never alone." [70]

Stipe's background was humble, even a bit confusing. His official birthday was January 2, 1951, but that's not when he was born. It was on a cold, snowy night on December 26 of the previous year that Stipe appeared, born next to the fireplace in a 16-square-metre stone hut. His parents delayed reporting his birth until the following year, gaining some small financial advantages in the process. Neda, his mother, had spent her childhood in the Sinai Peninsula, where she was sent as a refugee at the age of 7 during the Second World War. His father, Jože, fought as a teenaged Partisan in the war and later earned his living growing grapes and making wine. He raised goats and sheep, as well – an enterprise that brought no end of grief to poor Stipe, given the job of shepherding them. He particularly hated one finicky ewe called Gala, who was always escaping into the cabbage patch on Stipe's watch. Thankfully, Gala was eventually slaughtered and eaten.

When he wasn't herding sheep, Stipe scrambled around the mountains near his home, and even a bit further afield along the Bosnian border. Troglav, highest peak of the Dinaric Alps, still remains his greatest love, even after a long and successful career in the Himalaya. Just 60 kilometres from Split, where he eventually settled, Troglav was a good training ground, with steep, rocky faces and good winter climbing. When Stipe climbed Afghanistan's 7492-metre Noshaq in 1975, his career was launched. Four years later he was chosen to join the cream of Slovenian climbers on Everest.

◆ ◆ ◆

The 1979 expedition was a massive affair: 19 Sherpas, three cooks, three kitchen boys, two mail runners, 700 porters and 18 tons of equipment. The 25 climbers marched to their mountain like champions, their bodies firm and strong. They assembled at base camp on March 31. The climb became interesting when the team started hauling six tons of supplies up to Camp I, using a winch system for the last two hundred metres below the Lho La. Together with the Sherpas, the climbers bored holes in the wall, mounted ladders and competed with each other to see who could crank the winch hardest and haul the most cargo in a day. The Sherpas cranked while belting out "My Darling Clementine," and the climbers resorted to dirty versions of popular Slovenian songs. The monotonous days sped by in a flash.

A strong feeling of camaraderie infused the team as the joking continued up the mountain. Šrauf chased Marjan Manfreda up the wall. "Marjan, slow down. It's for your own sake!" But everyone knew that Šrauf couldn't keep up with Marjan, the greyhound. The other climbers terrorized Šrauf with their teasing, but it was all in good fun. He retained his reputation as a straight-shooting guy, never mincing his words, confident that his opinion was always on target. With his picturesque vocabulary, his original cuss words and his expressive face, he was totally absorbed in the present.

Aside from the joking around, there was a serious element. Tone Škarja's strategy for getting up the ridge wasn't based solely on past experiences on big mountains. His strategy was about performance on this particular mountain. And he was watching. If a climber couldn't reach Camp V without supplemental oxygen, he wasn't a summit candidate, as it was only above Camp V that oxygen would be used. The teams kept changing: as one climber became ill or too tired to go on, another would replace him. No partnership was sacred; everything depended on performance. Viki Grošelj had climbed under the leadership of both Aleš Kunaver and Tone Škarja, and he noticed significant differences in style. "Kunaver was a diplomat," Viki said. "We respected him enormously because he never said bad words about people. He just made suggestions…and we tried three times harder." Not so with Tone. "Nothing was good enough for Škarja," Viki recalled, but then he added, "But if he was quiet, you knew it was good. Silence was an enormous prize from Škarja."

Viki Grošelj and Marjan Manfreda pitched Camp V at 8120 metres, and it was Viki and Marjan who earned the first chance at the summit. Not far above Camp V, at around 8300 metres, reared a difficult rock chimney – the crux of the entire climb (UIAA Grade V).[71] The chimney was so narrow that Marjan, who led the pitch, couldn't carry a pack because it jammed in the narrow cleft of rock, stopping his upward progress. Without a pack to carry oxygen bottles, he couldn't use supplemental oxygen. The climbing was so difficult and the handholds so small that he couldn't use gloves. As Marjan's crampons raked against the smooth wall, it took all of his skill on rock and all of his experience earned on Makalu's South Face to keep moving up. At first his fingers were on fire, as if they were being boiled. Later, not as much.

Viki stood below, belaying him. "I just took care for Marjan, who fell three times. The fourth time up, he attached a fixed rope and said it was too late, and tomorrow we would continue." Marjan rappelled down. They were about to return to Camp V to try again the next day when they noticed his hands. Frozen, like stone. They headed down, Viki to Camp III and Marjan as fast as possible all the way to base camp for treatment.

The next day, Dušan Podbevšek and Roman Robas moved into position for a summit bid. They lost their way in the rock towers along the ridge above Marjan's chimney and had to return as well.

Now it was Nejc and the Štremfelj brothers' turn. The winds roared down, tossing the climbers to the ground, almost sweeping them off the mountain like unwanted dust. Their lungs were choked with snow and ice crystals as they cowered behind rocks and clipped themselves to pitons, clinging to the ridge. Near Camp V the powerful winds forced the climbers to crawl. They finally retreated from the hopeless conditions.

Down in Camp IV they huddled in the tent, which flapped with such violence they worried it would be swept away. When the wind suddenly stopped, the frame sprang back, snapping the canvas so loudly they were almost deafened by the noise. During the night, which they spent awake and on edge, Nejc resolved that Everest would be his last summit. But almost as soon as he made the decision, he knew he was fooling himself. There would be no end to his climbing in the big mountains: "My way is without an end."[72] With gusts as high as two hundred kilometres per hour penetrating their very souls, the climbers were forced down after several days without rest. Desperate for shelter, they crawled along the endless Lho La back to Camp I, and finally to base camp, where they regrouped and recovered.

On May 13 Nejc, along with Andrej and Marko Štremfelj, was back in Camp V, again in position. What a team: Nejc and Andrej had established themselves as a formidable duo on Gasherbrum I. The brothers were inseparable. As a threesome, they couldn't be beat. But there are many factors that contribute to a climb of this magnitude: climbing conditions, weather, illness and technology. And on Everest, it was technology that let them down.

It was Saturday evening, and they were poised at Camp V. After preparing the oxygen bottles, they finished drinking their last cups of tea. They crept into their sleeping bags, put on their oxygen masks and set the ventilators at a half-litre per minute. Now it was just a matter of waiting for morning. Outside the tent the night was desperately cold, and the sky was heavy with stars so bright they felt within reach. A light wind rustled the tent. Nejc tried to rest but his mind was racing.

> Tomorrow a great day will dawn. I have thought a lot about this moment but now I cannot think any longer. I am ready for anything. I know we will risk a lot. A long time ago I decided that, for Everest, I am even willing to give up my toes. Hands were another matter, or so I thought then, but now I am convinced that no sacrifice is too great. Even my life! Perhaps you don't believe me! Andrej certainly believes me. And I believe myself, which is the most important thing. If only you could see my friends' weary faces. If you could have seen them, their eyes glowing as they staggered with fatigue, you too would believe it![73]

Nejc wasn't the only one thinking along these lines. Andrej was uneasy, wrestling with his ambitions. "I only saw the summit," he said. "How to be the best on the mountain and to climb as high as possible. It didn't feel competitive. It felt like a team. It felt like solidarity." Although Andrej understood that if one person reached the summit, the expedition would be deemed a success, he understood himself even better. "For me, there would be no success if I didn't reach the summit. I would be happy for the expedition, but personally it wouldn't be a success. I was ambitious."

At two in the morning, Andrej began heating water for tea. Nejc woke from his oxygen-assisted sleep. Sometime during the night, Marko's oxygen system had failed, and he was now using his backup ventilator. They laced up their boots, prepared their cameras and ropes and packed two bottles of oxygen per person in their packs.

They strapped on their crampons and at 5:00 am crawled out of the tent. When Andrej opened his ventilator, however, it cracked, hissing louder and louder. He unscrewed it and returned to the tent for a backup replacement.

The climbers knew what to expect early on the route because of Marjan and Viki's description. Nejc was out front when Andrej called him back. Unbelievably, Marko's backup ventilator had also failed. Now he had none. Useless tears welled up in Marko's eyes as he waved goodbye and started down off the cursed mountain. As he watched his brother disappear, Andrej's stomach dropped. "I lost interest in the summit," he said. "I was trying to find a reason to go down."

Andrej was now faced with a soul-destroying situation like the one Nejc had faced four years earlier on Makalu, torn between loyalty and ambition. Nejc wrote about that internal struggle in *Pot*:

> Two of us will have to turn back because of equipment failure. We keep postponing the decision…The only ones left are Den [Danilo Cedilnik] and me. We all know there is no time for discussion. Den vigorously insists that I should be the one to go on and claims that he will not change his mind. His voice breaks when he says it but his decision is made. He speaks faster than me. I cannot choose between a great goal and a great friend. I feel like crying and find that I cannot get one word out. I want to suggest that we choose by lot but I can't bring myself to say it. As soon as I try, I imagine the sad descent with the shining summit of Makalu disappearing into the blue skies far above me, lost forever. Yet how much is the summit worth when I see tears in my friend's eyes? Something dies inside me. An emptiness opens up in my heart. My faith in the humanity inside me has been destroyed. The only thing left is this terrible alpinist's longing. I am aware that Den should be the one to go on…He is older than me and will probably not get another chance like this, while I have my whole life before me…Tears fall inside me and burn me more than if they were real tears, freezing on my cheeks…Thank you, Den. You thought you had lost the summit. But you won a friend forever.[74]

When Nejc saw Marko turn and start down, he swore and slammed his axe against a rock. He felt like smashing the entire damnable oxygen apparatus. Instead, he turned around and started climbing, with Andrej right behind him. They were making rapid progress toward the gully when there was a sudden loud hiss. Andrej's backup ventilator had failed. Instead of raging and cursing, Nejc sensed that the situation had reached a critical point. He remained completely calm and replaced Andrej's backup ventilator with his own backup. There were no more backups.

Crack. Another hiss.

Now Andrej and Nejc both lost their calm, cursing as only Šrauf, their cursing mentor, could curse. Nejc unscrewed the broken ventilator and flung it down. Andrej remembers that Nejc said, "Andrej, take my ventilator and the bottles. You will climb on with the oxygen ahead of me and I'll climb behind you without it."[75]

Andrej refused. "That's crazy. You know the price that Marjan paid for his effort."

"Okay, then I'll climb it alone," Nejc announced.

"No, Nejc. You can't," pleaded Andrej.

But Nejc wasn't in a frame of mind to go back. The only acceptable path was the one that went to the summit. He was prepared to give his life. "We have been through too much. Our yearning has been too great for me to turn my back on the mountain now. And back home there are people who love me, who trust me and respect me much more than I respect myself. For them, too, I am prepared to go all the way."[76]

In a moment of intuitive brilliance (or luck), Nejc retrieved the broken ventilator and screwed it back onto Andrej's oxygen bottle and spit on it. His reason for doing so was to test the extent of the leakage, but miraculously, the hissing lessened. Astonished, he realized that the saliva was freezing, filling up the tiny leak in the ventilator. He licked the icy metal like a puppy, losing the tip of his tongue in the process, until the hissing stopped completely. He looked up at Andrej. The saliva bandage seemed to be holding. "We just said, 'Okay, it works again.' We didn't think ahead," recalled Andrej. As they moved on, Andrej's thoughts of descending receded. "I got in the mood, and I forgot about my brother, and I became focused on the summit."

They continued up a gully until they were faced with the smooth, vertical chimney. On the slabs to the left of the chimney a white rope dangled, thanks to Marjan, who had climbed this crux section with his bare hands. Nejc attached his Jumars (ascending devices) to the ice-sheathed rope. His crampons scratched against the smooth rock. He adjusted his oxygen to four litres per minute and, panting like a racehorse, hauled himself up the chimney. Andrej clicked away with his camera below, documenting the effort.

For a brief moment Nejc let his mind wander to the future. A warm room full of friends, the smell of wine and cigarette smoke. Instead of screaming wind, the sound of a crackling fire. Crampons replaced by fleece-lined slippers. The friendly sound of climbers' voices, and images on a screen. Images of this unforgiving place. This magnificent mountain of their dreams.

He snapped back to the present and hoisted himself off the fixed line. Looking up, he could see two options in the gully ahead. The day before, Roman and Dušan had taken the wrong one and were stopped dead at the top of a gendarme. Nejc and Andrej chose the other way and ended up at a steep rock step directly below the ridge. It appeared completely smooth and covered by a thin layer of snow.

"Should we rope up now?" asked Andrej.

"No, it's better to go fast. We can go faster without the rope," Nejc replied.

Nejc crammed the end of his axe into a small cleft in the rock and hauled himself across the slab and onto the ridge. The wind slammed him with such a force that he was sure he would be swept into Tibet. Both men dropped to their knees as the huge blast of air screamed and moaned around the rocky corners of the ridge, sounding like an ethereal cathedral organ. Below them was the vast river of ice that forms the Western Cwm. Beyond the ridge of Nuptse, the plains of India shimmered in the distance.

With their goggles caked in ice, they crept up the sharp, exposed ridge, which was interspersed with frightening rock barriers. They were in the Yellow Band – a prominent layer of rock that encircles Everest between 8200 and 8600 metres. Nejc later lost all memory of the next stages of the climb. He would not remember how they moved from the Yellow Band to the Grey Band, where the rock changes character. He would only recall that things became easier for a time. That there were some snowfields and the occasional rock step. And that, at some point, they roped up. And then the Grey Band became cruel near the end, steep and terribly exposed to the wind.

Although they were above the hardest pitch – the chimney – Nejc and Andrej began to experience real difficulties at this point. They had benefited from the fixed line in the chimney, but now they were out front, leading on difficult and exposed rock, searching for a route to the top. At least they had supplemental oxygen, something Marjan didn't have when he had forced the route up the chimney.

They reached a steep, forbidding wall, a bit overhanging at the start. Andrej recalled that Nejc removed his gloves and crampons, preparing to climb it straight on. Andrej scouted around to the left and found an alternative route, steeper at first but then easing off. They traversed toward the South Face on a terrifyingly small, crumbling ledge with 2500 metres of space gaping below them. The exposure was almost too much to bear. But they forced themselves to think of other ledges that were just as narrow – in the Julian Alps – and safely crossed. They dug a small belay stance in the snow and pounded a piton into the fragmented rock. As Andrej belayed, Nejc began to climb barehanded on the next steep section. The frozen rock numbed his naked fingers almost immediately. He changed holds a few times, trying to get in balance, but he could feel nothing.

Suddenly the Western Cwm rushed toward him as a handhold broke off in his hand. Andrej held him with the rope. Back on the snow, Nejc waved his arms around like a windmill, adrenalin coursing through his veins, his fingers screaming in pain as the blood returned. Andrej said nothing, simply watching and waiting. His trust in Nejc was complete. Nejc tried again. A foothold broke a bit higher up, and he slid back down to Andrej. Leader-falls at 8500 metres. It seemed a bit extreme, even for these two.

"What time is it?" asked Nejc.

"11:45."

Scowling, Nejc replied, "That's late. Very late. We're moving too slowly."

"What are we going to do about getting down?" asked Andrej. "We can't down-climb this stuff. It's too difficult, don't you agree?"

Nejc didn't reply. They could worry about that on the summit.

For his next attempt at the rock step, Nejc made a small loop with a rope and slung it over a rock outcrop above him. He stepped into the loop, but it didn't provide the support he needed.

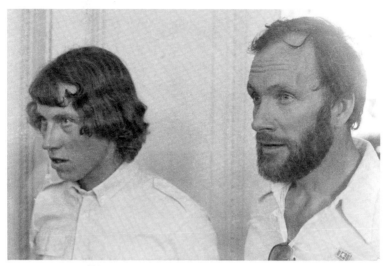

From top: Nejc Zaplotnik and Stane Belak (Šrauf). *NEJC ZAPLOTNIK COLLECTION*

Stipe Božić (far right) with his family in front of the stone hut where he was born. *STIPE BOŽIĆ COLLECTION*

Portrait of young Croatian climber Stipe Božić. *STIPE BOŽIĆ COLLECTION*

Aleš Kunaver, inspired leader of the first generation of Yugoslavian climbers to the Himalaya. STIPE BOŽIĆ COLLECTION

The 1978 Everest West Ridge reconnaissance team: Roman Robas, Tone Škarja, Stane Belak (Šrauf), Nejc Zaplotnik, "the little vampire" and Štefan Marenče. *Tone Škarja collection*

The mountaineering school at Manang – Aleš Kunaver's dream. *Aleš Kunaver collection*

Top: Nejc Zaplotnik at Everest in 1979. *NEJC ZAPLOTNIK COLLECTION.*

Below, left: Stane Belak (Šrauf) at Everest, 1979. *STIPE BOŽIĆ COLLECTION*

Below, right: This portrait of Stane Belak (Šrauf) showcases the horn on his forehead, which signified a rage that everyone wanted to avoid. *STANE BELAK COLLECTION, COURTESY OF SIDARTA PUBLISHING.*

Top: Marko Štremfelj, Marjan Manfreda and Franček Knez on Everest, 1979. *ANDREJ ŠTREMFELJ COLLECTION*

118

The complex cable and winch system used by the Yugoslavian team to move supplies and equipment up to the Lho La on Everest, 1979. *STIPE BOŽIĆ COLLECTION*

Top: Carrying loads to the Lho La, Everest West Ridge expedition, 1979. TONE ŠKARJA COLLECTION

Below: Marjan Manfreda climbing the chimney (Grade V+) at 8300 metres on Everest's West Ridge. His bold lead opened the route. VIKI GROŠELJ COLLECTION

Howling winds on the West Shoulder of Everest, 1979. *TONE ŠKARJA COLLECTION*

Top: Line of the first ascent of the Direct West Ridge of Everest, 1979. *Viki Grošelj*
collection

Below: The pulley system in action on the West Ridge of Everest, 1979. *Andrej*
Štremfelj collection

Andrej Štremfelj,
Nejc Zaplotnik and
Marko Štremfelj
before their summit
bid on the Everest
West Ridge Direct,
1979. *ANDREJ
ŠTREMFELJ COLLECTION*

Below: Andrej
Štremfelj and Nejc
Zaplotnik near
Camp 4 on Everest's
West Ridge, 1979.
*MARKO ŠTREMFELJ,
COURTESY TONE ŠKARJA
COLLECTION*

Andrej Štremfelj climbing below the Grey Band, near the summit of Mt. Everest, on his way to making the first ascent of the West Ridge Direct in 1979 with Nejc Zaplotnik. *ANDREJ ŠTREMFELJ COLLECTION*

Above, left: Nejc Zaplotnik on the summit of Everest, 1979, via the West Ridge Direct with Andrej Štremfelj. *Nejc Zaplotnik collection*

Above, right: Andrej Štremfelj and Nejc Zaplotnik in Camp I after descending from the summit of Mt. Everest in 1979. *Andrej Štremfelj collection.*

Left: Stane Belak (Šrauf) on the summit of Everest, 1979, after having climbed the West Ridge Direct. *Stipe Božić collection*

Below: Stipe Božić filming Stane Belak (Šrauf) on Everest in 1979. *Stane Belak collection*

The South Face of Lhotse with the lines of ascent by the Yugoslavian team of
1981. *Aleš Kunaver collection*

Top: Unconsolidated, fluted snow features high on the South Face of Lhotse, 1981. *ALEŠ KUNAVER COLLECTION*

Below: Climbing fixed lines on the South Face of Lhotse, 1981. *ALEŠ KUNAVER COLLECTION*

The South Face of Lhotse, 1981, raked by avalanches and unrelentingly steep. *STIPE BOŽIĆ COLLECTION*

Clockwise from top left: Franček Knez at Lhotse in 1981 – the man who would finally break through the barrier of the South Face to reach the ridge. *Aleš Kunaver* COLLECTION

Difficult climbing at 7400 metres on the South Face of Lhotse, 1981. *Viki Grošelj* COLLECTION

Andrej Štremfelj climbing without gloves on questionable snow-covered rock at approximately 8250 meters on the South Face of Lhotse, 1981. *Photo by Peter Podgornik. Courtesy Andrej Štremfelj collection*

Camp VI at 8000 metres on the South Face of Lhotse. *Aleš Kunaver collection*

He began slipping again. With the Western Cwm still haunting him, he held onto a minuscule hidden hold and scratched his foot onto a slight protuberance. He knee-jammed his body into position and held on. "Keep calm, keep calm," he said to himself. "You still have a lot of strength. You're not finished yet." He felt as if he were climbing with metal hooks for hands as he dragged himself off the rock onto a snow-covered ledge. He later wrote in *Pot*: "We shall win this battle! Not a battle with the mountain, but rather a battle with ourselves and our weaknesses. You cannot fight nature...You can only survive or perish in nature. These are the only options, and the choice depends on you alone. We choose life!"[77]

Nejc traversed along a narrow ledge, but just as he arrived at a cleft in the rock, the rope came tight. He could go no further. He nailed a piton into the shallow crack, a mere two centimetres deep. Two centimetres of doubtful protection. Now it was Andrej's turn. Hopefully, he wouldn't fall.

Nejc could feel Andrej's full weight on the rope as it stretched taut. Was he climbing? Ascending the ropes with his Jumars? With horror he looked at the piton, which was now bending from the weight. As the fog swirled around him, Nejc lost sight of the void below and suddenly felt confident. "I am not afraid. I trust in luck. I absolutely trust in my luck."[78] Thirty-five years later, Andrej laughed at his own memory of that moment: "Yes, I was jumaring at that point – good thing I didn't know about the bad piton."

When Andrej reached Nejc, their oxygen bottles were both empty, so they flung them off the mountain. The bottles clanged and bounced into the foggy abyss. With their second bottles deployed, Andrej started off and soon reached the top of the Grey Band, at which point they unroped.[79]

Nejc remembered that they hadn't checked in with base camp, and he hauled out the radio.

"Hello, Tone. Report back!"

"Receiving!"

"We are on top of the Grey Band. From here on, the climbing gets easier, and we might be on the summit in about three hours."

"Good job, boys. You won't turn back now, will you?"

"The wind is so bad here. We won't be able to descend on this side.

We'll probably go down the south side. We should maybe ask the Austrians if we can borrow their tents."

"We will arrange everything. You just be good and climb on."

"What time is it?"

"Twelve o'clock. Good luck. We'll be in touch at all times. Over."

Andrej and Nejc stared at each other. Only noon? Impossible! It was 11:45 three hours ago. Andrej shook his head in confusion, wondering how he could have made such a mistake. But such a wonderful mistake! The news gave them new confidence, not only that they could reach the summit but that they also might avoid a life-threatening bivouac. As Nejc fumbled with the radio, he noticed his hands. Pure white. And numb as marble. Gripped by panic, he rubbed them, flinging them around, banging them against his legs. Finally a familiar painful and stinging feeling returned to the digits. His fingers were still white, but he hoped he could save them. He also understood, however, that they might be the price of Everest's West Ridge.

Although the fog had now become impenetrable and the air was choked with falling snow, they were confident they would not get lost. They had studied this mountain for so long that they knew exactly where to go. They read the complex terrain with assurance. They knew that the snow slope steepened and narrowed into a gully that rose to the last rock step below the summit. Now climbing with their gloves on and without the rope, they scratched their way up the rock. Soon they were on a gentle snow slope covered in a thin layer of black sand that the wind had blown up from Tibet. And there, at the top of a sharp, snow-covered ridge, looming through the fog, was the tripod placed on the summit by the Chinese team in 1975.

Nejc stopped and waited for Andrej. Andrej hesitated, not wanting to go first. Nejc had been the engine on this climb – he deserved to be first. But Nejc thought otherwise. He had been first on Gasherbrum I. Now it was Andrej's turn. It became an irrelevant discussion as the two friends embraced on the top. They hugged and cried and slapped each other's shoulders. They took off their oxygen masks and sat down in the snow next to the Chinese tripod. Now what? Emptied of all the stress and gut-wrenching fear, they simply sat there. Then Nejc remembered. The radio.

"Hello, Tone. Hello, Tone. We are on the summit!"

A roar erupted, not only from base camp, but from climbers at every camp on the mountain. Šrauf, Stipe and Ang Phu, their sirdar, were on their way to Camp V when Stipe heard the news. He screamed down to Šrauf, who was struggling with lack of oxygen and black thoughts of doubt. "Šrauf, Šrauf, they are on the summit!" Šrauf's mood soared; he forgot his weariness as waves of relief washed over him. He leaned on a rock and began to sob and then, with a burst of energy, ran up to Stipe to share the joy together.

"Everest is ours! I feel like hugging the West Ridge above us," he yelled into the radio.

Base camp radioed in with questions about the descent.

Nejc answered, "We're sitting by the Chinese pyramid and don't know what to do. Motherfucker. What to do now, eh?"

He and Tone discussed their options. The first notion of going down the south side was discarded. (Andrej later expressed huge relief that this option had been eliminated. There were no expeditions on the South Col route, and after seeing the route in 1990 when he climbed it with his wife, Marija, he knew they would have died on that descent.) Finally, it looked as if the best choice was to descend the Hornbein Couloir. Although the couloir would probably require some rappels, it would bring them back down to easier terrain eventually leading to Camp IV, where their teammates waited. The lure of friendship and warmth was stronger than the promise of a less technical but unknown descent down the south side.

Still on the radio, Nejc and Tone erupted into a string of ecstatic expletives involving goddess mothers and intimate physical acts.

Tone Škarja: "Fuck...Oh, God! Amazing! Cheers!"

Nejc Zaplotnik: "Tone, don't you know that we are on top of her! Of Holy Mother! We are the motherfuckers!"

Tone Škarja: "Oh fuck it! Come, come, stop talking, boy!"[80]

With a start, Andrej and Nejc realized that they needed to pull themselves together and concentrate, because the route ahead was steep, exposed and difficult. They put on their oxygen masks and, before leaving, picked up a few rocks close to the summit. The first rock was for Marjan.

To save time and avoid a bivouac, they agreed to use the rope as little as possible. The mountain's features revealed themselves, one by one. Open book. Snowfield. Gully. Rock steps. They reached a vertical chimney in the Yellow Band, where they discovered a piton from the 1963 ascent. Climbing unroped down the steepening rock, they reached a narrow cleft from which Nejc exited across a boulder. Then, all of a sudden, Andrej's pack frame caught in the chimney and he tumbled head over heels. Flipping, he accelerated wildly, passing Nejc at high speed.

"Andrej, stop! Stop!"

After falling 50 or 60 metres, Andrej somehow turned himself around and slammed his axe into the slope with all his might. He came to rest and lay on the slope, covered in snow. His goggles and hat continued rolling downhill faster and faster until they disappeared. Nejc climbed down as quickly as he could.

"Andrej, are you okay?"

Andrej lifted his head and offered a weak smile. He stood up, brushed himself off and carried on, seemingly unfazed. "I put so much energy into this self-arrest that for 15 minutes I couldn't talk," he recalled. "I didn't feel any fear. But I was hyperventilating. I cut the fall out. It was done. Now I had to continue what I was doing before. It is a survival technique," he explained.

Focused like lasers now, they continued down the gully, which became increasingly benign, eventually opening onto a vast snowfield. The slopes leading to Camp IV seemed interminable to the two exhausted men. As night fell they began to lose their way. Their headlamps flickered and failed, and the temperature dropped. The cold began to seep into their bodies as surely as fear infiltrated their brains. Could they be too low on the mountain? Had they missed their camp?

Then, at 9:30 pm, they saw them. The tiny lights of Camp IV!

Their teammates came up to meet them, embrace them and help them complete the last steps to the tent. Suddenly there was warmth and tea and friendship. At last they could collapse into a dreamless state. But sleep was elusive for Nejc. "I have a feeling that I have experienced too much to ever sleep peacefully again." [81]

Days later, when they reached base camp, Andrej embraced his brother, Marko, who had only one thing to say to him: "Drejc, you are alive. You are alive!" Nejc went to Marjan's tent, where they talked for hours. About the crux pitch. About the Grey Band. About the summit. About Marjan's frozen hands. When Nejc could no longer control his emotions of gratitude and respect, he gave Marjan the small stone from the summit and left.

Meanwhile, up high on the mountain, Šrauf, Stipe and Ang Phu moved into position.

Ang Phu had become a climbing Sherpa at the age of 21 when he landed a job on one of the first international expeditions to Everest. He gained valuable experience, using equipment given to him by foreign climbers. Ang Phu was fearless and strong. His noble and fairly wealthy family from Khumjung was upset that he insisted on working on expeditions, but their concerns were in vain. He loved the work, the thrills and the mountains themselves. After he climbed Everest in 1978, he became famous. He even attracted an American mistress who wanted to wed and live with him in the United States. He declined. And now he had earned the chance to climb Everest a second time, by a completely different route. If he succeeded, he would become the first person to do so. Ang Phu was highly motivated.

The trio – Šrauf, Stipe and Ang Phu – waited out one day of bad weather in Camp V before setting out, following Nejc and Andrej's route to the Grey Band. Stipe filmed the entire climb. Their faulty oxygen bottles broke down as expected and were repaired with the same high-tech saliva method. They took a slightly different route at the Grey Band, traversing through less-steep rock steps into the Hornbein Couloir and up to the American Step. Here, Ang Phu wanted to stop, saying that his rock-climbing skills weren't good enough. Stipe helped him through the difficult bits, and before they knew it, all three were on top. With all the picture-taking, radio-calling and flag-hoisting, it was a full hour before they thought of descending.

Then the nightmare began.

During their 12-hour climb, a snowstorm had crept in. Down-climbing the American Step was difficult, and Stipe became pinned down in an exposed position by some strong gusts of wind. Stuck there for half an hour, he pounded the rock with his axe in a helpless rage.

As the storm gathered strength, the light faded and the fog thickened. Their oxygen ran out, and almost immediately the intense cold began to rob them of their body heat. Despite Šrauf's repeated calls to base camp, the radio remained quiet as a grave. They were completely on their own.

Šrauf pulled ahead of Ang Phu and Stipe, then stopped to wait. He could hear their voices high up in the murk.

"Stipe. Ang Phu," he called up. "What's happening? Are you okay?" No answer.

Frustrated now at their slowness, he tried to radio down again. "Base, come in. Base, come in." No response.

He descended the couloir, pounding in pitons and fixing the rope to ensure a safe descent for Stipe and Ang Phu.

Then Stipe called down. "Šrauf, I can't feel my legs. I think they're freezing."

Ang Phu said nothing. Realizing with horror that they would not reach camp that night, Šrauf scouted for a reasonably safe spot to reassemble. They would need to bivy above eight thousand metres, and they were completely unprepared. He screamed back up to the others to tell them what he was doing, but the storm swallowed his words.

Stipe arrived first, stiff from cold and moaning about the pain in his legs and hands. Ang Phu arrived at around midnight. Their tiny ledge was at 8300 metres. The wind ripped Šrauf's jacket apart and caked his goggles with ice. Haunted by the threat of freezing, Šrauf wanted to keep down-climbing, as a group. But Ang Phu, who had been silent so far, said in a calm voice and with complete certainty, "Šrauf. Stop. We will die this night." [82]

Base camp had been trying to make contact with Šrauf, to send up encouragement and advice. But as his radio began to die, Šrauf's voice came through more weakly with each transmission. The pauses between calls were longer and longer, until there was absolute silence. A wordless pall descended as base camp waited. Their fears smouldered as they relived that last desperate call from the indestructible Šrauf, screaming for a response.

But Šrauf, Stipe and Ang Phu did not die that night. They held on till morning. Šrauf relived hundreds of bivouacs in the Julian Alps – some almost as bad as this. If he could just survive the night, it would be like a second birthday. He could do it. They could all do it.

In *Pot* Nejc captured the emotions and thoughts climbers experience when bivouacking:

> As you start your bivouac, you imagine that it's going to be relatively comfortable. But then a never-ending night begins its destructive work. Wet clothes, horrible cold, chattering teeth, hunger, thirst, and a feeling that it will never end. Yet down below, somewhere on a different planet, people are sitting in warm rooms, with glasses full of wine that spill onto the table in merry, round splashes, heated faces, increasingly suggestive jokes, women starting to hug the men around the shoulders and unbuttoning their sweaty blouses, half-drunken songs mixed with cries of Dutch courage, rising all the way up to our little attic room. Then an accordion drowns everything out and the climax of the party goes on and on, like the endless minutes we are counting. But this doesn't lower our morale.[83]

They shivered and talked and moved their limbs, trying to stay awake, trying to stay alive. When Stipe began to drift off, Šrauf pummelled him, badgering him with orders to stay awake. They prayed for the dawn. After what seemed like an endless polar night, the blackness became slightly less ominous and the wind died down. A strange, silvery light slid over them as a new day dawned and the horrors of the night faded.

They unwound themselves from their frozen embrace and started down the huge snowfield, leaving the rope behind. As the temperature rose, they felt reborn. There were no more obstacles between them and Camp IV, just firm névé snow.

"We have survived, Ang Phu," Šrauf shouted. "You will come to Yugoslavia, Ang Phu…You will see our mountains. White mountains against the blue sky and our blue sea."[84]

Figures appeared at the bottom of the couloir, and the three men heard voices calling upward. Borut Bergant, Ivan Kotnik and Vanja Matijevec were on their way up from Camp IV to help them down. Instead of going to the summit, which had been their plan, they had chosen to help – another case of individual ambitions set aside for the good of the team. Vanja arrived with oxygen for Šrauf and then climbed up to Stipe, who had lost his crampon. Ivan and Borut waited at the end of the couloir with hot tea, radioing to base camp that the crisis had ended.

Ang Phu arrived and stretched out his hand to greet Borut. The next moment, he slipped. An awkward step, a moment of lost concentration. He fell on his back and began sliding down the slope. For a split second everyone froze. Then Borut reached out, trying to catch him. But Ang Phu was already a few metres lower, his hands and legs in the air, sliding faster and faster. A few metres stretched to 20 in a matter of seconds. Why didn't he self-arrest with his ice axe? What was he waiting for? Finally, when already moving at great speed, he twisted around in an attempt to stop his slide. His axe flew out of his hand. Now there was no chance unless he hit a patch of soft snow. He did, but only for a moment before he was back on the hard névé snow, tumbling faster and faster. A few hundred metres below, black rock ribs waited as his body fell, so naturally. He hit the rocks, bounced up in a great sweeping arc and then disappeared. All that remained were a few scratches on the snow and the blindingly white mountains. And silence.

His was a classic alpinist's death. Suddenly. Without goodbyes. Forever.

The climbers stared in disbelief. Then Borut started yelling into the radio. Numb, Šrauf began crab-walking down the moderate slope to Camp IV. Alone now, as the others were waiting for Stipe, his body was heavy as lead. Fatigue from the night and despair from the fall suffocated him. "Although I'm going downhill, I have to rest almost every 50 metres. Ang Phu is walking beside me, weighing on my conscience." [85] He reached Camp IV at 10:00 am on May 16, after 30 hours of effort.

Ang Phu's death signalled the end of the expedition and only added to Aleš Kunaver's commitment to the Manang mountaineering school. It was blatantly clear to everyone who saw the fall that Ang Phu didn't know how to self-arrest. A technique that every climber practises countless times was not in his arsenal.

◆ ◆ ◆

Everest 1979 was a massive success, but not everyone on the mountain embraced the big-expedition mentality. Franček Knez, one of the strongest technical climbers in the group and a man who would become a Slovenian climbing legend, was one. The endless hauling of loads and jumaring up fixed ropes didn't mesh with his style. Very slight – almost delicate in stature – he was more comfortable in an unleashed version of the vertical world. "I never had much time for summits, long ridges that dragged on forever," he wrote.[86] A philosophical man, he was thoughtful about what he did and why he did it. "Our body is a reflection of our thoughts and actions. We don't always live in our bodies. We aren't always at home. Very often we live in our memories and our longings. And then we are absent masters of our property."[87] He did his part on the mountain, and his efforts, like those of the others, contributed to the eventual success of the climb. But when he felt he could do nothing more, he asked Tone for permission to solo climb nearby 6639-metre Khumbutse. Tone agreed but added, "Just don't kill yourself."[88] Tone was later criticized for this unusual decision, but he reasoned, "Franček was a special man...He was a famous mountaineer, and if he wasn't going to climb Everest, he had to have something in his pocket."

Years later, Andrej retained strong memories of their team effort. "We were climbing for the team, not so much for Yugoslavia. We didn't have such a patriotic feeling. Of course we had flags in our packs, but we weren't so serious about it." Everest was a huge stroke of good fortune for Andrej, and he responded with energy and grace. And when he got home, he opened the little book where he recorded all his climbs and added one line: "JZ GREBEN – YU SMER – MT. EVEREST 19.3 – 13.5 79 I, II, III, IV, V, 30° - 50°. [SW Ridge, Yugoslavian route, Everest, duration of expedition, UIAA grades and degrees of steepness.]" That was it. A single line for Everest. And the only justification for the capital letters was that it was a new route. The understated entry was indicative of Andrej's modest response to having just completed one of the most iconic and difficult routes on the highest mountain on Earth.

When Nejc – the sickly child who had been such a worry to his family – arrived at the Ljubljana airport, his mother embraced him with relief. "My son, with whom I made pilgrimages from hospital to hospital, staying up endless nights by his bed, and whose life I feared for, has climbed the highest mountain in the world," she cried.[89] Even Nejc had tears spilling over onto his sunburned face.

But for Marjan the story was much different. The man who had opened the route at the critical moment, had climbed the crux chimney without oxygen or gloves, and had installed the fixed line for the teams that followed, came away with nothing but pain. Pain from his frostbite. Pain from not having reached the top. Pain from his lost fingers. He had given his toes for Makalu's South Face and had sacrificed his fingers for Everest. For Marjan, Everest was a bruising experience that took years to heal.

The West Ridge prize was a highly coveted one, and in the years that followed the Yugoslavian ascent, many attempts were made to repeat the route, still considered one of the most difficult on the mountain. The Bulgarians pulled it off in 1984, but their first summit climber, Hristo Prodanov, died on the descent, at which point the immensity of the Yugoslavian achievement loomed even larger.

♦ ♦ ♦

The team's return to Yugoslavia was triumphant even though the climb wasn't perfect for the political masters in Belgrade: it seemed a shame that they hadn't summited on May 25 so as to make President Tito's birthday celebrations extra special. Tito's health was in decline, and only one year later, he died, leaving Yugoslavia in a precarious situation.

Many likened Tito to a grand oak tree, whose shade was so great that nothing could grow under it. When he died, a massive outpouring of grief reverberated in every corner of the country. Albanian Communist Mahmut Bakalli later recalled, "We all cried, but we did not know we were also burying Yugoslavia."[90] The country took another ten years to die completely, thanks in part to the hopelessly inefficient system that Tito had put in place. Instead of appointing one head of state, he devised an eight-member, annually rotating presidency that consisted of representatives from each of the six republics and one from each of Serbia's autonomous provinces.

One of those provinces was Kosovo, where, on March 11, 1981, a seemingly minor incident triggered a titanic movement of unrest. It was lunchtime at the University of Prishtina. A student, angry at finding a cockroach in his soup, hurled his tray of food to the floor. Other students, equally fed up with the filthy conditions at the university, joined in the protest, which quickly grew to five hundred individuals. They burst out into the streets, and soon there were thousands shouting their frustrations about the living conditions in Kosovo. The authorities quashed the movement with brutal force, but the lion was out of the cage and its roar could be heard far beyond Kosovo's borders.

In a few years' time, Kosovo would play an even more important role in the future of the country when, on April 24, 1987, a man whose ambition knew no bounds – Slobodan Milošević – came to suppress another, much larger protest. The death of Yugoslavia would then enter its final, agonizing moments.

SEVEN

The Greatest Prize

Although Tone Škarja had inherited Aleš Kunaver's vision of climbing the direct Everest West Ridge and had risen to the occasion, Aleš continued nurturing even greater dreams. Climbing Lhotse's South Face, the most difficult and dangerous of Himalayan walls, had been his plan since 1962. Looking back, it's hard to fathom his audaciousness. Yugoslavians had accomplished little in the Himalaya before 1962. Most Himalayan teams were still climbing relatively straightforward ridges at that time. The great face climbs were still in the future, yet Aleš dreamed of the Lhotse South Face. His wife, Dušica, joked that their home was commandeered by the face: an enormous photo of it hung in their living room, and their lively dinner conversations were often about climbing it.

At 8516 metres, Lhotse is the fourth-highest mountain on Earth, linked to Everest by the South Col. In addition to its main summit, Lhotse claims two more summits over eight thousand metres: Lhotse Central and Lhotse Shar. The Swiss first climbed the mountain in 1956 by its western side. Numerous ascents followed, including the first winter ascent, by Polish ice warrior Krzysztof Wielicki on the last day of December 1988. But the south side is something else entirely. Lhotse's South Face rises 3.2 kilometres in just 2.25 kilometres of horizontal distance, making it the steepest face of this size in the world.

In 1981 Aleš assembled a 22-person team for the job, including a doctor, a radio man, two cameramen and a cook. He was convinced that an expedition-style approach was the only way to succeed on Lhotse's massive face. He planned to use Sherpa support on the lower slopes and fix ropes all the way up the wall, after which a chain of small climbing teams would leapfrog their way up the mountain.

Aleš chose the best and most experienced Himalayan veterans for the Lhotse team, with a special emphasis on technically proficient climbers. Climbers like Marjan Manfreda, Andrej Štremfelj and Nejc Zaplotnik. One of the most accomplished was the renowned rock climber Franček Knez. Franček had already done his bit lugging loads up to the Lho La on Everest in 1979, but he lost interest in that game soon after. Everest West Ridge just wasn't his style. Franček was a face man, and Lhotse's South Face didn't disappoint. "I am completely charmed," he wrote. "A cathedral of dark brown granite rises into the clouds. Sprinkled with snow, it looks like a pretty bride in white...Until this time it has never really been touched by the hand of a climber."[91] Franček said very little, but when he did, it was usually worth listening to.

◆ ◆ ◆

Born in 1955 in Selj, a small town in eastern Slovenia, Franček spent an idyllic childhood living and playing in the forests and fields near his home. He became adept at moving smoothly and swiftly through a wild environment, an important skill for his life in the mountains. "If you know how to walk in a steep forest, through rotting slippery leaves, then you know how to walk everywhere."[92] He became comfortable in the vertical world by ascending lofty scaffolding with his father, whose job it was to repair church steeples. He showed special talent on rock and was one of the first Slovenian climbers to actually train for the sport of climbing. He climbed fences and walls. He lifted weights and ran. He even trained while waiting for the bus, contracting the muscles in his calves and thighs until they screamed for mercy. But his favourite training exercise was scampering up a brick wall outside the local spa.

One day, when he was partway up the wall, a soldier with a Serbo-Croatian accent approached. "What are you doing?" he demanded.

"You can see what I'm doing," Franček called down.

The tall, pale soldier scowled. "Get down off that wall, now."

Being chased off his home territory by a foreigner made Franček angry. He reached further up the wall, grabbed a good handhold and stayed put.

"I said get down!" the soldier yelled.

Franček didn't move. The soldier opened his holster and fumbled with his heavy weapon, craning his neck while trying to aim it at the disobedient climber. Franček stared down. Was this guy seriously going to shoot him? Could he be bluffed? "My anger brought me into this dangerous game, but in every game there is a competition of strength. One of the competitors always loses the game," he later reflected.[93] After a moment he inched higher up the wall. When he glanced back down, the soldier had retreated a few steps. Franček had won the game.

But as obsessed as he was about training, Franček loved to climb even more. The 1979 Everest expedition provided him with his first exposure to the Himalaya, and probably came too soon in his career. Although he had climbed in the Andes, had made dozens of impressive ascents in the Alps and had winter experience in the Julian Alps, the West Ridge of Everest was a huge leap. And there was a lot of plodding involved. Franček wasn't good at plodding. It bored him to tears. Lhotse's South Face would be perfect for him.

◆ ◆ ◆

After establishing their base camp and studying the South Face, it wasn't long before the 1981 Lhotse climbers realized that their greatest challenge would be to survive the daily onslaught of avalanches. For no more than four hours each day was there even a remote chance of climbing safely on the face. Then the daily snowstorm would set in, followed by a shooting gallery of snow, ice and rocks that swept the entire face, all the way down to base camp. The only way to survive these conditions would be to retreat into some kind of shelter that couldn't be torn off the wall. The best option would be snow caves, sculpted out of the ice and snow. But snow caves take time to construct. With only four hours to climb and build camps, most of the teams would arrive at a potential site, erect their tents and only then begin excavating a cave before the avalanches began.

Camp V was the worst. Situated at 7800 metres in an unstable snow gully in the centre of Lhotse's yellow band, it was impossible to protect from avalanches. One terror-filled night began rather innocently when Marjan Manfreda and Borut Bergant arrived at what they thought should be Camp V. They had followed the fixed lines up until they disappeared. But where was the camp? After searching and shovelling, they finally spied the roof of a tent, almost completely buried by avalanche debris. Even before they managed to dig it out, two more avalanches hit them. After their third attempt at uncovering the tent, they gave up and simply burrowed in. Safely inside, they tried to make tea. But the matches wouldn't light, and the tent filled with smoke and gas. Already breathing heavily because of the altitude, they began to choke. They tried to light the stove with the gas lighter and that, too, failed. Meanwhile, avalanches continued to sift down over the tent, burying the two, centimetre by centimetre, locking them in an airless embrace.

Marjan passed out. In a dream, he heard his name being called. Desperate for oxygen, Borut flailed at the entrance of the tent, gasping and trying to escape. When he had finally clawed a tunnel through the snow, he grabbed Marjan and shoved him out into the fresh air. They had come very close to suffocating. A peaceful, but irreversible, fate. They took turns clearing the snow around the entrance with their hands, but the snow continued to fall and the avalanches kept slithering down. Marjan – possibly the toughest man on the mountain – began to lose heart. "I'm tired," he said to Borut. "I feel like going to sleep and forgetting about everything."[94] By ten that evening, Borut – called Čita by his friends – was frantic, for it was impossible to keep up with the quantity of snow that was threatening to bury them alive. He called base camp.

Čita: "Base, report back, Camp V calling. Over."

Aleš: "Base speaking. Čita, what's going on?"

Čita: "Aleš, there is no way to survive here, there's no air. We're suffocating here. We don't know what to do. We're digging our way out. Half the tent is snowed under. Should we cut it, or what?"

Aleš: "Don't leave the tent by night; you will retreat in the morning.

Whatever you do, don't leave the camp during the night! That
could be fatal, do you understand?..."

Čita: "The tent isn't much of a stronghold right now, Aleš."

Aleš: "I know, but it's considerably safer than anything else. Look,
we've had some snowfall here as well, but higher up the sky is
clearing. When the mountain is clear you can retreat." [95]

The crisis continued throughout the night. Camp V called base.
Base camp encouraged Camp V. While Camp V was being enveloped
by a fierce snowstorm, base stared up at a clear sky studded with stars.
After descending the next day, Marjan laconically remarked, "It was
clear to us that it wouldn't be at all crowded on the summit." [96]

It took seven weeks of hard labour in the most dangerous
conditions imaginable to establish the next camp, VI, at 8050 metres.
Rather high for a camp. Marjan Kregar and Viki Grošelj were the first
to stay there. The following day, Viki tried to find a route toward the
summit, but he progressed only 50 metres in a raging storm. Marjan
became frostbitten from the cold, even though he was belaying Viki
from *inside* the tent. After one more night, they retreated to base,
exhausted from their efforts. Viki's spine was so badly injured while
rappelling that he was hospitalized upon returning home.

But now that Camp VI was established in a slightly safer position
than Camp V, serious attempts could begin for the summit.
There were two possible routes: either left or right of the hulking,
overlapping shoulder, which was about four hundred metres below
the summit. The fear of avalanches persisted, however. Harrowing
stories came from everyone on the mountain, bringing into question
the soundness of their decisions to continue on in this war zone.

From Vanja Matijevec: "We were clipped onto the rope when we
[he and Franček Knez] were caught in an avalanche, which ran down
like a river and lasted for more than 15 minutes; but that was only the
beginning. When we descended into the chimney above V, another
avalanche of ice, rock and snow rushed downhill like a torrent and
didn't stop for almost an hour." [97]

From Nejc Zaplotnik: "I pull myself up the rope. Suddenly,
someone turns off the light; everything around me is in motion. The

whole world is sliding downhill…In a final effort, I grab the rope sling hanging from the piton and wrap it around my hand. I clench the rope in an iron grip. My heart stops beating in expectation of another jolt. Then daylight returns. Andrej [Štremfelj] and I dust off the snow and continue."[98]

From Ivan "Ivč" Kotnik: "It's hopeless trying to find yourself in this face. The wind and the avalanches blow away everything…Day after day, Lhotse topples our tents, covers the tracks we make. Only love and the will to survive are strong enough to keep us chained to this mountain…[The] Lhotse face is monstrous. When I stand on the glacier below it, I'm truly afraid."[99]

From Aleš Kunaver: "The part of the wall where we were supposed to descend is nothing but a huge snow waterfall. The face is over-hanging, so our ropes hang in the air for one hundred metres…During the abseil we're swamped by a waterfall of snow. I have a feeling we will be torn off the ropes…We slip and slide through avalanches of powdery snow on the steep slope below. We are saved by the fixed ropes. We are hanging from them helplessly, hoping this craziness will soon end."[100]

And so it went. Week after week the climbing teams fought with the avalanches, fought with their fears, fought with the face. Aleš had planned for 30 days on the wall. They were now approaching 60.

At each tenuous camp, during the long, tedious and terrifying hours when the mountain was too dangerous to climb, the alpinists huddled in fear. Entire lives were reviewed and relived, rewound from beginning to end, with pauses on the good times, fast-forwarding through the bad. Thoughts spiralled down to base camp, where this monstrous effort began: the place where, eventually, they would be released from this vicious cycle of danger; into which, like soldiers in combat, they had so willingly enlisted. Base camp, where the mail runners came and went with precious messages from home, where soon they would be able to behave like normal men, walking and whistling, talking and laughing, rather than burrowing their way up this mountainside like the mummified, helmeted and faceless, machine-like creatures they had become.

Feelings of solidarity with teammates vied with desperate longings for home and warmth and safety. They were united by danger, by their vulnerability to the forces of nature and by their complete reliance on each other. They knew they should treasure the intensity of these moments. But first they had to survive.

Andrej Štremfelj felt sure they would break through the physical and psychological barriers of the South Face. But he disagreed with Aleš's strategy. Aleš was mixing it up, pairing veteran climbers with less-experienced ones, shuffling the team configurations throughout the entire climb. Only near the end of the expedition was Andrej first teamed up with Nejc, his preferred and proven partner on previous climbs – his "engine." And it was the first time that the two were teamed up with Pavel Podgornik, who, to Andrej, felt like a stranger. "I don't think that was a good tactic," Andrej later said.

On May 14, Pavel Podgornik, Andrej Štremfelj and Nejc Zaplotnik made a serious summit attempt. It was 1:00 am, and their tent was abuzz with the clatter of cooking pots, jangling oxygen bottles and the hissing stove. Under the fluctuating glow of their headlamps and in the haze of their frosty-white breath, they guzzled tea and strapped on their crampons. They stepped out of the tent and looked up at the cold, merciless sky, heavy with stars. They glanced down at the magnificent face and up toward the summit ridge, with all of the mysterious, sharply delineated shadows in between.

"I felt small," recalled Andrej.

"I'm very tense. I've never taken such risk," thought Nejc.[101]

Above them rose a hundred-metre rock step, the last barrier to the summit ridge. Nejc hammered in a piton and stepped up from the crumbling rock at the base of the slab. His crampon slipped on the snow-covered slab. Although weak and exhausted, he scraped with his crampons and gained a delicate purchase while Andrej belayed him. Then Nejc's oxygen ran out. They were at 8250 metres. They looked at each other. No words were spoken, but the decision was unanimous. Andrej took out the radio: "We want to descend."

A difficult conversation with base ensued, in which Aleš struggled to maintain an upward momentum, at least for the benefit of the next rope team. But he needed Andrej and the others to agree to push through to the ridge. Andrej was blunt in his response. "That's how you see things from your position, but this ridge is fucked up. It would take a rope team one whole day to climb that rock step." Aleš again tried to persuade Andrej to climb through the rock step. It would open the route for the next team and would ensure the success of the climb. Andrej resisted, pointing out that the psychological strain of their position was even greater than the physical strain.

But Aleš was the leader, and after two months he knew that this was their last chance to succeed. "Listen, it's my duty to find combinations that could bring this mission to some sort of close," he pleaded. "I know that things are inhuman right now, as they have been up to now, but this is the only route still open to us and the only one that time still permits. Two of you can go down, but the one who's still strong enough could climb that step together with [Iztok] Tomazin. This is what I propose you do, if you're capable of doing it…This is my suggestion; it's up to you to make the final decision."[102]

Again, Andrej tried to convince Aleš as to how tenuous their situation was. "This terrain is killing me, Aleš, because you can't tell what's under your feet. We're literally swimming in snow."

Aleš signed off, accepting their decision.

They descended.

Nejc was devastated. "Everything in me has broken," he later said. "Have I crossed a boundary I shouldn't have? Have I crossed a line I've always been able to recognize until now? All I know is that we're fleeing, that a storm is raging and that we're freezing."[103] The tension of the long weeks of unbearable hardship and primal fear, the heavy feeling of responsibility for his rope team and his friends on the mountain, the sense of failure because of the trust everyone had placed in him – all of this came crashing down on Nejc as he descended from the rock step. But his will to survive was stronger. And he knew, just as Andrej did, that the only logical direction was down.

Until May 14 all of the expedition's efforts had been directed toward the ultimate goal: to climb the Lhotse South Face and reach the summit. After May 14 the objective shifted. Most of the climbers were exhausted, injured or ill. Franček had completely given up and was filling his time bouldering on a block of granite near base camp. Concentrating on the warm rock, on moving his hands and his feet and feeling the texture of the rock, he completely forgot about the terror of the wall. His mind cleared, filled now with the uncomplicated truth of sun on stone. For him, it was over.

Or so he thought. Aleš knew that the summit had receded from their grasp, but the top of the face might still be within reach. And Frančcek might be the man to do it.

And so Frančcek Knez and Vanja Matijevec headed up the mountain one last time. All the actors in this gigantic vertical performance had played their part. It was time for the final act. The ceaseless up and down on the mountain stopped. It became very quiet as the other rope teams watched and waited. Even Frančcek, who had fallen in love with the South Face at first sight, now expressed some reservations. "Here the mountain displays its magnificence, and as you gaze up into it you can magically feel your own smallness. The more you stare, the more you disappear into nothingness. Only a stubborn little niggling thought in your head is telling you, step beyond this eternal granite wall, if you dare."[104]

◆ ◆ ◆

Frančcek and Vanja left Camp VI at 5:00 am on May 18. They descended for about a hundred metres and began a long traverse, sinking into snow up to their waist and higher. They soon ran out of bottled oxygen. At 7:30 am they radioed in for the first time. The transmission was short and curt. They were making progress, but everyone sensed the tension in their voices.

The steep upper snowfields were pleated with parallel grooves of unstable snow. Crossing from one groove to the next was the most dangerous part. Cornices clung to the edges, hanging over fathomless precipices that were thankfully obscured by the dense fog. Frančcek lost traction and began slipping down toward a small rock pillar. He regained his footing and pounded two pitons into the loose rock before climbing over it. More treacherous snowfields lay in front of him, and then a huge funnel of perfect snow appeared, leading upward. But on his first step, he realized with horror that smooth slabs lurked underneath. Impossible to belay. The two had to climb simultaneously, trusting completely in each other. No slipping. No falling. No room for mistakes.

Aleš was standing alone some distance from base, his nerves frayed and worn. Radio in hand, he strained to see up the face, to glimpse anything at all. At 12:30 the radio crackled. The message was simple: "Permission requested to descend."

"No permission required. Do what needs to be done," Aleš replied. There could be no other response. But he was crushed. After days and weeks and months on the face, all their efforts had failed to achieve the goal. Not only the goal of the summit of Lhotse, but even to the edge of the face.

It was a bitter and difficult defeat.

With his radio still switched on, Aleš began trudging back along the rock-strewn glacier to base. Suddenly his radio sputtered again. The reception was spotty, and he struggled to catch the words. Then the radio exploded as climbers in camps strewn up and down the face began talking at once. They had changed their minds. Franč“ek and Vanja were continuing up! Aleš tried to interject and speak to the summit team, but Franč“ek and Vanja cut him off.

"I understand," he said. "They now exist in their own separate world."[105]

What had happened up there? Aleš later learned that it was a simple clearing of the fog that revealed how near the climbers were to the serrated summit ridge. Tantalizingly close, just a few rope lengths away. With tense directions back to Vanja, Franč“ek started up. He plowed up the steep, unconsolidated snow and then stepped onto a broad snow mushroom, which immediately caved in under his feet. After free-falling for about ten metres he was left dangling from the rope. He righted himself and clawed his way back up and into the next groove of snow. Then Vanja fell, losing his radio in the process. Two falls at over eight thousand metres.

The mists shifted again, revealing a rock tower and a small notch on the ridge. A short, steep traverse led to the notch, and they were there, at the rim of the face on the summit ridge, at 8250 metres. It was as far as they would go. They radioed base to report where they were and that they would descend the other side into the Western Cwm. Descending the South Face was out of the question; it was much too steep and dangerous. They asked base to arrange for a helicopter to pick them up above the icefall at the bottom of the Western Cwm.

When Aleš heard their request, he was shocked and deeply afraid for them. Descending the other side might seem like a good idea, but there were no teams on that side of the mountain; it was completely deserted. Neither Franček nor Vanja knew the route, and it was much too high for a helicopter to land. They would be completely on their own. Aleš needed to be sensitive with his response. In fact, the situation was even more complicated because the helicopter was Vanja's idea and Franček disagreed. It was now 6:00 pm, however, and their options were narrowing. Descending the South Face would be a nightmare. Particularly in the dark.

Ten minutes later another message came through: they would try to return the same way. Aleš was relieved. "To me, a rope team disappearing behind the mountain would feel like a satellite flying off its orbit into space. They would disappear from our horizon, possibly forever."[106]

Hours passed with no radio messages. Just heavy silence.

Franček and Vanja had no time for radios: they were fighting for their lives. As darkness fell, they were slipping and sliding, almost free-falling down the steep snow runnels, collapsing from fatigue, drifting off into a seductive stupor, waking with a start and forcing themselves to keep moving. Stopping meant dying. Avalanches slithered around them, but they hardly took notice. Around midnight the snowstorm abated and a feeble moon threw a weird, ghostly light.

Vanja recalled the rush of relief when they finally reached the fixed line leading to Camp IV. "I hurl myself down the rope and in another moment I'm racing toward Franček...I'm now certain that we've returned to life...Strength returns to us like life flowing to a fetus through the umbilical cord. It's a beautiful feeling. We've forgotten the suffering of yesterday and last night; we've forgotten all the doubts we've had on the rim of the face; we've forgotten everything but the thin thread that leads to a warm, comfortable hole in the ice in the middle of a vertical face."[107]

At 4:30 am, base received a message. The climbers were back at Camp IV. After 24 hours of continuous climbing, they were safe. They had made the right decision. As Franček later wrote, "Wisdom is the prize of suffering."[108]

The next morning Aleš sent a message home. "FACE CONQUERED, SUMMIT NOT, COMING BACK."

As if to taunt them, after almost two months of daily storms, the next day the weather cleared and the South Face revealed itself.

♦ ♦ ♦

Success and failure are sometimes strangely alike. Perception of either is personal. A magnificent line in the Himalaya had just been climbed. Yet there was little joy in it. Franček reflected that he and Vanja had chosen the only realistic option left to them: get to the top of the face. This they did. The summit was out of their reach at that point. "In the end, I can say we have probably accomplished more than anyone has ever achieved in the Himalayas," he said, adding, "If the weather had been good, we would have continued. We both felt great."[109] Years later, he admitted that the complex, dragon's back ridge was probably a project for the future.

But as Everest was to Marjan Manfreda, Lhotse was to Franček. It was years before he would speak about the climb, so deeply did it affect him. He kept this story buried deep inside, afraid that talking or writing about it would destroy its significance for him. Eventually he felt ready to reminisce about this most powerful experience. By that time, the ordeal's "forcefulness has waned," he said. "My friends on the expedition have been torn apart by the winds of time like powdery snow on the slopes of the south wall. Only bright bits are left, like the starry sky."[110]

An expedition of this magnitude is a complicated affair, with many different personalities and personal ambitions, and varying levels of skill, power and endurance. Even courage. Aleš tried to be philosophical about their efforts: "Every one of us has his personal peak – the point where one's strength runs out."[111] After 64 days on Lhotse's South Face and only four days of good weather, their combined strength had run out. Perhaps their greatest achievement – even greater than reaching the rim – was that nobody died.

EIGHT

Dhaulagiri Obsession

I grew to love this beautiful country where the gods invite you into their kingdom and demons put a spell on you so you forget your own transitory life and are ready to join them in an instant. I grew to love these cheerful people who squat before their hovels, pick each other's lice and greet you with "Namaste!" God is in you. God is in me and God is in you, you kind mountain people who still know how to waste your time with such kind serenity and still know how to curiously observe the bizarre habits of the foreigners who come to you, driven by strange, incomprehensible goals – to climb into the homes of the gods. I am returning back among the clouds, where everything I have pondered so far disappears, where all the truths lose their importance and all that matters is hard work and a burning will.

—Nejc Zaplotnik, *Pot*[112]

I t was no accident that Stane Belak (Šrauf) was not with Aleš Kunaver and most other top Slovenian climbers on the South Face of Lhotse in 1981. Like Aleš, Šrauf had an obsession. But it wasn't Lhotse. Šrauf was smitten with Dhaulagiri.

With Tone Škarja's help, a bit of financial support from the Alpine Association trickled down to support Šrauf's dream. The seventh-highest mountain in the world, Dhaulagiri rises seven thousand dramatic metres above Nepal's Kali Gandaki River, and its South Face is over four thousand metres high. Even though Tone thought that Šrauf had a "tendency toward masochism," he believed in the 1981 Dhaulagiri expedition and, in retrospect, felt it was one of the most important of all Himalayan expeditions – not only those undertaken by Slovenian climbers.

Šrauf's fascination with Dhaulagiri was inspired by Dinko Bertoncelj, a Slovenian lad whose life was transformed by the Second World War. After his father was killed on the doorstep in front of his eyes in 1944, Dinko fled to Austria, then eventually to Bariloche, Argentina. He was just 15 years old. There, he carved out a new life of skiing and climbing and healthy outdoor living. The rest of his family fared less well: his sister was sentenced to two years of hard labour, building roads in Austria, and his mother nearly starved after his father's death.

Dinko's talents earned him a place on the first Argentinian Himalayan expedition, to Dhaulagiri in 1954. A military effort, it was not averse to using military tactics when necessary, blasting inconvenient rock with explosives in order to create comfortable tent placements, for example. Despite the expedition's questionable methods, the Argentinian team reached eight thousand metres before being turned back by a fierce storm. And although it was a European team that made the first ascent of Dhaulagiri in 1960, it was Dinko, the brave young Slovenian boy, whose story remained in Šrauf's mind.

At first, Dhaulagiri, which means "dazzling, white and beautiful," seemed like too remote a dream. But after climbs in the Alps, the Hindu Kush and the Himalaya, Šrauf had gained enough self-confidence to seriously consider the peak. More precisely, the mountain's South Face. Because of its size, the objective dangers on the wall and the technical nature of the climbing required, the South Face was still unclaimed. It was while descending from the summit of Everest in 1979 that Šrauf decided on Dhaulagiri: "I thought I might take the lead where others had given up," he said.[113] He admitted that some of this desire was fuelled by raw ambition – the need to do something great.

Initially, it seemed that the mountain was rejecting Šrauf in every possible way. The first available permit was for 1984 – much too late, in his mind. The South Face would surely be climbed by then. It was one of the choicest Himalayan prizes still available, and he wasn't the only alpinist eyeing it. Even Messner had attempted the face, making a bid in 1977 before retreating. Then, like a miracle, the Nepalese officials released a permit for the post-monsoon season of 1981. Šrauf grabbed it.

When he went to Nepal to reconnoitre the face in the spring of that year, Aleš's Lhotse expedition was in full swing and Šrauf began to appreciate the full extent of the competition that existed within the Alpine Association. Lhotse was the priority for 1981. Šrauf knew he would need to build his modest six-man team with less-experienced climbers and with considerably less money. There would be no doctor. There would be little time for acclimatization climbs. Most important – and this was due not to the Alpine Association but rather to the nature of the objective – there would be no retreat down the wall in case of injury or illness. It was simply too steep. Once on the wall, they would need to descend the other side.

They pitched their tents at base camp on September 26. They were optimistic, despite the ceaseless thundering of falling rock, seracs and avalanches. Luckily, the fog was usually so thick that they couldn't see the enormous hanging glaciers and black rock walls that awaited them. When the sun finally came out, they climbed a nearby summit to acclimatize and study the wall rearing up before them. The conclusion: it was not only hopeless but insane! Particularly the western half of the wall, which they unanimously rejected.

They opted for a line slightly right of centre, hoping to top out on the southeastern ridge to join the Japanese route at around 7300 metres. They would continue up the ridge for another thousand metres to the summit and descend the northwestern side of the mountain. There were many problems with this route, but the most serious was that the first chance to descend was very near the summit. Until then, their only option would be up. "This ascent without the possibility of retreat was hanging over me like a bad dream," Šrauf admitted.[114]

The weather improved, and the forecast was promising. A full moon would bathe them with enough light to climb during the cold of the night – the safest time on this crumbling wall. They would have two teams of three climbers, separated by a few days. The first team, consisting of Šrauf, Emil Tratnik and Vincenc Berčič, began on October 15. They climbed as far as they could the first day, using the fixed ropes they had installed during the previous weeks. They rested while waiting for the moon to rise and started up again at 4:00 am. For the rest of the night they climbed up the fixed ropes, hauling 30-kilogram packs, playing a lethal game of Russian roulette, not knowing if the ropes had been damaged from falling rock and ice in the preceding days. By morning they were at the top of the black rock section. Now it was time to cut the umbilical cord with the valley. From now on they would be climbing alpine-style.

By 9:00 am the sun was wreaking havoc on the wall. Cascades of slush and rock and ice and water threatened to drown them. They dived under an overhang, gasping for air, and waited while the wall shed itself of debris. As darkness fell, they tiptoed up to a little ledge and waited for the moon to light the way. It rose later and shone more weakly than the night before, but there was still enough light to see. They climbed as if the devil himself were chasing them, racing up the mountain to reach safer ground above six thousand metres.

While the first team ducked and wove on the face, the second team waited its turn down below, puzzled by what appeared to be agonizingly slow progress. They couldn't imagine how difficult it was to make headway up the wall. They had no idea how frustrating it was to waste so many precious daylight hours while waiting for the mountain to cool down and stabilize. Šrauf's team could climb for only five or six hours per day. As well, now that they were higher on the wall, their lack of acclimatization began to show. Šrauf, Emil and Vincenc struggled to keep their balance on 70° ice, making delicate moves on the points of their crampons with heaving lungs and reeling heads.

The second team began to climb up the face but soon retreated because of rock and icefall. Šrauf and his team were now the only prisoners trapped on the wall. They felt terribly alone as they crawled upward, knowing that their teammates at base were now reduced to the role of helpless observers.

Climbing unroped to save time, they reached the Japanese ridge on their sixth day on the face. Not yet the summit, but the face was theirs. What a victory! The South Face of Dhaulagiri! While setting up their sixth bivouac they studied the ridge, which they assumed would be much easier than the wall they had just climbed. They would be disappointed. That night the wind raced at one hundred kilometres per hour and the temperature plummeted. The ridge was fully exposed to the raging winds. The next day they struggled to climb across smooth rock slabs and sheets of steel-hard ice, compromised by exhaustion, lack of decent food and the relentless wind. They gained only two hundred metres of height.

During the night the temperature dropped again. It was −30°C inside the tent. Frost feathers everywhere. They had sketchy radio contact with base, but just enough to learn that the weather was changing – for the worse.

On the eighth day of climbing, Šrauf finally glimpsed the summit floating just beyond the undulating ridge. He remained optimistic and climbed unroped, trying to save time. When he turned around to talk to his partners, he realized he was alone. Just before sunset he began chopping and digging out a bivouac site on the ridge at around 7900 metres. As dusk enveloped the mountain, Vincenc appeared, moving slowly, deep creases lining his face. There was no sign of Emil. Šrauf retraced his steps for a few hundred metres and found Emil crouched behind a rock.

"Come on, let me take your pack. It's not far," Šrauf offered.

When they reached the bivouac site, there sat Vincenc, staring at his fingers. He held them up to Šrauf in terror. "I think they're frozen."

Their bodies were starting to fail. But at least they were still together. And tomorrow would be summit day, at which point they could start heading for home. That night the temperature dropped to −40°. "I can still remember the dry coughing and the ice crystals in the air," Šrauf recalled. "Our thoughts were confused and the situation seemed hopeless and hopeful at times."[115]

The next morning, whatever luck had been with them vanished. The wind-drifted snow crushed the tent, destroying the poles. They lost radio contact. They ran out of gas. Vincenc could do nothing but stare at his frozen hands. Šrauf crawled out of the tent to see if he could salvage it but realized there was nothing worth keeping. When he noticed a monstrous storm brewing on the south side of the mountain, he finally grasped exactly how desperate their position was. "After nine days of extreme efforts, we prepared ourselves to flee for our lives."[116]

They jettisoned the empty gas cylinder and any food that required cooking. The ruined tent was already buried, so there was nothing left to do but escape. The summit was so close, a stone's throw away. But it was too far. They still had days of descent to endure, and wasting time on the summit would only decrease their chances of survival. Šrauf looked at Vincenc's terror-filled eyes and knew that the only humane direction was down.

At 5:00 pm they discovered a small, half-buried tent from a previous ascent. At first they thought they were hallucinating. But it was real. And inside were two gas cylinders and some food. Emil and Šrauf installed Vincenc in the tent and prepared to bivouac beside it. But even this bit of good luck turned on them. When Šrauf accidentally bashed one of the gas cylinders, it exploded in flames. Within moments, only a few scorched tent fragments remained. Their beards and eyebrows singed from fire and their stomachs aching from hunger, they faced another night out in the open. The next morning, their 11th on the mountain, they lurched down toward the glacier plateau 1300 metres below them. The storm continued without mercy.

On the 14th day they straggled in to the village of Khalipani, exhausted, starving, dehydrated and severely frostbitten. Here, there were people. There was fire and food. Everything should have been fine. But it wasn't. The climbers had no money, and the villagers demanded payment for their food and their help. They dragged themselves from village to village, begging for food. The blisters covering Vincenc's hands and feet burst and became infected. They began to reek as gangrene set in. For Šrauf, the man who had single-handedly taken on the impossible task of teaching sanitation to every Nepalese villager, watching his friend's hands rot – in part, from the bacteria surrounding them – was heartbreaking.

The men waited seven excruciating days for a plane to Kathmandu, to a hospital, to food and to cleanliness. Twenty-four days after entering the wall, they were back in the capital. Theirs was a lightning-fast expedition compared to the ponderous 65-day effort on Lhotse's South Face or the weeks spent on Everest's West Ridge.

Yet the suffering had been enormous. And sadly, they didn't seem to glean much pleasure or pride from the astonishing accomplishment of having climbed Dhaulagiri's South Face, even though many in the international climbing community understood the magnitude of their effort. Šrauf and his little team had done something incredible – a climb for the future.

But they had missed the summit. Even as he was flying home from Nepal, Šrauf knew he would be back to settle the score on Dhaulagiri.

Šrauf's obsession drove him to organize three more expeditions to the peak: in 1985, 1986 and 1987. Not once did he consider a straightforward or previously climbed route. In 1985 his team climbed a 3400-metre-high new route, alpine-style, on Dhaulagiri's East Face, reaching the Northeast Ridge route at 7600 metres. But after 45 days on the mountain, hurricane winds destroyed their chances, and the summit again eluded him. He tried the following year, this time with Marjan Kregar, but they were forced to give up at 7650 metres due to bad weather. His last expedition, in the late fall of 1987, placed Iztok Tomazin and Marjan Kregar on the summit just before nightfall on December 4. Although not officially a winter ascent – the Himalayan winter calendar starts on December 21 – they climbed the peak in winter conditions. (They were credited with a "meteorological" winter ascent.)

Dhaulagiri remained Šrauf's mountain of suffering, even though he never stood on its summit. It did not lose its allure for him, and had he lived long enough, he most certainly would have climbed it. Nejc understood that summit obsession, which sometimes borders on insanity. As he wrote in *Pot*:

I want to reach the summit more and more badly. It's all I am still living for. I have reached the point where I can't imagine returning without summiting. Most people don't understand what drives us to these extreme efforts and risks, but every bit of effort gives the goal more value. The more effort and risk you've invested, the more exalted the goal and the more fervent your desire to attain it. Your willpower grows stronger, too, and sometimes this strength of will, which in normal circumstances can help you survive, prevails over all signs of danger, even your instinct for self-preservation. It can drive you to extremes and beyond. This is why alpinists depart toward summits and never return again.[117]

NINE

Fallen Stars

By 1983 Nejc was at the top of his game. He had three of the 14 eight-thousanders under his belt: Makalu, Gasherbrum I and Everest, all climbed by impressive new routes. He was a member of the local mountain rescue team and was reaping unprecedented accolades for his recently published book, *Pot*. Happily married, with three beautiful sons, he trained and climbed and delighted in his good fortune. He could have felt blasé about his success and entitled by his fame, but he didn't. He retained his sensitivity toward the natural world around him and empathy for the people whose lives intersected his, however tangentially.

> I am running on a nearby hill above Kranj. The wonderful rhythm of panting and footsteps is driving me up the path. On top of the hill stands a hotel that has been remodelled into a retirement home. Shuffling their feet, the shadows of forsaken people move about, looking for the early warmth of the spring sun. A little man stands by the fence, his spine erect and his enflamed red eyes fixed on a distant view. Far away the white peaks of the Julian Alps are outlined against the sky. I don't know...his old eyes can probably not even see these far-off mountains any longer. His weakened heart doesn't even sense that they are there. But his absent-minded and enraptured contemplation of the distant horizon, his unmoving gaze, fixed on the object of my own desire, creates an invisible bond between me and that little man. Before I know it we are both staring into the distance,

his heart full of memories and mine with longing. As if I have opened the gates of knowledge, I enter the world of wrinkled faces, crooked limbs, red-rimmed eyes and shuffling feet. I am ashamed of my own strength and health and youth and dreams, while the toothless faces offer me their all-comprehending smiles, offer to take my hand.

I look to the other side of the hill, where the smoke pours from the town and from where the rumble of heavy industry can be heard. My hometown, which I love, and which I always look for from the summits, now seems like a torture chamber that twisted the bodies and killed the longings of these old men and women. They gaze absent-mindedly into the distance that awaits them, calmly and coldly. So this is how all struggles end – love, fame, wealth and everything we consider to be of value in this world – with this fixed gaze into the distance! A little old man with an unshaven face and lively eyes asks me for a cigarette. Although I stopped smoking ages ago, I decide I will always take cigarettes with me when I run up here.[118]

Even when halfway around the world, Nejc remained open and receptive to the people around him. His observations often led to increased self-awareness and wisdom. He wrote in *Pot* about one experience in a Nepali hospital.

A wizened little man was squatting on the floor in the beautiful new hospital in Pokhara. A tiny boy with his hand in a plaster cast was brought from the surgery and laid on the rags that the man had placed on the floor. He squatted by the boy, gazing steadily at his face without turning his eyes away for a single moment, stroking his hair and waiting for him to wake up. Who knows where they were from? Who knows how far he carried him on his bent old back, full of trust that the men in white coats would cure his pain. He went on squatting, stroking his hair and waiting for him to come back from some other place, from some world unknown to his father. And then great, dark eyes opened, bewildered, searching for his father, and enormous tears slid down his brown cheeks. He took him into his lap and kept on squatting and stroking the boy.

The son was crying with fear, pressed against his father, who, oblivious to the world around him, spoke comforting words to him, stroked his hair, all the while squatting in the middle of those dirty rags on the cold cement of the corridor of the beautiful new hospital. I understood the drift of the father's words. I understood them with my heart rather than with my mind. "Have a good cry, my boy. It will all pass. When you wake we will go to a tea shop and have a big bowl of fragrant rice. And you will grow up to be as strong as a mountain." The boy stopped crying. The father wiped his tears with dirty rags, lifted him with his worn-out hands and took him somewhere to eat that mountain of warm, fragrant rice. And I kept sitting on the floor, watching the empty corner just vacated by my two teachers of love and trust.[119]

When Stipe Božić, Croatia's leading alpinist, agreed to join the Yugoslavian expedition to 8163-metre Manaslu in 1983, he invited two of Slovenia's top Himalayan climbers along to bolster their chances of success – Nejc Zaplotnik and Viki Grošelj. As early as 1956, Yugoslavia had aspired to launch an expedition to the still-unclimbed Manaslu. Eighth-highest mountain in the world, it is located in the west-central part of Nepal. But the political and economic conditions at the time prohibited it. Instead, Manaslu was first climbed that same year by a Japanese team, and again by the Japanese in 1971 and 1974. Manaslu became known as a Japanese mountain. The year 1972 saw Messner on the summit with a Tyrolean team, but it was also the year that 17 people died on the mountain, most in an avalanche. Manaslu had now earned a reputation as a killer. The goal of the 1983 Manaslu expedition led by Croatian Vinko Maroević was to climb the lower part of the difficult South Face along the Tyrolean route and then continue to the summit along the yet-unclimbed South Ridge. Once again, the goal was not to repeat a known route, but to forge new ground – by now, a Yugoslavian specialty.

It was immediately apparent that the approach to the face was extremely dangerous, exposed to horrific risk of avalanches from both snow and ice. Huge seracs towered above them. But the greatest threat lasted for only 30 minutes, and they all agreed to this game of Russian roulette. It was a simple process: turn off your brain and climb. The team made excellent progress and within three weeks was above seven thousand metres on the route. On his way back to base camp for some well-earned rest, Nejc observed the landscape around him and speculated about the days to come. He wrote in his diary: "We come again to the endless glacier and the precipitous muddy moraines from which a constant fusillade of boulders keeps coming in our direction. And there, standing on a lovely grassy ledge, we spot the tents in base camp above the lake, huddled together like frightened chickens."[120]

On April 15 the entire team assembled in base camp to celebrate Nejc's 31st birthday. It was to be his last.

On April 24 Stipe and his team were in base camp. Viki was several hundred metres up the face, and Nejc, along with Srečko Gregov and Ante Bućan, was plodding up toward Viki. A loud crack shattered the silence. Viki saw a huge teetering serac break off between Camps I and II. At first it seemed to float, as if miraculously suspended in the high, thin air. But when the miracle ended, it roared down the mountain with lightning speed. He jerked around, craning to see if anyone was in its path. He saw three climbers scatter like scampering rabbits. But the avalanche engulfed them in a flash.

When the cloud of snow and ice dispersed, Viki could discern that one person was still moving. Screaming, he plunged down the slope while Stipe began racing up from base. They first spied a battered pack, and then a pair of climbing boots protruding from the ice. Both belonged to Nejc. They slashed at the avalanche debris with their ice axes, their efforts useless because the snow and ice had hardened into a cement-like casing. More unstable seracs threatened them from above. Only after 40 minutes of scratching and chopping at the unforgiving surface did they finally free Nejc from his icy tomb. His face was strangely peaceful, but his neck was completely crushed. Nejc was dead. Stipe turned his attention to Srečko, who was seriously injured, but despite more searching, Ante's body was not found. It took two days to carry Nejc's body down to the edge of the glacier, where they buried him among the rubble.

The climbers were in shock. Nejc was one of those people who simply seemed indestructible. Viki couldn't begin to fathom how they would explain this great tragedy back home. They were destroyed by their grief, drowning in a pool of sadness. Of course, Nejc had been their climbing partner and dear friend. But he was much more than that. He was their voice. He had understood their dreams and desires, their fears and doubts, and he had articulated those emotions for them through his writing. Losing Nejc was like losing a part of themselves. The climbers left the mountain, and Stipe vowed never to return to the Himalaya, so great was his guilt for inviting Nejc to join the expedition.

But gradually guilt turned into remorse, and Stipe and Viki felt they had to do something to honour Nejc's memory. Something grand. They returned to Manaslu the following year, four months after its first winter ascent by Polish climbers Maciej Berbeka and Ryszard Gajewski. They would climb it in Nejc's honour. Together with Edo Retelj from Split and Aleš Kunaver, leader of their four-man team, they knew from cruel experience that the slow pace of an expedition-style climb was too dangerous for this mountain. Instead, they would attempt it alpine-style. The pundits gave them no more than a 1 per cent chance of success. At first, it appeared that those critics might be right.

After lugging 60 kilograms of food and equipment up to a cache at 5700 metres, they descended to base camp to rest before the final push. But on their way back up, they were horrified to see that a huge avalanche from neighbouring Peak 29 had buried the cache under several metres of snow. All was lost: food, a tent, down jackets, ice axes and stoves. Now they had just one stove for four, and minimal climbing equipment. They moved to plan B.

Edo returned to the valley, and Aleš remained in the tent, giving up his place on the summit team to Viki. Publicly and officially, Aleš understood his role: "The leader's duty isn't to summit but to enable his friends to summit safely!"[121] But in his diary he confided with sadness that this was his last chance to summit an eight-thousander. He was 48 years old.

Since Viki and Stipe had the only functioning stove, Aleš needed to fabricate one. He cut the bottom out of a gas cylinder and placed a lighted candle inside, creating just enough heat to melt snow for drinking water, vital to his survival.

As Stipe and Viki began their ascent, Stipe shattered his ice axe on a patch of bullet-hard ice at 6400 metres. When they radioed Aleš with the bad news, he promised to leave his tent at 4:00 am the next morning and climb up with a replacement. He arrived three hours later, laden with two axes, 30 metres of rope, one bolt, some packaged soup and sugar. Now the two could continue their ascent.

For three days Aleš huddled in his little tent, melting snow with his candle, writing letters home and battling the spindrift avalanches that threatened to wipe him off the face. On the third day, May 4, Stipe and Viki reached the summit. "We were overjoyed to be standing on it, for Nejc, for Ante, for Aleš and for friends from both expeditions who had sacrificed so much in order that we might succeed," Viki wrote.[122] A few days later the climbers were back in the valley, where Stipe laid a small stone from the summit on Nejc's grave. It was a humble, final resting place for a man of such talent, such fame, such promise.

Nine years before, Nejc had stood on the summit of Makalu, contemplating his life stretching out before him. He couldn't have foreseen how short it would be.

> Shall we find other Makalus, or is this to be the first and only one? At the age of 23! The end of longing. The end of planning. Is this really the end? Will we really drown in the grey monotony of everyday existence?…We will return home, and our daily struggle will begin anew: school, jobs. However, new goals will present themselves as we go along. This is how it has always been. This is how it will remain for a long time yet, until we some day become feeble old men and are drowned among the crowd.[123]

In Aleš's official report of the climb, he wrote, "There were no difficulties except for the loss of one ice axe."[124] His understated words concealed his altruistic behaviour on this, his last expedition. Tragically, only a few months later he was killed in a helicopter crash near Lake Bled, in one of Slovenia's most beautiful valleys.

Aleš had been part of that first postwar generation of Slovenian alpinists, the ones who wore hobnailed boots, used their mothers' laundry lines for ropes, borrowed ice axes and made their own pitons. They dreamed of the Himalaya and, of course, dreamed of standing on the summits of the eight-thousanders. Aleš never fulfilled that dream for himself. Even so, he is the man most often credited for guiding the direction of his fellow alpinists in the 1970s. He was strategic with his plans, built on his trust in the skills and motivation of Slovenian climbers. He was courageous, publicly declaring his intentions for those grand objectives. An educated man, he respected individuals and worked with them to form a cohesive whole. In this way he built powerful teams. He never lost a climber on any of his expeditions. His legacy of leadership, vision and teamwork was unparalleled. He led by example, and he led with elegance. Most important, he led with compassion. His performance on Manaslu was the perfect example.

But for Nejc's widow, Mojca, the commemorative climb did little to ease the pain. Just 29 years old, with three young boys, she was a nurse and the main breadwinner for the family. It was soon clear that nursing wouldn't pay the mountain of bills, so she opened a small hair salon to earn some extra cash. That sideline became her main occupation and one that later morphed into several offshoot businesses for her sons Luka and Nejc Jr. She eventually married Tomaž Jamnik, a close friend and former climbing partner of Nejc's.

Thirteen years after the fateful 1983 expedition to Manaslu, Viki returned, this time with Mojca and her three sons. The lonely grave with its faded wooden cross was still there. It had survived 13 Himalayan winters, 13 years of thundering avalanches, 13 years of tender summer flowers. "My father was king!" shouted Nejc's youngest son, Jaka, spinning around in awe of the landscape. "Just look what land he chose for his cemetery."

Luka, who was 23 years old at the time, wept with his mother and brothers, overwhelmed by the magnitude of the spot. "Although we were all in the mountains a thousand times before, we'd never been in such a high and beautiful place," he said. "I guess we needed that trip to see why our father loved the mountains so much, especially the Himalaya."

TEN

The Loner

N ejc Zaplotnik had provided inspiration and companionship
for young climbers from Kranj in the last years of his life.
Climbers like Andrej Štremfelj and, later, Tomo Česen. Born
in 1959, Tomo began climbing in 1972, the same year that Aleš Kunaver
and his team forged new ground on the South Face of Makalu. His
first adventures were on the rock crags near his home in Kranj, but
it wasn't long before he was in the Alps, testing himself on snow and
ice. Tall and slender, dark and handsome, he looked more like a model
than a climber. After four years of dating, Tomo married Neda, his
high-school sweetheart, at the tender age of 20. Two years later their
first son, Aleš, was born.

A natural athlete, Tomo progressed quickly under the guidance
of Nejc. The two went to the French Alps and romped up the Bonatti
Pillar of the Petit Dru, the North Face of Les Droites and others. Nejc
possessed the experience, the skills and the intelligence required to
keep up with his talented and curious student. Tomo recalled that
he also had great self-confidence – too much at times. "I think he
believed that nothing could happen to him," Tomo laughed. "He was
often saying 'Don't worry, everything will be okay.'"

Tomo earned his keep as a steeplejack, working high on exposed
rigging, towers and ladders. In his free time, he rock climbed, often
solo. And in the winter, when the rigging jobs dried up, he perfected
his winter skills on the brooding north walls of the Julian Alps and
the classic lines around Chamonix.

Tomo gained his first experience at altitude in 1983 when he climbed the North Face of Peak Communism in the Russian Pamirs. At 7495 metres, it convinced him – and the Alpine Association's expeditions commission – that he was ready for the Himalayan giants. Two years later, in 1985, he was invited to join an expedition led by Tone Škarja to 8505-metre Yalung Kang, a subpeak of Kangchenjunga, which straddles the border between India (Sikkim) and Nepal. Of the several turning points in Tomo's career, Yalung Kang was possibly the most important. With Tomo away for three months to climb, Neda went to her parents' with three-year-old Aleš. Pregnant at the time with a second child, she was stoic, never showing fear or worry about her husband.

The 15-person team approached the North Face in traditional expedition style, using Sherpa support, supplemental oxygen and fixed ropes, and establishing four camps in preparation for a summit bid. Tomo was teamed up with Borut Bergant, an experienced high-altitude climber who had been on Everest and Lhotse, as well as other Himalayan expeditions. Tomo learned a lot from Borut, simple little routines with his equipment and in camp that at sea level would seem unimportant but that, at altitude and in storms, could mean the difference between life and death.

Tomo became ill at Camp IV, vomiting everything in his stomach. The next morning was no better. He felt weak and shaky.

"Borut, I need to go down," he gasped, careening out of the tent.

"You will be fine," Borut reassured him. "Once you start climbing, your dizziness will disappear. Give it a chance."

Tomo indulged in some bottled oxygen and agreed to try. Borut was right. The higher they went, the better Tomo felt. It was as if the thinning air energized him with its purity. Fourteen hours later they reached the top.

By 5:00 pm it was clear that most of the descent would take place in the dark. As the night wore on, Tomo grew stronger while Borut withered. "He became exhausted," Tomo explained. "His psychological preparation was not good...He was concentrating only on getting to the top, and when he got to the top, he relaxed."[125] Tomo's analysis has a ring of truth and characterizes many high-altitude ascents where all the energy and drive are focused on the summit, leaving little in the tank for the return trip.

At around 8400 metres they arrived at a 20-metre pitch of steep ice and technical rock. Tomo rigged the rope for rappelling and Borut went down first. After a short time he called up. "Okay. You can come." Tomo doubted that Borut had reached the bottom of the pitch, but he rappelled down anyway to find him standing on a ledge, ten metres above the bottom of the steep step. Still hanging on his rappel ropes, Tomo began to place another piton from which he could set up a second rappel.

While Tomo was pounding in the piton, Borut fell. Not a sound. Simply gone. "I think he died, and then fell," Tomo later said. "Because when you fall and you are still alive you do something to stop yourself. He didn't do anything."

Now Tomo was alone on the little ledge. It was his first high-altitude bivouac. Completely unplanned. He didn't know what to do. He spent the night moving his extremities and trying to stay awake. He locked his core against the cold and prayed for the dawn. "I was there and I had to survive," he explained. "It's that simple or that complicated."[126] He later admitted it was the closest he came in his entire career to crossing the edge between life and death.

Meanwhile, base camp was watching. They saw Borut and Tomo reach the summit and, later, only one climber descend. At first it was unclear. Franček Knez, who was part of the team, walked away to be alone in the nearby meadow. Instinctively, he knew that a tragedy was being played out on the mountain. He had watched as the events unfolded, one ruinous incident after another. He later wrote about his feelings at that time. "I can feel the strength in this place. It blows through me, and in a moment it blows away all the dreams of my heart. An emptiness opens up, heavy and deep. Emptiness and sadness."[127]

How do you process a day like that? Success on the mountain. Tragedy on the mountain. Which emotion prevails? Pleasure? Pride? Grief? Anger? A chill settled over the camp, and as they waited, the destructive worms of reproach and blame and guilt burrowed into every climber's psyche.

Two days later and safely back at base camp, Tomo crumbled. He could barely walk. He couldn't sleep. He couldn't even stand. When the expedition doctor injected him with a sleeping potion, Tomo slept for

20 hours. He woke, ate a little, and slept for 15 more. He had stretched his physical and mental limits on Yalung Kang.

◆ ◆ ◆

One year later, Tomo had his next big chance, this time in the Karakoram. There are four eight-thousand-metre peaks in the Karakoram region of Pakistan: 8611-metre K2, 8051-metre Broad Peak, 8080-metre Gasherbrum I, and 8034-metre Gasherbrum II. Although remote, their close proximity makes them attractive targets for climbers wanting to climb more than one mountain in a season. Acclimatizing on one of these giants and then relocating to a nearby base camp and tagging another is now a fairly common practice. But it wasn't in 1986 when Viki Grošelj arrived, leading a 14-member team to climb Broad Peak and Gasherbrum II and do a reconnaissance of K2. There were some newcomers on the team. Andrej Štremfelj's wife, Marija, a talented and energetic alpinist with dozens of impressive ascents in the Julian and French Alps, was here to test herself at altitude. Her slight stature concealed a formidable strength and steely determination.

This was Silvo Karo's first exposure to the Karakoram, as well. Powerfully built, his arms thick as logs, Silvo looked as if he could devour eight-thousand-metre peaks for breakfast. Born in 1960 near Domžale, he was a farm boy who hated farm work. He started climbing in 1977, first introduced to the sport by his priest. Luckily for Silvo, as had been the case for other climbers, his army stint was in Bovič, a mountain town in the Soča Valley. His 18 months of mandatory duty were spent running, climbing and training. No more pigs or cows. The hard work paid off, and within a few years Silvo had amassed a remarkable number of difficult rock routes in Yosemite, Colorado, the Dolomites, the Alps and Patagonia. And now he was itching for Broad Peak. The other young member of the team was Tomo, whose renowned speed in the mountains meant that he now often climbed alone.

Viki was confident that Broad Peak, with its 1.5-kilometre-long summit, would be a straightforward first objective for this extremely strong team. On July 28, Viki and Bogdan Biščak left their camp at 5:00 am, plowing through the deep, powdery snow until they reached an exposed ridge above the 7800-metre col. Only after 20 gruelling hours did they reach the summit, becoming the first Slovenians to do so. In the next days, ten more climbers reached Broad Peak's summit, including Tomo, Silvo and both Štremfeljs. This was Andrej's second Karakoram eight-thousander and, for Marija, a new record for Slovenia as she became the first woman to reach that height. Tomo soloed the route in 19 hours.

One of the visitors to their Broad Peak base camp was Polish climbing superstar Wanda Rutkiewicz. She had just become the first woman to climb K2, and although she was physically and emotionally destroyed, having lost two of her three companions on the climb, she was determined to add Broad Peak to her resumé. Tomo recalled that she created quite a stir as she negotiated for the use of their tents and ropes. "Some of our climbers were prepared to climb with her and even carry her backpack," he marvelled. In the end, she abandoned her plan.

Next up for the Slovenians was the ice-clad, pyramid-shaped Gasherbrum II. On August 2 Bogdan Biščak, Pavle Kozjek, Andrej Štremfelj and Viki headed for Gasherbrum II base camp, a two-day walk away. They reached it in one day and, being well acclimatized, began climbing at 6:00 am the next morning, carrying the bare minimum of food and equipment. Five hours later they were at the base of the Southwest Arête at 5900 metres. They erected two tents and enjoyed a nice long rest while waiting for the unstable slopes above them to freeze. They began climbing again that evening at 9:00 and continued through the night. It wasn't until they reached 7400 metres that the sun's rays first touched them. There, they met a group of Pakistani climbers on their way down, having summited after 32 days on the mountain. The Pakistanis were a little stunned at the audaciousness of Viki and his crew, shooting for the summit the day after arriving at base camp.

As the sun continued its arcing ascent, the day became pleasantly warm. Then somewhat hot. Finally, almost unbearable. "The last few hundred metres were horrible. The sun was shining through white mists and I could never have believed that such heat could be possible at 8000 metres," Pavle Kozjek complained.[128] Bogdan and Andrej powered ahead and summited first, followed a few hours later by Pavle and Viki. With such a fast ascent, and the balmy, almost tropical sun, it would have been nice to tarry on top and enjoy the view. But a storm had broken out on K2 and was fast approaching the Gasherbrum group. Before they even stepped off the summit, the first snowflakes appeared in the air. Now the race was in the other direction – down. They squeaked out an impressively fast alpine-style ascent of Gasherbrum II just in time. The storm lasted for days, wreaking havoc in the area.

While the boys were running up Gasherbrum II, Tomo Česen wandered over to K2 and soloed up to 7900 metres on the Southeast Spur. Officially on a "reconnaissance" of the mountain, Tomo later admitted that he was sorely tempted to go to the top. He explained, "We had permission to 'look at something.' And 'looking at something' is not so specific." Asking for forgiveness from the Pakistani authorities would have been much easier than waiting for permission, so Tomo kept going up. After 17 hours he reached the Abruzzi Spur, looked up at a bruised and threatening sky and saw that a fierce storm was moving in. He fled the mountain.

Others on K2 weren't so lucky. In a horrifying series of events, 13 climbers from the United States, England, Poland, Italy, France, Pakistan and Austria perished on the mountain during that climbing season. In several cases, they had spent much too long at altitude. On this mountain, on this day, Tomo's speed kept him safe.

One year later, in 1987, Tomo was back in Nepal, invited to 8383-metre Lhotse Shar (one of Lhotse's three summits) with a team of stars – 13 of them. They were unsuccessful, but for Tomo the expedition was another important learning experience. After several weeks on the wall, he and Andrej Štremfelj climbed from base camp to 7500 metres and back again in a single 12-hour push. "This was a sign for me that you can climb in a different style," he said. "Of course, you have to be fit," he added, stating the obvious.

Tomo rationalized that by spending less time on the wall, he could significantly reduce his risk. He was now certain that, once acclimatized, he was much better at climbing continuously without sleep than moving his way up the mountain slowly, sleeping in camps along the way. This would be his style in the future.

ELEVEN

Next Wave

Not far from Tomo, in the town of Kamnik, another major player in the next wave of Slovenian alpinists was emerging. Born in 1965, Marko Prezelj showed early signs of a strong, pragmatic character. He was only 13 when he launched his first business: beekeeping, an enterprise his father eventually took over from him. In school Marko excelled in the classes that interested him – biology, physics and math – and studied only as hard as necessary in those that did not. "I was sort of an opportunist," he reflected. He revelled in subjects that presented opportunities for problem-solving, but the abstract world of philosophy and psychology didn't interest him. "I was interested in real things," he said.

Life was good for the young Marko. With both parents working and two boys in the family, they had everything they needed. Living in the country provided them with an abundance of fresh food. Health care, school, even university was free. "Anyone who was keen to study and was motivated could progress to any degree, from any village in the country," he explained. Like many who grew up in the Socialist era, Marko looked back with fondness on that time, with its simplicity, lower taxes, fewer roads, smaller houses, less infrastructure, no mobile phones and stronger friendships. He ignored any signs of oppression imposed by the government and focused instead on his immediate environment: family, friends and neighbours. "You knew that you could count on people," he said. "Everything was simpler." Alpinism later replicated that simple and honest way of life

Marko craved. "I cannot transform myself back to that time – to that mental state. I value that time, but at the time I was not even aware of it."

Marko's first mountain experiences were in the Kamnik Alps at the age of six. He would go with his family for three or four days at a stretch, sleeping in the mountain huts, hiking, scrambling up summits and running back down the other side. Sometimes they would wander along an unmarked hunter's trail. On one such excursion, Marko heard shouts from the fog above, climbers yelling, giving commands. As they called back and forth – "On belay...Climb on..." – he became intrigued. "I understood that there were people who knew more about mountains than we did," he recalled, and the first inklings of wanting to become an alpinist were stirred.

But he was only 14. You had to be 16 to go to climbing school, so Marko and his brother took up road-biking. Their first trip was a ten-day excursion to the coastal region of Istria. On the second trip they travelled further south down the coast, all the way to Dubrovnik in southern Croatia. Then they pedalled to Rome.

By this time he was old enough to join the climbing club, and Marko progressed through the training program, taught by an experienced alpinist, Bojan Pollak. Looking back, Marko admitted that he had some issues with Bojan and his style: "He was a man made of stone." Bojan forbade climbing shoes in the mountains, for example, only allowing mountaineering boots. He insisted that all the young climbers wear red socks and wool knickers, both of which they abhorred. Marko hated the rules as much as anyone, but he was pragmatic. "If I can't change the system, I can work with it," he shrugged, adding, "I didn't want to fight a battle that I knew I would lose."

After three years of training and a series of exams, Marko was declared an alpinist. His network of partners soon included foreign climbers, a small, rebellious victory that raised some eyebrows. But Marko was more interested in climbers who shared his values than in just any climber living next door. Even at this early age, the strength of his character was evident; he was practical, precise and selective.

His army stint was, in his words, "a waste of time." Posted on the plains east of Belgrade, he soon ran into trouble with his superior.

Nejc and Mojca Zaplotnik with Viki Grošelj at the Zagreb airport before Nejc and Viki headed off to attempt Manaslu in 1983. *VIKI GROŠELJ COLLECTION*

Above: April 15, 1983. Nejc Zaplotnik celebrated his 31st birthday in Manaslu base camp. It would be his last. From left to right: Boris Siriščević, Ivo Kaliterna, Ante Bučan, Igor Žuljan, Nejc Zaplotnik, Gordan Franić and Vinko Maroević. *Viki Grošelj collection*

Left: Nejc Zaplotnik working on his next book in Manaslu base camp, 1983. *Viki Grošelj collection*

Top: Climbers carrying the body of Nejc Zaplotnik to his final resting place at the base of Manaslu in 1983. *Stipe Božić collection*

Below: In 1996, Viki Grošelj returned to the base of Manaslu's South Face with the Zaplotnik family to visit Nejc Zaplotnik's final resting place. From left to right: Nejc (Jr.), Mojca (his widow), Luka and Jaka. *Viki Grošelj collection*

Edvard Retelj climbing in 1984 at around 5000 metres on the lower section of the South Face of Manaslu. This was the second, and successful, attempt on the face. He died nearly thirty years later in an avalanche on Mt. Kamešnica – 60 kilometres from Split. *STIPE BOŽIĆ COLLECTION*

The North Face of Dhaulagiri, the mountain of Stane Belak's (Šrauf's) obsession.
TONE ŠKARJA COLLECTION

Top: The final resting place of Stane Belak (Šrauf), one of Slovenia's greatest alpinists. *Stane Belak collection*

Below, left: Stane Belak (Šrauf). *Stane Belak collection. Right*: The spot at the base of the North Face of Mala Mojstrovka in the Julian Alps where Stane Belak (Šrauf) and Jasna Boratanič were killed by an avalanche on December 24, 1995. *Stane Belak collection*

Top: Two climbers (see faint shadows) climbing the fantastic North Face of Cho Oyu, 1988. *Viki Grošelj collection*

Above, right: Borut Bergant, who died while descending with Tomo Česen from the summit of Yalung Kang in 1985. *Stipe Božić collection*

Left: Viki Grošelj ascending Everest in 1989 with Stipe Božić. *Stipe Božić collection*

Above: Andrej Štremfelj on a difficult new route on the Southwest Face of Shishapangma, 1989. *ANDREJ ŠTREMFELJ COLLECTION*

Left: Pavle Kozjek at the first bivouac on the Southwest Face of Shishapangma, 1989. *ANDREJ ŠTREMFELJ COLLECTION*

Marija Štremfelj on the summit of Everest in 1990 after having climbed it with her husband. They became the first married couple to reach the top. *Andrej Štremfelj collection*

Top, left: Stipe Božić, Croatia's leading Himalayan climber. *Stipe Božić collection*

Top, right: Marko Prezelj. *Tone Škarja collection*

Below: Tomo Česen. *Tone Škarja collection*

Top: The Tomo Česen Lhotse South Face team of 1990: Dr. Janko Kokalj, Kami Sherpa, Tomaž Ravnihar and Tomo Česen. *ALEŠ KUNAVER COLLECTION*

Below: Tomo Česen back in base camp beneath the South Face of Lhotse, 1990. *ALEŠ KUNAVER COLLECTION*

Top: View from Lhotse at approximately 8300 metres, looking toward the Western Cwm. The photo was taken by Viki Grošelj in April 1989 when he climbed Lhotse by the normal route. It was this picture that Tomo Česen used as proof that he reached the summit via the South Face. The photo was published in *Vertical* magazine, reversed. *VIKI GROŠELJ COLLECTION*

Below: Kangchenjunga with routes of the 1991 Slovenian expedition. Main Summit: Stipe Božić and Viki Grošelj; Middle Summit: Uroš Rupar; South Summit: Marko Prezelj and Andrej Štremfelj, alpine-style. *VIKI GROŠELJ COLLECTION*

189

Top: Marija Frantar and Jože Rozman on their tragic bid to climb Kangchenjunga in 1991. *ANDREJ ŠTREMFELJ COLLECTION*

Below, left: The new route on Kangchenjunga's South Summit climbed by Andrej Štremfelj and Marko Prezelj in 1991. *ANDREJ ŠTREMFELJ COLLECTION*

Below, right: Andrej Štremfelj and Marko Prezelj (in red circle) on the lower part of their route on Kangchenjunga South, 1991. *TONE ŠKARJA, COURTESY ANDREJ ŠTREMFELJ COLLECTION*

Marko Prezelj climbing a rock step on the Kangchenjunga South Summit ascent, 1991. *ANDREJ ŠTREMFELJ COLLECTION*

Top: Marko Prezelj on the South Summit of Kangchenjunga with Yalung Kang in the background. *Andrej Štremfelj collection*

Below, left: Marko Prezelj leading above 8000 metres on the last day to the South Summit of Kangchenjunga, 1991. *Andrej Štremfelj collection*

Below, right: Andrej Štremfelj on the last night of the descent from the top of Kangchenjunga South Summit, 1991. *Andrej Štremfelj collection*

Marko Prezelj on the summit of Melungtse in 1992 after he and Andrej Štremfelj made the first ascent of the mountain, in alpine style. *ANDREJ ŠTREMFELJ COLLECTION*

The punishment? Twenty laps around the stadium. Perfect training, he thought. He ran them with pleasure, but when he was done, the officer scolded him. "You don't count very well. You cheated. You will need to run another 20." Even better! "I started to practise this kind of pragmatism, playing with the system," Marko admitted.

After his initial three months of training, Marko was sent to the officers' club as a drinks waiter. He became a kind of animateur, running the sound system for their musical needs, organizing movies and taking photographs. His compact frame, neat appearance and broad, open grin appealed to everyone. Despite his lacklustre experience as a soldier, Marko benefited greatly from the army, later working as a professional army alpinist and trainer for 17 years. This coveted position required the highest level of recognition within the country, a level that was determined by an evaluation system invented by Marko's old nemesis, Bojan Pollak.

The Alpine Association of Slovenia, like other sports organizations, relied on the central government for financial support. Evaluating competitive sports such as skiing was easy. But the less easily rated sport of mountaineering also required some kind of measurement, and Bojan was just the man to create one. He invented a complex system of points, differentiating between summer and winter ascents, with winter earning higher marks. Winter was from December 21 to March 20, and one day later didn't count as winter, despite a route being done during a severe snowstorm. Climbs that were one hundred metres were worth more than shorter climbs, even one that was 98 metres and devilishly difficult. This points system was not unfair, but climbers began choosing their objectives based on it. Why climb on March 22 when you could do it a couple of days earlierand get double the points? Why bother with an incredibly challenging 95-metre rock climb when a less interesting one of five additional metres would earn you more points? This strategizing was unavoidable, because the number of points determined the type of climbing licence an alpinist could claim: a state licence, a national licence or an international one. There was even a kind of *super* licence for climbers who had done something exceptional – a "master of disaster" licence, in Marko's words. Climbing Everest would qualify. Marko understood the system and used it to his advantage, reaching that highest level. But he was also a motivated alpinist whose values remained intact. And those values more than anything made him aspire to climbs that were even harder than those undertaken by the alpinists who preceded him – climbers like Nejc Zaplotnik and Aleš Kunaver.

After reaching 7300 metres on Lhotse Shar in 1987, Marko was invited by Roman Robas the following year to join an expedition to Cho Oyu. At 8188 metres, Cho Oyu is the sixth-highest mountain in the world. It lies on the border between Nepal and Tibet, 20 kilometres west of Everest. The first ascentionists climbed it in 1954 in impeccable style. Two Austrians followed Pasang Dawa Lama into Tibet, set up a base camp and climbed alpine-style with neither bottled oxygen nor a permit. The first Slovenian team arrived in 1984. Although they didn't reach the summit, the group of Styrian climbers, including Franček Knez, reached 7700 metres on a dangerous and technically challenging face on the Nepalese side. The most difficult climbing was below them, but deep snow, storms and exhaustion turned them back.

The 1988 team of eight included Marko, Viki Grošelj and Tone Škarja. Their goal was the mysterious north side of the mountain, up a route that had never been climbed. When they reached the end of the valley, there it was: Cho Oyu's North Face, a wall of rock and ice more than two kilometres in height and twice as wide. Completely untouched. They were speechless with excitement.

They placed three camps on the face and fixed two kilometres of rope on the lower part of the mountain, where there would be difficult mixed climbing. Seven climbers reached the summit by various routes, including the first complete traverse of the mountain by Iztok Tomazin. It was a rousing introduction to the eight-thousanders for Marko.

◆ ◆ ◆

While climbers like Marko were realizing their dreams in the Himalaya, tensions had mounted to unprecedented levels in Yugoslavia. Orthodox Serbs, in particular, felt under pressure. Much of their distress originated from an ancient grievance dating back to a humiliating defeat in the Great Battle of Kosovo in 1389.

Although both sides sustained incredible losses, the Ottoman Empire annihilated the Serbians. After this turning point, over the centuries, the heartland of Kosovo changed from a mostly Serbian Orthodox population to a predominantly Muslim one. Bit by bit, Serbs had lost their foothold in this, the poorest of Yugoslavian regions. When they organized a protest in the town of Kosovo Polje in 1987, Yugoslavian president Ivan Stambolić took little interest and instead sent his deputy, Slobodan Milošević. In retrospect, it's hard to measure the magnitude of his mistake. As the influence of Communism declined in the late 1980s, Yugoslavia, more than almost any other Communist state, was best equipped to transition to a multi-party democracy. Thanks in large part to Milošević, however, this was not to be.

Milošević was ambitious and strategic. He had wanted to step into Tito's shoes as leader of all Yugoslavia, and when he failed to achieve that goal, he adjusted his expectations to lead a new, enlarged Serbian state. In Kosovo he saw an opportunity to fan the flames of Serb nationalism. He stood before the crowd, donning the mantle of protector of all Serbs, encouraging them and promising them his undying support. "Slobo, Slobo!" they responded. Overnight he became a Serb hero, and before the year was out, he had ousted Ivan Stambolić from power.

He spent the next two years consolidating his grip in Serbia, in Montenegro and in Kosovo. He harnessed the enormous clout of the Yugoslav National Army until, finally, individual Yugoslavian republics had two choices: join "Greater Serbia" or fight a war against one of the largest standing armies in Europe, the army Milošević had commandeered for his own ambitions.

Meanwhile, Slovenian authorities were relaxing their hold on citizens; under the leadership of Milan Kučan – famous for his big blue eyes – the country was ready for change. The Slovenian intellectual community lobbied for massive reform, and on September 27, 1989, Slovenia declared itself a sovereign state. Milošević initially showed little interest, concentrating on a much bigger prize, Croatia. Although Croatia was also flexing its independence muscles, its government was less well organized than Slovenia's and was mired in postwar revelations connected to the state's notorious death camps. The relatively calm Tito years were history. Yugoslavia roiled and heaved with turmoil, ambition, confusion and, ultimately, death.

There was even more reason now for climbers to leave the country and go to the Himalaya to climb. As Nejc wrote, "I am sentenced to freedom."[129]

◆ ◆ ◆

Viki Grošelj and Stipe Božić were still among the most active climbers during this time, along with the new wave of emerging alpinists. In 1989 Viki and Stipe joined a large Macedonian expedition to Everest and Lhotse. They received but a lukewarm welcome when they first got to base camp. Because Tibet's doors were closed at the time, the Nepalese side of the mountain was crowded. Viki and Stipe had arrived almost one month later than most other climbers and were told they would need to pay to go through the Khumbu Icefall, the treacherous jumble of towering and unstable seracs and gaping crevasses through which all climbers attempting the South Col route must pass. An American commercial team had equipped the icefall with ladders and fixed lines and wanted recompense.

Since the Macedonian team was already at Camp III, the pair rushed on up as soon as they had paid. The commercial teams on the mountain were further irritated at their speed and complained to the liaison officers at base camp. Did they have a permit? For Everest? For Lhotse? Which route? Viki and Stipe presented their permits and expected the affair to blow over. Not yet. There was an alleged rock-throwing incident, and tempers flared. More than 20 years later, Stipe shook his head in amazement. "They accused us of being illegal, without ethics…This was a new experience for us…my first meeting with such ways of thinking – the first time I met a situation where Sherpas fixed ropes for clients."

Their first order of business was Lhotse. They climbed together to 8090 metres, where Stipe began getting frostbite in his feet. Viki carried on and summited, assisted by Stipe on his descent. The next day they traversed over to Everest, which they both summited. The climb made Stipe the second European after Messner to have climbed Everest twice and by two different routes, earning him international celebrity status. The expedition was also a significant coup for Viki, who had summited two eight-thousanders in one expedition.

Their success was also proof of having chosen the right partner. Of all the partnerships from the many Yugoslavian and Slovenian expeditions during this time, Viki Grošelj and Stipe Božić were together the longest. Starting in 1979, they joined forces on ten expeditions. With such different personalities, it's a miracle they survived. "We are not alike," Stipe admitted. "I am a Mediterranean type – I like improvisation. Viki is systematic – he likes to plan in advance. But somehow we found our way together." They may have had differences, but they shared similar dreams and understood that they were stronger together than apart. Viki reflected that their partnership was less about equal climbing abilities and more about strong feelings of friendship and ethics. "When I remember the best climbs everywhere, my first memory is not where the face was or how beautiful it was," he said. "I remember who I climbed with."

As always, Nejc said it best in *Pot*: "I cannot bear obligations in the mountains except those that arise from friendship." [130]

◆ ◆ ◆

Slovenian climbers were on fire, and the expeditions headed out, one after the other. During the autumn of 1989, Viki was back in the Himalaya, this time on 8027-metre Shishapangma. Located in Tibet, Shishapangma is the lowest of the 14 eight-thousanders. The expedition was led by Tone Škarja and included seven living legends – Silvo Karo, Andrej Štremfelj, Pavle Kozjek and Šrauf among them – and one "greenhorn," as Marko Prezelj referred to himself. Unfortunately it didn't turn out well for Marko, who later vowed to avoid large expeditions in the future. "I lost a kind of virginity there," he said of Shishapangma.

The plan was to set up base camp, acclimatize and then send roped parties of two or three climbers up several different lines alpine-style. Andrej and Pavle were the first to summit, via a difficult new route on the Southwest Face. As Andrej described it, "The face did not give up easily...We climbed steep rock until we were 50 metres from the top."

Viki and Filip Bence climbed the mountain the next day, giving Viki his eighth eight-thousander and his fourth within one year. (Cho Oyu, Lhotse, Everest and Shishapangma.) Meanwhile, Marko, Šrauf and Iztok Tomazin were working on a third line up the mountain.

Marko and Šrauf – it should have been a dream team. The formidable Šrauf, a legend in the Himalaya with years of experience, and Marko, the talented younger climber. Marko had nothing but respect for Šrauf. He recalled the first time they met in the winter of 1985. Marko and two companions were climbing a route on the west face of Vrana in the Kamnik Alps. "I could hear him before I could even see him," Marko laughed. Marko and his friends were late, and it looked as if they would need to bivy on their route. They could see a lone figure descending a faint hunter's trail not far away.

The lone climber yelled, "Hey, what are you climbing?"

Marko recognized the voice in an instant. It was Šrauf. "Once you know it – the intonation – his voice was also his personality…quite strong and super-special," Marko explained. The three decided to play a joke on Šrauf.

"Oh, you don't know this route?" they taunted, knowing full well that he did.

"Who are you?" Šrauf barked back at them.

"Who cares who we are?" they yelled back.

Taken aback, the gruff and dominant Šrauf took a moment to digest the disrespectful attitude of these youngsters, obviously having a good time at his expense. But he liked to joke around, too. So, what the heck…

"Okay, good. Do you have bivy gear?" he called back.

"Yeah, no problem. Don't worry," Marko answered.

"Okay, guys, take care."

Marko recalled that the inflection in Šrauf's voice had shifted, from the "king of the mountains, keep the riff-raff out of my territory" tone to one that acknowledged the young climbers as people he actually cared about – his tribe. "He used to call us young climbers 'puppies,'" Marko explained. "It was his way of saying that we didn't have his experience. It was just to keep a distance."

With this fond memory in mind, what could top climbing a new route on Shishapangma with the legendary Šrauf? Šrauf had proven himself many times: Makalu South Face, Everest West Ridge, Dhaulagiri South Face, and more. But now he was 20 years older. Twenty more years of fighting, often with himself. "He was the one who kept pushing himself to the limits, and over them, and then rescuing himself," Marko said. "He lived in the moment all the time," he recalled, adding, "I'm not capable of that."

But on Shishapangma, Šrauf was not living in the moment. He was distracted. He became ill, but he didn't take care of himself. He was cold, but he didn't dress properly. It was almost as if he had lost his self-respect. Marko watched him deteriorate and thought, "Fuck, what kind of a legend is this?" On that expedition to Shishapangma, some alpinists were on their way up in their careers and others were on the decline. Šrauf was on the latter path, and he and Marko made little progress on Shishapangma. It is impossible to know what internal battles Šrauf was fighting: personal issues, aging issues, competitive issues. Regardless, Marko's final analysis of the man was: "Šrauf was the best."

◆ ◆ ◆

Internal battles are often the most difficult, and Slovenia was facing one of its own, reeling with shame and shock at a horrifying discovery that went back to the days immediately following the Second World War. When tens of thousands of Yugoslavians – Slovenians, Croatians and Serbians – were sent back to Yugoslavia from Austria, they faced certain death. Some were collaborators, some were pacifists and many were simply confused and war-weary citizens. On May 26, 1945, the *Slovenski poročevalec* newspaper predicted their destiny: "We have imprinted revenge in our hearts as a program and a core, in order to shatter and destroy this company of traitors and executioners…Victims must be avenged. Revenge must reach down to the deepest roots. We shall not only cut down the rotten tree, we shall dig up its roots and burn them, and the soil in which they grew we shall plow ten feet deep, so that not the least sprout remains of the tree." [131]

That revenge took place in 1945, mostly at two mass execution sites: the first at Hrastnik in eastern Slovenia and the second in the peaceful wooded hills near Kočevski Rog. More than 11,000 people were lined up at the edge of deeply excavated pits and shot in the back at a rate of seven hundred per day. Explosives were later thrown in to fill the sites with dirt and rocks, to hide the evidence. The areas were then sealed under the pretext of being top-secret military bases, and for 35 years, the slaughters were taboo subjects. There was no way to even *begin* to comprehend the truth. Were the executioners heroes or villains? Were the victims martyrs or criminals? A few brave writers began approaching the topic, and grief-torn relatives made timid forays into the woods to light candles or lay flowers near where they suspected their loved ones' bodies might lie.

Over time the death pits were unearthed, revealing thousands of corpses. Four hundred mass graves in Slovenia alone, including Teharje, Slovenj Gradec, Slovenska Bistrica, Podutik and many more. On July 8, 1990, a reconciliation ceremony was held in the forest near the Kočevski Rog cave. Twenty thousand people showed up. The air was heavy with grief, shame and untold stories. A feeling of closure began to percolate the collective consciousness, but the healing was incomplete. For who were the executioners? Were they still alive? Had they left the country? Were they in power? Were they living next door? Nobody could answer those questions, and so the distrust lived on.

TWELVE
Seismic Shift

A lthough Yugoslavian climbers entered the Himalayan arena late, the international climbing community was stunned by their accomplishments on Makalu and Everest and awed by their near successes on the South Faces of Dhaulagiri and Lhotse. There were many more: Kangbachen, Trisul, Cho Oyu, Shishapangma, Gaurishankar South Summit, Annapurna, Gangapurna, Yalung Kang, Ama Dablam, Lhotse Shar – the list of ascents went on and on. As their triumphs accumulated, confidence grew. So did national pride.

As head of the expeditions commission of the Alpine Association from 1979 to 2014, Tone Škarja – the man who led the 1979 Everest West Ridge expedition – was a powerful individual in the climbing community. Although he had first accepted the leadership torch from Aleš Kunaver with reluctance, he eventually carried it with dogged determination. He tapped into national pride and squeezed precious financial support from the central government for expeditions. Not surprisingly, he had the final say on which expeditions were funded and who was on them. Tone was a savvy manipulator of the old-boys'-network style of getting things done. Yugoslavia's political system may have been called socialist, but it was actually a network of contacts. Tone aspired to some kind of national climbing legacy, and although Yugoslavian climbers had yet to climb all the eight-thousanders, he knew they were well equipped to do so; it was simply a matter of checking them off. The eight-thousanders undertaking took 20 years and included a combination of normal routes, new routes, alpine-style ascents and ski descents. He led an entire generation of expeditions, but his tenure was full of turbulence. Still, despite severe criticism of some of his priorities, the results are remarkable.

Tone Škarja faced many challenges in his years as a leader: funding issues, political wrangling with the Belgrade bosses, and the conflicting goals of the top Slovenian climbers. His greatest test was navigating the sea change in attitude among the alpinists who depended on him for funding. For at the height of his eight-thousanders program in the late 1980s, many young Slovenian climbers had aspirations other than chasing eight-thousanders: difficult routes, small teams, individual rather than national goals. The concept of leadership was changing, too. Modern alpinists weren't interested in taking orders or joining large, unwieldy teams. They wanted independence. They preferred nimble, lightweight expeditions with three or four climbers. Marko Prezelj's advocacy for this approach was known far and wide, not only within Slovenia. "Style matters" was the mantra of this elitist alpinist, who railed against anything commercial, public or "impure."

There were already a few early signals of a more individualistic attitude back in 1921 when disgruntled young Slovenian climbers went off and started the Touring Club Skala, grumbling about "style." They were interested in personal goals and difficult lines rather than nationalist objectives. And there were many more-recent examples of the attitudinal shift: Franček Knez abandoning the Everest team in 1979 to wander off and do a first ascent on neighbouring Khumbutse; Šrauf taking a small team to Dhaulagiri's South Face in 1981 instead of joining the Lhotse team. This evolution eventually led to a cataclysmic explosion within the climbing community, an eruption that would revolve around one charismatic and impossibly talented climber from Kranj – Tomo Česen.

♦ ♦ ♦

Tomo Česen first spied the North Face of 7710-metre Jannu in 1985, on his way to Yalung Kang. The soaring shaft of rock and ice at the western end of Kangchenjunga initially attracted him in a hypothetical way, since the direct route on the North Face seemed unclimbable. Jannu was first climbed in 1962 by a French team led by Lionel Terray. The French route was a circuitous one via the South Ridge. Alpinists from Japan and New Zealand had also climbed portions of the North Face, but the line that attracted Tomo was the direttissima, straight up the middle, solo. When he approached Tone Škarja for support, he met with resistance. A couple of other climbers were also interested in the face, and Tone felt they should go as a team. Tomo disagreed. He was training and climbing full-time at this point and felt that solo was the safest way to go. He had also attracted the attention and support of some private sponsors – taking the first steps toward being a professional climber. He didn't need Tone's approval.

Together with Dr. Janko Kokalj, a liaison officer and a cook, Tomo established base camp on April 22, 1989, at 4600 metres. After five days of studying the face, Tomo knew that climbing at night would be the key. That, and climbing fast. His pack held the bare minimum: extra clothing and gloves, sunglasses, a headlamp, a sleeping bag, a bivouac sack, a bit of food and liquid. He carried no stove. He prepared his equipment, attached a few pitons and a spare ice-axe blade to his climbing harness and strapped on his crampons. Together with his rope, helmet and two ice axes, he walked to the edge of the glacier, said goodbye to Janko and started up. In an interview with American alpinist Mark Twight, Tomo explained where his super-lightweight confidence originated. "I knew…that I could go for three to four days without food and two or more days without sleep." [132] The wall was steep from the beginning. After four hours of climbing near-vertical ice, he stopped to rest. Just for ten minutes. His mood was euphoric. "Alone on the glacier, I felt exhilarated, a good sign, and I was already in complete control of my feelings." [133]

Down in the valley the shadows had lengthened into a solid wall of darkness, but up on the face it was light enough to climb. Tomo climbed through the night, when, thanks to the cooler temperatures, rockfall and icefall abated. By morning he had reached the top of the icefield. More steep ice and tricky rock steps led to a final slab of granite that almost stopped him. A stretch of rock that would have been a fun romp in climbing shoes at sea level was incredibly challenging in plastic double boots and crampons. But it was the key to the last icefield, so it had to be climbed. Carefully. He described his technique: "I leaned unhappily with my hands on the slab and my crampons in the thin ice below. I clawed with an ice axe at some small ice crystals. Eventually I felt enormous relief when my axe at last hit solid ice. This section was definitely not for the faint-hearted!"[134]

He was finally on the last part of the face. But it was now a one-way ticket. There was no way back down what he had climbed: vertical gullies; glassy, fragile ice; black, metal-hard ice; surreal, green-tinged ice; rock cliffs; and always that gaping void below the points of his crampons. Technical climbing on mixed terrain at this altitude is only possible if one has the highest level of skills, a superb sense of balance and singular concentration as well as having undergone merciless training. At one point Tomo was forced to pendulum from one ice gully to another. He described the process in his official report: "I hammered in a piton, threaded the rope, descended a little and swung to the side. Thus, I reached the continuation of the ice gully to the left."[135] His account of the manoeuvre elicited scathing remarks from many climbers who scoffed that what he described was impossible.

He described reaching a soft, snowy ridge at the end of the gully and continuing up to the summit, arriving at 3:30 pm, just as a sea of roiling charcoal-grey clouds appeared. The descent down the unfamiliar Japanese route was epic, and his concentration didn't falter until he reached the glacier below. Almost immediately, he began to stumble and sway, now completely spent.

The ascent, as he recounted it, had been staggering in its serious-ness and its difficulty. Tomo climbed Jannu in 23 hours and descended in 18. He had acclimatized for less than a week. It was hard to believe. Many didn't. Tomo had no photos to prove his ascent and didn't seem much bothered by the disbelief he encountered. He shrugged off their doubts, saying, "I also learned that the limits of risk and impossibility are very different for different people."[136] As proof of his climb, he referred to a single piton placed in a crack high on the mountain – but someone would have to go up there to find it. No one did. Tomo's thoughts were already focused on the future. He felt he had pushed his own physical and psychological limits on Jannu and was ready for an even greater challenge.

◆ ◆ ◆

Tomo spent the next year learning everything he could about Lhotse's South Face. He singled out the 1981 expedition as his most valuable source of information. One year before that trip, Aleš Kunaver had sent two climbers to base camp to watch the face for two months and sketch every avalanche and rockfall path they saw on a photo of the face. Tomo studied the marked-up photograph and consulted with climbers who had been on the 1981 team, including Viki Grošelj. He studied slides from Viki's extensive collection and plotted and planned his route. He consulted Andrej Štremfelj, who advised him not to descend the other side, should he reach the ridge. He learned that the face was notoriously unstable, particularly in the afternoon when the daily snowstorms rolled in, raking the face with avalanches, rockfall and icefall. He studied the point at which the 1981 team left the pillar and traversed right, the point where they ran into horrendously loose rock overlaid with snow. "These guys did 90 per cent of the job," Tomo said. "They had bad conditions. They were unlucky. I'm sure if they had gone straight up the pillar they would have finished it."

But it may have been more than bad luck that kept them from their goal. Aleš had assembled the best climbers in the country, and there were a few who stood out. This was the time of socialism, however, where a team was a team and the players were equal. Tomo and others felt that, had Aleš saved his best technical climbers from the gruelling trips up and down the face over those many weeks, they might have been less exhausted and more motivated at the end to push through that last difficult barrier. "They didn't have enough power to try a few more times," Tomo reflected.

After 1981 there were a number of attempts on the face from several countries, including one led by Reinhold Messner. And in 1989, the man who probably came closest to cracking the face – Polish alpinist Jerzy Kukuczka – fell near the top, tragically ending his brilliant career. Kukuczka's death added fuel to the fire that fed many ambitious high-altitude climbers. The South Face of Lhotse was still up for grabs.

Tomo arrived at Lhotse's South Face on April 15, 1990. Nothing about his climb was conventional, including his choice of base camp. Much lower than normal at 4850 metres, it offered a convenient source of water and protection from the aggravating winds that swept down off the face each afternoon. True, his camp was one and a half hours from the base of the climb, but for a greyhound like Tomo, that was nothing to worry about. To acclimatize, he romped up and down the slopes of Lhotse Shar four times in six days. From his high point on Lhotse Shar at 7200 metres – a full 2300 metres of elevation gain from his base camp – he could view the South Face and map out his route. What he saw from Lhotse Shar confirmed what he already knew: the bottom of the face was the most dangerous because of avalanches and rockfall; the real difficulties began at eight thousand metres; and night climbing would be critical.

Tomo began the climb on April 22, only seven days after arriving at base camp. It seemed incredible – almost impossible – that he would launch the climb of his life after such a short acclimatization period and such a significant output of energy on Lhotse Shar.

He took very little: a sleeping bag and bivouac sack, two ice axes, crampons, a helmet, a harness, ice and rock pitons, extra gloves, socks and goggles, a camera, a walkie-talkie, one hundred metres of six-millimetre rope, clothing, a bit of food and three litres of coffee. He left camp at five in the afternoon, intending to climb the most dangerous part of the lower face at night. Apart from a few tricky vertical rock steps, he recalled that conditions were good, and he made swift work of the snow and ice slopes. After 15 hours of climbing, he bivouacked at 7500 metres just as the sun was beginning to rise.

The bivouac site was protected from the daily barrage of snow, ice and rock, and the day was warm, so, confident that he was safe, Tomo took a nap. In the early afternoon he vaulted up a narrow couloir that led to a few rocky steps, then across a long snowfield ending in a rock buttress. It was late in the evening before he reached his second bivouac site, at 8200 metres. Although safe from rockfall, it was bitterly cold. "You can't describe such a night with mere words," he recalled. "Cold! Loneliness!"[137] And without doubt, anxiety, as the night fear set in. The next day would be the most difficult on the face and would determine the outcome. The rock buttress above 8200 metres was the crux – the mystery that had lured Tomo to Lhotse's South Face. The North Face of Jannu had perhaps been more difficult, but it was not as high. This rock buttress had turned back some of the world's best high-altitude climbers. Tomo wanted it badly.

The morning of April 24 was calm and clear. His official report written later described the following scenario. Leaving every bit of unnecessary equipment at his bivouac site, he began to climb. He took three hours to climb 60 metres of steep, snow-covered rock; for a few moves he needed to use artificial aid. In anticipation of his descent, he left a fixed rope at the top of the rock step for a rappel. In thickening clouds and a freshening wind, he gained the ridge, from which he could see the South Col toward Everest, and Cho Oyu further along to the west. To the south was a sea of cloud. He descended a bit into a saddle and then climbed on up.

At 2:20 pm he radioed base: "Janko, I cannot go any higher."

"Why not?'

"I'm on top!"

In his report, Tomo made no mention of photographing the summit moment, only that he felt immense pressure to descend. He ruled out descending much easier ground to the Western Cwm between Everest and Lhotse because he didn't know the way and was convinced he would get lost. Instead, he retraced his steps as far as 7800 metres, then rappelled over a rock step, using pitons left by the 1981 expedition. He made no mention of the rappel rope he had left on the way up, nor the extra equipment he had stashed at his last bivouac site. He descended amid continuous waves of spindrift avalanches until finally the air became choked with snow. His third, nerve-racking bivouac was at 7300 metres. "They say I'm cool-headed but in that third bivouac my nerves nearly cracked...I felt that the whole of Lhotse seemed to be trembling from avalanches."[138]

Around midnight the storm abated and the avalanches became less frequent. He looked up and saw what he was hoping for, the twinkling of stars. Not wanting to chance the morning's weather, he roused himself and raced down the rest of the face as if in mortal fear of the white monster he knew was lurking. By 7:30 am he was down. He described his mental state as "incapable of thinking"; the concentration and strain had destroyed him. Yet photographs of Tomo show him looking surprisingly unfazed when he strolled into camp. Fresh and healthy, even well-groomed – a sharp contrast to his appearance after descending Yalung Kang. Many would wonder about this seeming dichotomy in the days and months, and even years, to come.

As compelling as Tomo's Lhotse climb was, it paled in comparison to the furor that followed. His 64-hour round-trip, solo ascent of the "last great problem" of the Himalaya shocked the mountaineering community. Journalists flocked to interview him. He earned a Slovenian national medal. Reinhold Messner nominated him for his second Snow Lion Prize, worth $10,000. Gear companies vied for his attention and his expertise. His profile was complete: devoted family man, classically handsome and a Himalayan superstar.

Then came the first grumblings. Elite French alpinists huddled in their drafty alpine huts and overpriced Chamonix bars. *"Ce n'est pas possible! Où sont les photos? Nous demandons preuve!"*

But Tomo had little evidence to offer. And not only for Lhotse. His camera had frozen on Jannu, and nobody from base camp had seen him on the summit. He had nothing from K2. His photos from Lhotse were confusing at best: various views from the wall that were impossible to pinpoint. He produced one summit photo that showed Everest and the Western Cwm, and it was this photo that was published in the French climbing magazine *Vertical*.[139] At first Tomo ignored the whiners, chalking it up to jealousy. Then, in October of that year, a big Russian team climbed the South Face up a direct line to the summit using siege techniques: 20 climbers, seven camps, thousands of metres of fixed lines, bottled oxygen and two solid months. When they reached Kathmandu, they claimed the first ascent of the South Face of Lhotse.

The first to protest was Pierre Béghin, one of France's most respected high-altitude climbers. When he questioned why they weren't acknowledging Tomo's ascent, they answered, "He didn't get to the summit." But what about the summit photo? he countered. "You can't see the Western Cwm from the summit of Lhotse," they announced. According to the Russians, the curvature of Lhotse's West Face blocked the view of the Western Cwm. They were certain about that.

Emboldened by the Russian claim, outspoken French alpinist Ivano Ghirardini wrote a searing article in *Vertical* titled "Alpinism in Perdition." Ghirardini ranted at a multitude of sinners: sponsored climbers, helicopters, media and, finally, Tomo. As a professional climber, Tomo should have provided proof, he averred. Simple and final. On a climb like the South Face of Lhotse, he should have anticipated doubt. He should have been prepared.

Tomo fought back in a scathing letter to *Vertical* in which he made fun of Ghirardini and accused the Russians of taking a giant step backward in the evolution of alpinism. Tone Škarja supported him with a letter, stating, "Lhotse became a milestone in the development of alpinism, and only dogs piss on milestones."[140] He added more fuel when he said, "The French like to hate and look down on others, and in particular the first-class alpinists," and then topped it with this: "Their alpinism is not developed and they don't have any concept of modern alpinism."[141] Tomo added that his route would one day be proven because he had left all his pitons. The flurry continued in the climbing press, particularly in France. At times it became embarrassing, even for the French, as a number of top alpinists sprang to Tomo's defence.

Then, in the summer of 1992, Messner invited Tomo to give a lecture in Vienna. Messner, a consummate alpinist and a stickler for detail, was a big fan of Tomo's, but he noticed some inconsistencies in his story. Was the weather good, or was it bad? When Tomo mentioned that he had left no pitons on the route, Messner recalled that he had earlier said he *had* left pitons. Pitons or no pitons? And when he saw the film footage of Tomo returning to base camp, he could not fathom the fresh-faced young man loping down the hill. Surely even Tomo would look a little wearier after climbing the South Face of Lhotse? Things didn't add up, and Messner withdrew his endorsement.

But back in Slovenia support for Tomo was solid. Rock solid, until February of the following year.

Viki Grošelj was, and continues to be, a public personality in Slovenia, giving lectures, writing books and making films. His craggy good looks are well-known throughout the country. His slide collection and mountaineering library are extensive. While preparing for an exhibition of climbing literature, he came across a copy of *Vertical* – the same issue that showcased Tomo's climb. As he flipped through the pages, he was surprised to see a number of photographs from Lhotse. Surprised, because Tomo had returned to Slovenia claiming to have none. His word was his honour. Everyone in Slovenia had accepted that.

Viki continued looking at the images and then turned to his own

Lhotse slide collection from the 1981 expedition. Two of the slides in the *Vertical* article, attributed to Tomo, were his. "I nearly fell down," Viki told Greg Child, who was doing an investigative piece on the climb. Tomo's "money" shot was the photo of Everest and the Western Cwm. "I took this from five hundred feet below the summit on April 30, 1989, when I climbed the West Face of Lhotse," exclaimed Viki. That explained the appearance of the Western Cwm.

The mystery of how Tomo acquired the images was soon solved when Viki's wife, Cveta, explained that Tomo had appeared at their house a couple of days after returning from Lhotse, asking for photos. He had none of his own and wanted to show his sponsors his route. He said nothing about taking credit for the photos. Cveta trusted him as a close friend so never thought twice about it. He returned the photos a few days later.

As Viki digested this stunning information and continued to study the photos in the magazine, he began to doubt some of the other images as well. The angles weren't right. They looked more like the 1981 route, which was to the right of Tomo's alleged line. He began to wonder if Tomo had *any* photos from high on the mountain. His faith in the wunderkind of Slovenia began to crumble. Dušica Kunaver had also lent Tomo slides before he left for Lhotse, but she remained (and remains) firm in her belief that he used them strictly for research in order to complete the route he named in honour of her husband.

Furious, Viki demanded an explanation. Tomo admitted that he had borrowed the slides but he insisted that he had not claimed them as his own. That was the fault of the folks at *Vertical*. Sheer incompetence. *Vertical* staff disagreed, recalling in detail the various meetings and conversations about the article, with nary a word from Tomo about the origin of the slides. Finally, Dominique Vulliamy, who worked on the article for *Vertical*, said what she had been thinking all along: "Knowing the challenge of the wall, he decided to play his cards as well as he could, by using someone else's photos to prove an ascent he did not make."[142]

♦ ♦ ♦

As the uproar about Tomo's Lhotse ascent raged on, another dramatic storm arose in Slovenia. Actually, two storms.

Under Tone's leadership, it was obvious that the Alpine Association wanted to collect all the eight-thousanders. It was equally apparent that this was also Viki Grošelj's personal goal. During this time, a national sports lottery was allocating funds for sports organizations and the Alpine Association put up its hand for a slice of the pie. They received enough money to fully support one alpinist for a year. A highly coveted position. Tomo Česen had enjoyed the honour – and the salary – the previous year. Now it was Viki Grošelj's turn.

Many young Slovenian alpinists scoffed at this decision and grumbled among themselves that climbing eight-thousand-metre peaks by normal routes was passé. It was true that Slovenia had not yet climbed them all, but so what? It would happen eventually. In their minds, this project – and by extension this man, Viki – was completely disconnected from the direction that "real" alpinism was taking. It infuriated them that much of the association's funding was going toward chasing eight-thousanders, but what could they do? They felt powerless against Tone Škarja. They felt this high-profile award to Viki would only cement the program's misguided direction.

The Alpine Association and the sports lottery decided to hold a press conference live on national television. The young moderator was both skilled and knowledgeable. He invited Viki to the studio and asked him pertinent questions about his eight-thousanders project. Viki answered with aplomb, being a consummate communicator. Marko Prezelj, who was watching the program on television, laughed with contempt as he recalled that day. "Fuck, he is talking bullshit. It is his personal project and he's using national interest to cover the costs." The journalist thanked Viki and then turned to a pre-taped interview with Tomo, the previous year's recipient, who had been asked to comment on the coming project. Marko described what happened next. "Tomo said what most of the climbers at that time were thinking: 'This is a good personal project but it has nothing to do with the general direction of alpinism.'" The cameraman swung the camera back to Viki, who turned red and lost his composure. How could he respond to something so blunt, so personal, particularly on national television?

Within a week every newspaper and magazine in Slovenia had published the story that Tomo Česen had used Viki Grošelj's photo to prove his ascent of the South Face of Lhotse. What had happened in those seven days? It's all a bit murky, but it appears that Viki sent a letter to the expeditions commission of the Alpine Association, chaired by Tone Škarja, explaining the photo debacle and asking for an internal review by the ethics committee. What was supposed to be an internal affair was mysteriously leaked to the press. For an organization renowned for the glacial speed at which it moved, the letter's appearance was shockingly swift.

What was *not* mysterious, particularly to the younger generation of Slovenian alpinists, was what Tomo had said to the interviewer; they agreed with him but were too afraid to speak out. At the same time, Tomo was being crucified in the press for the misuse of Viki's photos. The whole affair was messy and added to the huge cloud of doubt being cast over his ascent. But the underlying issue was much bigger than a few photos: it was a split in philosophies between the two generations of climbers.

Another press conference was organized, and a letter appeared:

The opinion of Tomo Česen is our view – top alpinism can no longer be the climbing of eight-thousanders along the easier routes. Top alpinism consists of solving the increasingly difficult problems on the walls in the great mountain ranges of the world, in alpine style, by solo ascents, winter ascents, extreme ski descents…This means reaching the limits of the possible and pushing the limits upward…The Alpine Association of Slovenia, which is supposed to direct and support Slovenian alpinism, has been focused on collecting eight-thousanders at any price…We don't downgrade any of these results, but the current attack on Tomo Česen is more than anything an attack on the criteria of top alpinism and on us as individuals, on our athletic achievement, as listed below.[143]

Many alpinists signed the letter, not fully understanding that their support would be interpreted as support for Tomo's Lhotse climb. By now it was impossible to separate the two issues.

Tone Škarja scoffed at the letter and the signees, averring that many had no idea what they were supporting. Then he lashed out with a letter of his own. "Without the Commission for Foreign Expeditions, there would be no Slovenian ascents in Pakistan, Nepal...

nor successes on Makalu, Everest...The commission can't please everyone...In response to the open letter, it's worthwhile to support everyone who wants and is willing and able to climb in the high Himalaya. It's only those who have never experienced it who can talk about 'walking up eight-thousanders.'"[144]

To be fair, Tone had worked hard to organize and fund expeditions to the greater ranges. He had nurtured and supported many of the young climbers who were now attacking his leadership. "I was very hurt by this affair...It was individual alpinists who benefited from the Alpine Association...but I tried to make sure everyone got what they wanted...It was a burden...I didn't have to work so hard...This was like whitewashed graves...You are white on the outside but stinking on the inside – Slovenian alpinists are like whitewashed graves."[145] Tone was more than hurt. He was humiliated by this "blot" on Slovenia's brilliant Himalayan record, much of which he had orchestrated. The Lhotse scandal was a dark moment for all Slovenian alpinists. "It deeply affected them, more than they think," he later insisted.

And what about Viki, the man who had been humiliated on national television, accused of being a "walk-up" man? How many had taken the trouble to examine his climbing resumé? South Face of Makalu. New route on the North Face of Cho Oyu. Partial new route on the South Face of Shishapangma. South Face of Manaslu, and more.

Tomo Česen's contested South Face of Lhotse climb and the changing ideology of Slovenian climbers morphed into one convoluted mess. The issues became so entangled that eventually neither could be identified as separate concerns. And the fissure that appeared between the generations grew as wide as the Grand Canyon. Many look back at this moment as a turning point in the development of alpinism in Slovenia, for it now became polarized – a condition that would last for another ten years.

The halo of Slovenian alpinism was now tarnished. In Marko Prezelj's opinion, it was about time. "It was too big," he said. "If you went to France and said that you were a Slovenian alpinist, they would say, 'Oh boy, you must be really strong.' It was too much. For that generation, at one particular moment, it was no longer good. It had to happen. It was like in Poland; they lost one generation. Now we are struggling to restore the image of alpinism in Slovenia."

As for Tomo, judgment was inconsistent. Some of Slovenia's best climbers and most foreign climbers categorically dismissed him as a fake. Not just on Lhotse, but on Jannu and other solo climbs in the Alps. Some referred to him as a "Monday climber," doing his solos on Mondays when nobody was around to witness them. But many other Slovenians stood by their man. Perhaps it was simply a case of national pride. Dušica Kunaver was horrified that anyone would doubt his claims. She felt close to Lhotse's South Face, since her husband had envisioned its ascent first, had spent years planning for it. If he were alive, she believed he would have been extremely proud of Tomo.

The most common response from climbers who were most qualified to have a knowledgeable opinion, not just an emotional one, was that Tomo was *capable* of climbing it. Whether he did or not was his problem. Because of the complicated terrain on the summit ridge, it was possible that he had reached the top of *something* in the western summits area, mistakenly thinking it was the real summit, or conveniently assuming it was. But even those climbers most capable of expressing an opinion were rarely completely qualified, since few had climbed the Lhotse South Face.

Marko stated with conviction: "I believe him. Of course, I have to. In alpinism there are many cases that don't have proof. Even now, photography is not a real proof. You can photoshop it. If you want to fake something, you can do it so well that most people will believe it. It's his problem. It's not my problem. I don't care." He added that, although there was no proof that Tomo did it, there was also no proof that he didn't. As for many landmark climbs – Messner's ascent of Nanga Parbat, Ueli Steck's ascent of the South Face of Annapurna, and others – there was simply no proof. Despite the number of extremely questionable aspects to Tomo's story, Marko added, "If I stop believing him, I will have to stop believing every other climber who claims something…There are a few summit claims that I don't really believe, but I don't want to go into it – it's like shit, the more you stir it, the more it stinks. The [Alpine] Association still recognizes it as an ascent – what else can they do? I'm not saying it's true. I'm saying that I believe. I believe in the fundamentals of alpinism, which is trust. And from this perspective, it's not my problem. He has to live with whatever is true."

In addition to living with whatever was true, Tomo had to live with his voracious ambition. At first the pressure was internal. "You know how it goes...you start with some activity, you train, then you want more...You just always want to do something more," he explained. Tomo was rewarded handsomely for his climbs, which fuelled his drive even more. He was whipped into a frenzy of performance – greater and greater feats – until even *he* couldn't meet his own expectations. Sadly, he seemed to be missing a critical message about the importance of the alpinist's path – not only of the arrival at the summit. Nejc wrote in *Pot*:

> We hungered for great deeds but were not aware that the greatest deeds, achievements – just like a humdrum existence – are composed of little moments. We were not yet aware that there is no such thing as heroic acts, that people invent them so they can kneel before them and forget their own insignificance...How many disappointments and how many mistakes we have to experience to learn how to wait...Many times I have set out by myself, across rock faces and snow-capped mountains, quietly listening to the pulse of energy bubbling up inside me and releasing itself into endless open space.[146]

Tomo retired from Himalayan climbing after Lhotse. There were many reasons, but one was certainly his need to escape from the pressure to perform. As he recalled, "You know, you do something, and then this small community asks you in the next sentence, what is your next plan? This was crazy to me. What is your next plan?!" He felt increasing pressure from his private sponsors and after Lhotse decided the sponsor relationship was lopsided: "You put together everything – how much they give you, how much you get from this – when you put one and one together you realize that you are a loser." He had entered the rarefied world of the professional climber, and it no longer worked for him. He called it the "magic circle": the magic circle of climbing, sport, sponsors and media. "This magic circle is not so easy to get into, and it's even harder to get out of," he said. "I was in it and...when I calculated everything, I said, 'I don't want to play this game anymore.'"

Part of the magic circle was fame, and it turned out that Tomo didn't enjoy it as much as he had expected. Fame wasn't a sensation that came from within but was external, born in the eyes and minds of others. "If your character is not good to be a public person, you will see hell. I was not a natural public person," he admitted. His wife, Neda, concurred. "We had no private life. We couldn't even go out for a coffee without being inundated by strangers, either asking for autographs or accusing him of lies." Tomo defended himself for a while but eventually gave up. "Finally I said, 'Listen, guys, if you say so, I don't care. I really don't care.'" By 2014 his resignation was complete. "I can tell you now, after almost 25 years, it's not important at all," he said. "When you have some particular project, then you are concentrated on this project. But after a while it's not so interesting anymore," he explained. "Climbing is only one part of life. I'm sure it's not as important as it once looked…and I imagine that it will be even less important after one hundred years. After two hundred years, nobody will care."

But the Lhotse South Face was, and continues to be, important to alpinists, and most feel that he lied about his climb. At least for the moment, there is still only one person who knows the whole truth about where Tomo went on Lhotse.

◆ ◆ ◆

It's tempting to speculate about what might have been on Lhotse, had Nejc been alive. Not only on Lhotse, but for the entire generation of alpinists who were challenging the old ways. Nejc, although part of that older generation, was a modern thinker. He understood the conflicted complexity of the alpinist's life. He could have provided a precious link to bridge the widening gap. He might have smoothed the transition, defused the bitter battles and mended the strained friendships. As he wrote in *Pot*: "This is what our life is like: full of joy, full of sadness, full of longing, full of successes, and of bitter disappointments. So full of happiness and suffering at the same time, that sometimes there is just too much of everything. It is then that we grow old."[147]

THIRTEEN

A Most Beautiful Summit

J ust one year after the Lhotse affair, an expedition of another sort was about to take place. One that would firmly cement the reputations of Slovenian alpinists as leaders in the Himalayan arena. But although the 1991 Kangchenjunga expedition was one of Slovenia's most successful, it was also tragic. With Tone Škarja as leader, the goal for this multi-summited giant – third-highest mountain in the world – was three-pronged. Viki, Stipe, Marija Frantar, Jože Rozman and several more Slovenians planned to climb the 8586-metre summit via the standard route. Marija already had about six hundred ascents to her name, including one eight-thousander. She, like the others, was well equipped for the job. Marko Prezelj and Andrej Štremfelj were after a new route to the South Summit, and Vanja Furlan and Bojan Počkar were going to try the east wall of nearby Jannu.

Polish climbers Wanda Rutkiewicz and Eva Pankiewicz had also joined the expedition, adding a competitive dynamic. Wanda, the Pole, and Marija, the Slovenian, both wanted to be the first woman to the top of Kangchenjunga. Despite this, Viki felt later that the two Polish women integrated well into the team. Stipe disagreed, insisting that Wanda was particularly difficult, argumentative and easily riled. "One time she hit the local cook with a Thermos bottle," he said. Many on the team criticized Tone for accepting Wanda and Eva on the team, but he felt pressured. "We thought we had no power to say no," he said. Then he added, with a weary voice, "It was the reason that many things happened."

◆ ◆ ◆

At first, Andrej didn't know which route to try on Kangchenjunga; he only knew that it had to be new. Then he saw a photograph of an enticing couloir and long ridge leading to the South Summit. "This line looked quite safe to me," he said. Then he clarified with a grin, "It wasn't *very* safe, but it looked *quite* safe." Andrej knew it would be an important climb, a difficult climb, one that would push him to the very edge of what was possible, but hopefully not beyond. "On such an ascent, you are walking for a very long time just on the border," he explained years later. "That is the art of alpinism – to be close to the border but not to go over it."

Marko Prezelj was not Andrej's first choice as partner for the climb, but two others were disqualified because of poor performance and illness. Marko was next on the list. Andrej picked up the phone and called him.

"Will you go with me to Kangchenjunga?"

Silence. Then, "Ahhh, I don't know, I have to finish my studies," Marko finally answered.

"Hey, Marko, your studies can wait. Kangchenjunga is now."

Marko replied that he would think about it and call Andrej back. He took ten minutes. The answer was yes. Andrej hadn't even specified which route, so Marko had no idea what he was getting into, but he was game to try.

Marko and Andrej arrived at base camp later than the rest of the team and camped separately, planning to acclimatize on whatever nearby peak looked interesting rather than hauling loads with the other climbers. From the outset, Andrej insisted that they remain apart as a stand-alone, two-person team, concentrating on their goal and solidifying the bonds of their partnership. He didn't want to get caught up in the group dynamics of the larger team. He wanted no distractions. Their first acclimatization climb was Boktoh East, a 6114-metre peak that they raced up in one day. Next was 7349-metre Talung Peak.

They climbed to a bivouac at 6300 metres and started for the summit on the second day. Climbing unroped, they became separated in the howling wind. Finally, Andrej thought it was too dangerous to continue. "I saw Marko coming from around a corner and I thought, 'Okay, he feels the same and he is coming back,'" he recalled. But Marko was *not* turning around: he was descending from the summit. Without a verbal exchange, Andrej turned around and they both descended. Big misunderstanding. Talung was a great acclimatization exercise, but Marko tagged the summit and Andrej didn't. Had he known how close he was – only 50 metres – Andrej almost certainly would have continued. It was a tentative beginning to the partnership.

Six days later, still apart from the rest of the team, they started up their main objective, the 8476-metre South Summit of Kangchenjunga. Vertical tongues of ice and expanding rock flakes made for extremely difficult climbing and took many hours to solve, one pitch at a time. After ten hours they had ascended the first 650 metres of the climb. (UIAA Grade VI, A1, and ice that varied from 60 to 90 degrees.) Although they had planned to climb through the night, the weather changed and it began to snow, so they stopped and set up a bivouac at 6200 metres. Lightning split the sky, and the entire mountain range reverberated with thunder.

Freshly fallen snow added to the challenge the next day. They moved off the ridge, searching for easier ground, scraping their crampons on the steep, snow-covered slabs and placing the picks of their ice axes into minuscule cracks. Eleven hours of delicate, nerve-racking climbing later, some of it in the dark, they found a spot tucked into the bottom of a crevasse that was safe enough to set up their second bivouac. When they stuck their heads out the next morning, the winds were screaming. Marko began to have problems with his feet. Then his stomach. He vomited what little fluid he had managed to get down, and Andrej worried about their chances of continuing. They had only one litre of liquid between them and were now out of fuel.

Despite Andrej's worries, they must have felt confident, as they left everything in that last camp: their food, the tent, the stove. Although the two were solo climbing, they were prepared to rope up and belay if the need arose. A while later, Andrej looked back at Marko and noticed that his harness looked rather bare.

"Marko, where are your pitons?" he asked.

"Oh, they were so heavy I left them down on a ledge."

"Oh, okay."

After a couple of hours, Andrej glanced back again and noticed that Marko was no longer carrying the rope. "Marko, where is the rope?"

"Oh, the rope was so heavy I left it down below."

Half an hour later they faced the hardest pitch on the route. They had neither rope nor pitons. Luckily they discovered a length of tattered Russian rope, rotten from many years in the sun. It held together well enough for them to climb the difficult section, but they knew it wouldn't be strong enough for a rappel. Now they were truly committed. They would have to descend an easier way. But where?

The treacherous climbing continued until the junction of the Russian and Polish routes, only 250 metres below the summit of Kangchenjunga South. Andrej plowed on, ahead of Marko. Very near the end, Marko could see Andrej, and the top, so close. Yet he later admitted, "I [could] almost touch it but [had] to fight back a strange wish to quit and turn back."[148]

They reached the summit on April 30 at 4:45 pm. Marko felt only relief that the exhausting ascent had ended. They rested and took a few photographs. "I [was] in no particular hurry and enjoyed the solitude around me," Marko recalled. "The sunset [was] magnificent."[149]

The only problem with sunsets is that they quickly turn into nights, and eight-thousand-metre summits are not great places to spend them. Andrej started preparing some of the least-damaged fragments of the old fixed ropes to use for rappels. They began descending the other side of the mountain, where the rest of the team was climbing. They encountered bits and pieces of old fixed ropes and radioed Camp III to get some directions, but their batteries were so weak they couldn't decipher the reply. They had just started down a steep couloir at around 7900 metres when Marko dropped his ice axe. It cartwheeled down, miraculously slamming into a snowdrift just metres before it would have plunged into the void. In something of a daze, Marko retrieved the axe and continued down-climbing, since there were now no fixed ropes and they had used the last of their Russian remnants. Their only headlamp died. Down steep rock and then hard, polished ice. Down, down, down, through the night, they held on.

Marko slumped on a snow ledge and watched Andrej descending ahead of him. He knew instinctively that he must not stop, must

keep moving, must not sleep. As Andrej's figure receded, five red tents appeared. Wonderful! Marko closed his eyes, sure that he was hallucinating. He opened them. The tents were still there. Andrej, too, was resting nearby. Marko stumbled down, drawn by the colourful tents and Andrej. Then two teammates appeared, laden with hot tea and refreshing beer. He could actually smell the beverages. Which would it be? A tall mug of frothy lager or a steaming cup of sweet black tea? In an instant he knew that it was all a dream, a cruel hallucination. The only reality was the endless descent. The only sound was the thrumming of his pulse, like waves on a distant shore.

Near dawn, Marko saw another tent. He shook his head, trying to clear his vision. But this time it was real and directly in front of him. He dived in, wrapped himself up in a sleeping bag and fell into a coma-like sleep. Even Andrej, in retrospect, admitted that the descent had been tough. Technically difficult, and more so because of their advanced state of exhaustion. Andrej reached base camp the next day, and Marko one day later.

♦ ♦ ♦

The rest of the team was also doing well: Uroš Rupar reached Kangchenjunga Central, and Viki and Stipe, Kangchenjunga Main. On the way down they spent the night in Camp III with Marija and Jože, who started climbing toward the summit two days later. But the weather was beginning to deteriorate. Despite base camp's efforts to dissuade them, Marija and Jože continued. Most on the team felt that Marija was making the decisions at this point, intent on winning the race with Wanda.

When the two climbers eventually radioed base, it was clear they were in trouble. Exhausted, frostbitten and snow-blind, they reported that they were about 150 metres short of the summit but were unable to continue and were returning. The truth was much worse. They were hopelessly lost. Then radio communication broke down completely.

Wanda Rutkiewicz found their bodies a few days later. The two climbers had fallen all the way to Camp IV, probably due to exhaustion. Tone called the expedition off, infuriating Wanda, who felt strong and confident that she and Eva would make the summit. The following year, she returned to the mountain with Mexican mountaineer Carlos Carsolio. She too died on Kangchenjunga.

The team was shattered by the loss of Marija and Jože. Marko, the youngster, the future of Slovenian alpinism, searched his soul for answers:

> How can I learn from what happened to them if in a year's time I'll want to hear the gusting of wind, the thunder of avalanches, the hissing of drifting snow, the crackling of ice in an icefall, the striking of crampons onto the slope, the dripping of water into a crevasse? Am I any wiser? There is so much that I experienced that I don't understand: daring, desire, fear, climbing, wind, snow, doubts, hope, risks, uncertainty, the summit, the moment of freedom, descent, relaxation, falling, hallucinations, sleep, dreams about Marija and Jože, stumbling in the mist, joy, anxiety, death, indifference, confusion, sadness. Why all this chaos of thoughts? What did Andrej and I achieve in those six days? Only a line on a photograph of the mountain. But all this I experienced so intensely that I will never be able to forget or repeat.[150]

An adventure experienced at just the right moment can inform the rest of your life. Although Marko refused to name his *best* climbs, he admitted that Kangchenjunga was surely great. "It had elements of friendship and the unknown," he later explained. "I knew only 10 per cent of what might happen on this monster...At first it looks shit, and then you begin to solve the problems. Without complexity I am not challenged." He wrote in the *American Alpine Journal* that Kangchenjunga "took a lot from me but gave me back even more."[151]

Andrej Štremfelj, when asked about his most important climbs, named two. The first was Everest 1979, when he and Nejc climbed the West Ridge direct. Andrej referred to this as the climb that best represented his expedition-style climbing career, even though once the majority of the route had been prepared in expedition style, he and Nejc did the most difficult climbing above 8300 metres in alpine style. He named Kangchenjunga as his most important post-Nejc climb and his most important alpine-style climb, although this, too, was a complicated affair in terms of style. They climbed their new route independently and in pure alpine style, but there were teammates standing by in case of problems during their descent down the other side of the mountain. Alpine style, expedition style – subtle nuances, indeed.

Andrej felt drained by Kangchenjunga, suggesting that he, and most climbers, are not capable of making another such effort for several years – if ever. He felt that his and Marko's first ascent of 7181-metre Melungtse the following year simply couldn't compare, despite calling it one of his most beautiful Himalayan ascents, executed in pure alpine style.

Viki Grošelj rated Andrej and Marko's new route on Kangchenjunga as the single most important Slovenian Himalayan ascent.

Kangchenjunga was also important to Andrej for a more personal reason, one that had to do with partnership. When Nejc died on Manaslu, Andrej's climbing compass disappeared. "As I tried to discover my true self and my own way through the labyrinth of top alpinism, I felt lost and alone," he recalled. "It wasn't untilmuch later that I found the second highpoint in my climbing career. Kangchenjunga."[152] And for this second great climb, his partner was Marko. Even though the partnership began somewhat tentatively on their acclimatization climb, they found their stride as they worked their way up through the complex and difficult terrain, drawing on each other's strengths and building trust along the way.

For someone with a climbing career as long and distinguished as Andrej Štremfelj's – 40 years and counting, including eight eight-thousanders, four by new routes and two in pure alpine style – his number of partners is equally extensive. But Andrej insists that he had only four important climbing partners: "My brother Marko, Nejc, my wife Marija and Marko Prezelj."

Andrej credits his brother for his early adventures, particularly in the Julian Alps. Nejc began as a mentor, but they evolved into a powerful team. Still, Andrej admits that Nejc was the engine; his enormous energy and drive and confidence electrified Andrej and inspired him to perform his best. Both their Everest and Gasherbrum I ascents were ahead of their time. After the Everest West Ridge climb, Andrej – and others – began to think that all of their training and experience would protect them in the mountains, that they were incapable of making mistakes. That they could dodge death. "We thought we were untouchable," Andrej said.

Then Nejc died.

Andrej struggled to accept that, even though Nejc had been smart and experienced and skilled, even *he* wasn't completely immune to danger. When Nejc was killed, Andrej's confidence was shattered. "My house of experiences broke down…I needed one year or more to build the house again, but never again was that house quite as strong as before."

"I lost a lot of friends in the mountains, and also Marija's sister died on my rope," he said with sad, haunted eyes.

Together with Marija, Andrej climbed four eight-thousanders and countless routes in the Julian and French Alps. But climbing with Marija was fundamentally different from climbing with other partners. "If we had no children it might not be such a big difference," he said. They do have children, however: two daughters and one son. With Marija, his tolerance for risk is lower.

In retrospect, Andrej believes that coming face to face with mortality in the mountains was a valuable lesson. "I have to be 100 per cent prepared. I have to think for myself. To be faster." Nejc, in his own way, agreed with Andrej when he wrote in *Pot*: "Mountains are beautiful and safe. I know no cruel mountains. It is we who are dangerous because we doubt our path."[153] Still, on the descent from Kangchenjunga, Andrej, a devout Christian, admitted, "I had a bit of help from my God."

Andrej partnered with many great alpinists, but he saved his signature climbs for Marko Prezelj. The two made their best ascent together on their very first try. Their new route on Kangchenjunga's South Summit remains one of the iconic climbs of that era. Their style and ethics were in sync.

Both Marko and Andrej could recall only the bare-bones details of their achievement. They remembered that it was cold. That it was hard. That the descent was the most difficult. That they survived. They remembered that it was a challenge and that they made a good team. Like Nejc, who wrote about the frailty of memory, they remembered the important things.

Top, left: A young Silvo Karo and future rock master. *Silvo Karo collection*

Top, right: Three Musketeers on Fitz Roy, December 1983. Franček Knez, Silvo Karo and Janez Jeglič. *Silvo Karo collection*

Below: Janez Jeglič descending on frayed ropes on Fitz Roy, December, 1983. *Silvo Karo collection*

Top, left: A very determined-looking Franček Knez in Patagonia in 1986. *Silvo Karo collection*

Top, right: Janez Jeglič confronting a Patagonian storm on the South Face of Cerro Torre. *Silvo Karo collection*

Below: Three Musketeers in a celebratory mood in Buenos Aires after climbing Cerro Torre. Janez Jeglič on piano, Silvo Karo on lead guitar, Franček Knez singing backup and Dr. Borut Belehar on air guitar. The piano apparently did not survive the night. *Pavle Kozjek, courtesy of the Silvo Karo collection*

The beginning of Silvo Karo and Janez Jeglič's adventure on the West Face of Bhagirathi III, September 1990. *SILVO KARO COLLECTION*

Janez Jeglič on the West Face of Bhagirathi III, September 1990. He and Silvo Karo reached the summit on September 7 after six days on the wall. *SILVO KARO COLLECTION*

Above: Croatian climber and journalist Stipe Božić with his fellow soldiers on the border between Croatia and Serbia in 1991. *STIPE BOŽIĆ COLLECTION*

Left: Croatian soldiers in winter camouflage uniforms in the war with Serbia, 1992. *STIPE BOŽIĆ COLLECTION*

Top: Stipe Božić, young Croatian soldier, in the war with Serbia. *Stipe Božić COLLECTION*

Below: Ratko Mladić, Bosnian Serb former military leader, who was accused of committing crimes against humanity and genocide, being interviewed by Stipe Božić. *Stipe Božić COLLECTION*

Top: Stipe Božić after climbing K2 and losing his partner, Boštjan Kekec, high on the mountain. *Stipe Božić collection*

Below: Slavko Svetičič, one of Slovenia's most talented alpinists and a soloing specialist. He died high on the West Face of Gasherbrum IV in 1995 while soloing the wall. *Slavko Svetičič collection, courtesy of Sidarta Publishing*

Above: Stipe Božić filming below Jannu East. *Tomaž Humar collection*

Left: Šrauf and Tomaž Humar enjoying hot springs on their return from Ganesh V in 1994. *Tomaž Humar collection*

Above: Viki Grošelj self-portrait on Annapurna I at approximately 7500 metres. *Viki Grošelj collection*

Left: Self-portrait of Tomaž Humar on the summit of Annapurna, 1995. *Tone Škarja collection*

Top: Arjun Tamang and Tomaž Humar returning to Annapurna base camp from Humar's solo summit climb, 1995. *TONE ŠKARJA COLLECTION*

Below: Celebrating the first ski descent of Annapurna in 1995. Janko Oprešnik, Tone Škarja, Davo Karničar, Tomaž Humar, Viki Grošelj and a staff member from the Rum Doodle Restaurant in Kathmandu. *TONE ŠKARJA COLLECTION*

Above: Jeglič family photo: Janez, Mirjam and Irena, with Ana in Irena's lap. Filip was born shortly after Janez's death on Nuptse. *JANEZ JEGLIČ COLLECTION*

Left: Janez Jeglič and Tomaž Humar before climbing Nuptse. *MARJAN KOVAČ, COURTESY OF JANEZ JEGLIČ COLLECTION*

Top, left: View of the South Face of Dhaulagiri, with Messner, Polish, Humar and Šrauf routes indicated, left to right. *Tomaž Humar collection*

Top, right: Self-portrait of Tomaž Humar on the South Face of Dhaulagiri at approximately 5700 metres. *Tomaž Humar collection*

Below: Tomaž Humar's triumphant return to Slovenia from the South Face of Dhaulagiri. *Stipe Božić collection*

Above: Tomaž Humar, greeted at the Ljubljana airport after his return from the South Face of Dhaulagiri. From left to right: Viki Grošelj (partially hidden), Stipe Božić, Reinhold Messner and Tomaž Humar. It was this photo that irritated many of Tomaž's contemporaries in Slovenia. *STIPE BOŽIĆ COLLECTION*

Left: Tomaž Humar, in obvious pain and distress, back in base camp after having been rescued by helicopter off Nanga Parbat's Rupal Face. *TOMAŽ HUMAR COLLECTION*

Top: The North Face of North Twin in the Canadian Rockies, taken from the south end of Mt. Alberta. *RAPHAEL SLAWINSKI COLLECTION*

Below: Stipe Božić and Viki Grošelj at the base of Annapurna I, North Face, 1995. The two formed possibly the longest-standing climbing partnership in the history of Yugoslavian alpinism. *VIKI GROŠELJ COLLECTION*

Above: Andrej Štremfelj climbing the Klin route on Anića Kuk in Paklenica, Croatia. *ANDREJ ŠTREMFELJ COLLECTION*

Left: Vlasta Kunaver, alpinist and paraglider, and daughter of Aleš Kunaver, preparing to fly off the summit of Trisul in 1987. *ALEŠ KUNAVER COLLECTION*

Top: Andrej Štremfelj indicating the first page of a book where he recorded every one of his climbs, and continues to do so – a precise, handwritten (and minimalist) record of a prolific alpine career. *Bernadette McDonald collection*

Below: Marjan Manfreda relaxing on his front porch, 2013. *Bernadette McDonald collection*

From *Pot*: "How many times were my rope mates disappointed with me for failing to remember a single detail from a climb, just one day later? But how well I remember what I felt inside, which was both messy and tidy, agitated and calm, hungry and sated, greedy and content. How well I remember the handshakes, the flashing eyes, the beating hearts of those rare people who became close to me."[154]

◆ ◆ ◆

A few months after summiting Kangchenjunga, Andrej received a call. Could he and Marko go to Autrans, France? There was something called the Piolet d'Or – a kind of prize for alpinism – and they had won it. Andrej responded with the only question that made sense to him: "Will you pay us, or what?" The guy on the phone assured him that it would be worth their while. It was the first Piolet d'Or ever awarded and the beginning of a long relationship with the prize for both Andrej and Marko, although Marko's was much stormier than Andrej's.

In 2007, when Marko Prezelj and his partner, Boris Lorenčič, won the same prize for their first ascent of Chomolhari's Northwest Pillar, Marko refused the prize. Publicly and loudly, he stated that it was impossible to compare worthy climbs. He explained on his website: "Every climb is unique...Judging an ascent is senseless. The essence of a climb burns out in the moment of experience."[155] His strict ethics and focus on style clashed with the world of media and prizes and publicity. He became labelled a "purist" and was accused of being intolerant of anyone less talented than he. Up on that pedestal, the view turned out to be quite a lonely one.

Even now he refuses to be on the Piolet jury, convinced that it's simply a commercial enterprise, a marketing exercise, not an alpinism exercise. "Come on, it's not for alpinists," Marko scoffs. Russian alpinist Pavel Shabalin expressed similar sentiments: "Alpinism was exceptional and sacred because it was closed to the masses. And now it finds itself in the same historical situation as love. When love was poetry, it was exceptional and sacred. When mass media put love in TV and magazines, it became pornography."[156]

But it's not only the commercial nature of the Piolet that bothers Marko. "The Piolet is a symbol of vanity," he says. He suggests it would be better to organize a party, invite a group of climbers who had done some good climbs, and celebrate. It's unlikely that Marko's approach would excite the sponsors, though, because what would they gain? A big bill for a party. Without winners and losers there is no excitement, no spectacle and no publicity.

Marko's climbing partner, Andrej, feels differently about the prize and the activities that surround it. He feels that the Piolet can positively influence what young people choose to climb. He sees value in the prize's gathering, with its exchange of ideas on values and style. Former president of the jury, he recalls the animated discussions: alpine style versus expedition style; weather forecasts – yes or no; satellite phones – yes or no. He believes the competition will help direct the future of alpinism. Andrej looks at alpinism with a long view, pointing out that every ascent influences those that follow, but he adds that the influence of an individual climb depends largely on media attention or support. The Piolet combines both.

If Andrej is right, the first Piolet prize was indeed awarded to the best climb, for his and Marko's technically demanding and elegant alpine-style ascent of Kangchenjunga surely influenced the future of Himalayan climbing. Andrej was the transition figure – an alpinist who was schooled in the previous generation but whose vision of climbing embraced the new wave's approach. Marko exemplified that new wave, and together they formed a powerful team.

FOURTEEN

Three Musketeers

Another signature team from the golden era of Slovenian alpinism combined the wisdom and experience of an older climber with the infectious enthusiasm of youth. Only this time it was a threesome. The three musketeers – Franček Knez, Janez Jeglič and Silvo Karo – climbed massive rock walls together in India and Patagonia, and they valued their friendship as much as the climbing. They were part of the Slovenian climbing saga that had less to do with high mountains and more to do with steep mountains. Their journey took them to ranges like the Andes, which are dominated by sheer rock faces and soaring towers.

◆ ◆ ◆

Born in 1961, Janez Jeglič spent his first 13 years on a farm, but when his parents divorced, he moved with his mother and two siblings to Domžale, a city near Ljubljana. Here, his academic performance spiralled downward, and he refocused on sports: ski jumping, road biking and climbing. When he returned from mandatory military service in Serbia, he turned to mountaineering full-time.

Janez first met Irena at a Catholic youth gathering. He was 21 and she just 17. She fell in love almost immediately with his sapphire eyes and rugged jaw, and only later grew to appreciate his Christian spirit. With his calm and positive attitude, he seemed like a man who could protect her. He seemed trustworthy. After dating for several years, they married in 1987.

Janez and Irena had a great deal in common, including their church, but the most important was their desire for children. Five long years passed as they were handed from doctor to specialist to naturopath, always with the same results. They thought their problem was solved when they took in a baby boy named Daniel, whom they cared for and loved for three months. Then his birth mother appeared, begging to have him back. Devastated, Irena made a pilgrimage to Lourdes in France. She prayed. She immersed herself in the sacred waters, and the miracle she yearned for took place. She became pregnant. Not just once. The couple's daughter, Mirjam, was the first of three children.

By the time Mirjam was born, Janez was a professional alpinist employed by the army, as well as climbing on international expeditions. Irena was the homemaker and caregiver. It wasn't easy, but her extended family stood by, eager to help. Nothing about this lifestyle was a surprise to Irena. She knew what Janez was before they married, and she knew what to expect.

◆ ◆ ◆

In 1983 Janez joined Silvo and Franček in Patagonia to climb a difficult new route on the East Face of Fitz Roy, a stunning chunk of granite usually shrouded by cloud and wind, and sheathed in a film of ice. Older than Janez by six years, Franček Knez already had a formidable resumé. First ascents, new routes, speed ascents and solo ascents in the Julian Alps, the French Alps, the United States, South America and the Himalaya. In 1982 he had soloed the North Face of the Eiger in six hours. There were very few days in which one route sufficed for Franček; he devoured routes. The man whom Silvo Karo referred to as the "guru of Slovenian mountaineering" lived a simple existence: he trained, he worked and he climbed. He owned neither a car nor a phone. He hitched rides to the mountains or took the bus. "It was easy," he laughed. "It was not a problem. Only for the mind."

Franček was famous for downgrading the difficulty of his routes for a logical – and personal – reason. In the UIAA system at that time, VI+ represented a climb where the climber was "on the edge of falling." Franček could climb VIII or IX, so his grading of a climb reflected his own abilities. If he wasn't on the verge of falling, it surely wasn't a VI+. He simply graded it lower. In order to fully understand the true difficulty of a Knez route, one needed to consider not just the grade but also the length of climb and the number of hours he took to climb it. He moved quietly and lightly on rock, like a spider. His unique approach to route finding seemed instinctive: he could find a way through a labyrinth of wild, loose and unknown rock with little fuss. The wilder the better for Franček. Like Andrej, Franček was a transition figure from the older generation; his methodology was that of the future: light and fast. It was with younger climbers that he formed his most memorable partnerships – climbers like Janez and Silvo.

The three often solo climbed the easier sections of multi-pitch routes in order to be fast and efficient, and once climbed 19 new routes together in two days. Franček explained the technique: "We made fast work of it because we climbed straight up and down and only belayed when absolutely necessary."[157]

On Fitz Roy, after days of climbing overhangs, ice-filled cracks and smooth slabs, they were forced back to base camp by storms. When the weather improved, they headed back up their fixed ropes, moving their mechanical ascenders up the ice-covered lifelines. Franček hoisted himself up and across an overhanging edge, hanging freely in the air, "like a spider on a string, a barely noticeable thread."[158] Suddenly he began slipping down the rope into the depths. He stopped, staring in shock at the weathered and torn rope sheath in front of his face. Slowly, every so slowly, he spun in circles, nothing but air below him and only a few shreds of rope holding him in place. Very carefully, he reached up the rope as high as he could, reattached one of his ascenders onto the undamaged part and carried on up. He later described the sensation: "The threads of life are thin, and whoever steps onto the thin rock edge that separates the here from the hereafter is able to see the true dimension of life."[159]

Although the musketeers were up for the fiendishly difficult climbing, the ropes were a serious problem. The shards of falling ice lashed at them, and the hurricane-force winds frayed them as they whipped back and forth across the rough granite walls. At times it felt like playing Russian roulette. But they won the deadly game, and eventually all three stood atop that glowing piece of rock.

"There are moments when you touch happiness, just for a moment," Franček later said. "Every touch is part of eternity. It's a golden dew on your immortal soul."[160] Their partnership was sealed. The three musketeers had tasted the sweetness of life and the inner calm that follows an intense climbing experience. Nejc Zaplotnik understood and wrote about the feeling: "When you bend down to drink water out of a cold stream, you feel the goodness of this clear drink, and happiness that this water is along your path. In those moments, things that people take for granted and don't even notice anymore bring you immeasurable richness…You eat because you are hungry. You drink because you are thirsty. You sleep because you are exhausted…Every fibre feels your eating and drinking. You sleep like the dead."[161]

◆ ◆ ◆

The three musketeers returned to South America in 1986, hoping to climb a new route on the mythically beautiful East Face of Cerro Torre. They were part of a nine-person team that included several rock stars: Franček, Silvo, Janez and another master, Slavko Svetičič. With the team was Irena. This was her first expedition outing with Janez, and it seemed a little daunting. Foreign country. Foreign language. Wild weather. To add to her stress, she was alone, stuck in a tent at the base of the wall, studying for her teaching diploma. The infamous Patagonian weather threatened to drown them. Weeks of rain, drumming on the tent. After a month they managed to fix ropes up 750 metres of the most difficult sections on the wall, which slashed upward like a twisted knife. But the summit was still a long way up, and it was now coated in rime ice and snow. When the storm let up, the mountain reappeared in its full majesty, wrapped in a shimmering white veneer. Unfortunately all of that whiteness needed to come down, and as soon as the sun hit, it did exactly that – in a series of sloughs, careening chunks of ice and hissing avalanches. The climbers inched up the wall, fighting with their fixed lines, now coated with multiple layers of ice. But on January 16, 1986, nine climbers stood on the top of Cerro Torre: six by a new route, Devil's Direttissima, on the East Face; and three by the Maestri route.

Upon their return to Slovenia, each one of the three musketeers was interrogated by the security police. The authorities seemed to know everything about their trip: where they had been and on what days. There had clearly been an informant on the team – a normal practice in those troublesome times, when everyone's loyalties were suspect. Silvo was particularly nervous because he had brought back a book written by a Slovenian in political exile and he was worried it would be discovered. If so, it would only add to the "official" government file on him, which included information about every aspect of his life.

◆ ◆ ◆

Franček's Patagonian adventures consolidated his preference for climbing in small groups. The Everest and Lhotse expeditions had given him valuable experience in the high mountains, but they had been long, dragged-out affairs. As a high-precision performer on steep terrain, he abhorred what happened to his body on those big expeditions. He became weak and run-down. His finely tuned rock-climbing skills deteriorated to a shocking degree. It took months to rebuild his body to its former standard. Franček hated those wild swings in performance. Another challenge was the social interaction. He disliked the constant negotiating and group-think that permeated those expeditions. And perhaps the most important consideration was the actual climbing objective. Slogging up ridges and snow slopes, regardless of how steep, just wasn't his thing. He was most comfortable on vertical ground, preferably rock. He loved the feel of rock in all its forms: limestone or granite, loose or solid. And it was on rock that he shone brightest, solving micro-route-finding problems and tracing elegant lines like a true rock master.

A year after Cerro Torre, Franček went to northern Pakistan with Slavko Cankar and Bojan Šrot. The Trango Towers are a group of dramatic granite spires located on the north side of the Baltoro Glacier. Although not the highest in the group, Trango Tower (sometimes called Nameless) soars to 6239 metres and was first climbed in 1976 by a British team that included another legendary rock master, Joe Brown. Franček and his partners were there to try a new route on the South-Southeast Face. From the first moment Franček saw the monolithic pillar piercing the indigo sky, he was spellbound. This was the mountain for him. As they settled into their base camp, they couldn't keep their eyes off the walls. When the evening sun slid low in the sky, light burnished the tops of the spires like fire, even as the lower reaches of the walls retreated into shadow.

Trango didn't disappoint them. They used every technique in their arsenal: friction climbing, crack climbing, tiny pinch holds and dancing up hard alpine ice. The unknown route on the looming wall offered countless route-finding problems. It looked so smooth at first, but the cracks were there, as was one shallow gully. "It rises across a lonely vertical wall as a mysterious seductive abyss opens up below my feet," Franček recalled.[162] When they slid down their ropes on the final descent to base camp, their satisfaction was complete. "Very few things are truly well done," Franček later wrote. "For me, Trango was one of those things."[163]

Nejc had described this sense of complete happiness at one perfect moment in time: "This is neither greed nor melancholy. Rather, a peaceful experience of moments that are gathered into a mosaic, without knowing what the final picture will be."[164]

The team headed directly to nearby Broad Peak, a Karakoram eight-thousander. Franček didn't summit, once again frustrated by the mundane plowing through deep snow. Instead, he forged a partial new route, both steep and dangerous, while descending to Camp II. Although Broad Peak interested him, it wasn't in Trango's league.

Franček travelled next to India to climb fantastic new rock routes on 6660-metre Meru Peak in the Garhwal Himalaya, and an impressive pillar on nearby Bhagirathi II, both in alpine style. He tried Bhagirathi IV but failed, in part because he refused to compromise on style. India gave him both success and failure, equal amounts of intense joy and pain, as he forged new ground on steep, unknown terrain. Franček was probably one of the best examples of a "purist" climber in all of Slovenia at that time. In his own words: "There are tempting goals, yet when you reach your goal, you often remain empty-handed. The goal is just the inspiration; the path is its own purpose. It is important to believe in your path."[165] The words are Franček's, but they could have been written by Nejc, so similar was their approach to the mountains, and to life.

◆ ◆ ◆

Three years later, two of the musketeers, Silvo and Janez, returned to the area for a bold objective: a new route on the West Face of 6454-metre Bhagirathi III. They started up the face on August 27, 1990. They made short work of the first 450 metres and began setting up their portaledge for their first bivouac. The climb – and their lives – almost ended that afternoon. As they scampered up onto the portaledge, the bolt anchoring their hammock broke. They plunged down and were left dangling on pitons. Now one metre below their ledge, they felt their hearts pounding. "We were shocked," Silvo later said, with some understatement. "We saw our food and equipment falling down the face. Luckily for us, we did not."

After descending to base, collecting their treasures and repacking, they went back up the face. During the day the overhanging wall above them wept with melting ice, but at night the plunging temperatures turned the rivulets into dangling shards. Now climbing up ice-filled cracks, they changed to rock shoes, uncomfortably cold but necessary on this difficult terrain. Further up the face the rock deteriorated into a disintegrating black mess. "It was a vertical wall of coal," Silvo said. Handholds collapsed at their touch. Pitons were useless. They finally reached the end of this dangerous stretch and set up a bivouac on a comfortable ledge. While the men were preparing their meal, two ravens appeared out of the gloaming, somehow sensing the possibility of food. They circled and waited. But Silvo and Janez had nothing to spare. Still, the soaring black beauties provided a distraction from the reality of what lay ahead.

On the morning of their fifth day on the wall, the weather continued to be bad. They left most of their equipment at the bivouac, intent on reaching the top that day. Almost immediately they were faced with a section of rock as loose as a newly plowed field. Silvo described the terror as they waded upward: "What we go through in the next few hours cannot be described. One can only live through it to know what it is like. Falls of ten metres, poor protection in rotten rock, technical grade of A4, the feeling that we won't survive if we don't reach the top of the face by night!"[166]

They did not reach the top that night. Caught by darkness in a steep ice chimney, they rolled up together in a single sleeping bag on a narrow, snow-covered ledge. Bruised and exhausted, they were soon soaked to the skin as the bag absorbed the snow that fell throughout the night. The wind picked up and reached hurricane force by morning. Horrified by their situation, they had no option but to move. They chose to move up. After a few more pitches of steep climbing, they reached a large snowfield at the top of the face. They continued up the gentle slope, pressing their reluctant bodies into a biting wind that lashed their faces with shards of ice and snow. At 9:00 am on September 7, their sixth day on the face, they reached the top of Bhagirathi III.

Their first thought was how to get down.

As dangerous as the climb up the face had been, the descent was even worse. Many accidents happen on descent, in part due to fatigue. It's also more difficult to route-find in a downward direction. Rappelling down steep ground is the obvious way to make rapid progress, but the technique is fraught with uncertainty. Where will you build the next anchor? Will the rock be firm enough? Will there be solid ice? What if you reach the end of your rappel ropes and are suspended above an overhang? Will the ropes get caught when you try to pull them down? Silvo and Janez encountered all of these problems on their descent.

Their rappel anchors were frighteningly wobbly, some just a single piece of protection, an absolute no-no under normal circumstances. But this was not normal, and they were running out of equipment. Even when they used two pieces, the supposed "bomber" piece of equipment would pull, forcing them to rely on a questionable backup.

Finally there was no equipment left. No pitons. No camming devices. No ropes. On flatter ground now, Silvo tumbled into a crevasse, but he managed to extricate himself. The snowstorm became mixed with a cold rain that plastered their clothing to their skinny frames.

After 15 more kilometres trudging across the Chaturangi Glacier, they arrived at base camp, hungry, drenched and cold. Their porters had departed for the valley but had left food for the climbers in the hope they would return. They tucked in as best they could, yet it wasn't easy, as their bleeding and battered hands were so swollen they could barely remove their boots or hold a cup of tea. All night long, they drank and drank. Tea had never tasted so good.

With no time to spare, Silvo and Janez travelled via Delhi to Kathmandu, where they rested just three days before heading directly to Everest, joining an Italian-Slovenian expedition. Among the group were Andrej and Marija Štremfelj. Janez and Silvo were confident that their acclimatization from Bhagirathi III would hold them in good stead on Everest, and their plan was to make a traverse from Camp II over to the West Ridge, climb the route and return on the South Col route: a partial new route and a complete traverse of the mountain.

They climbed as high as 7500 metres, but Silvo became ill and remained sick with angina for ten days, all of which were good weather. During that time, Janez and the Štremfeljs climbed the South Col route, a more modest objective than their original plan. Although he had to miss the climb, Silvo seemed not to care too much, since it was the traverse that had attracted him most. Besides, the fresh memories of 1300 metres of climbing in super-alpine style on Bhagirathi III were too much of a contrast to the South Col route on Everest. The latter route could not give him the kind of intensity that Bhagirathi III had provided, an intensity Nejc had described years before when climbing in Yosemite:

> All that is left is one metre, then one centimetre of reality, and your own body. Your concentration and strength maintain your body in an impossible position and slowly move it toward the edge of the granite flake. Your concentration is so complete that everything disappears, everything becomes unimportant. Only when you climb do your body and soul form a whole and help each other. Your mind enables your body to move, and the strength of your body gives your mind experience and confidence in the work you are doing and faith that you will do it well. Only when I climb are my thoughts completely concentrated on one single square centimetre of reality. Even sexual intimacy with the woman I love allows my thoughts to drift, but now, in this moment, a harmony that we have almost forgotten has been reached: nature, body and mind have become one. They mutually serve each other and complete each other. Climbing is a school for life, a school for love.[167]

Bhagirathi III was Silvo and Janez's last big climb together. Although they still climbed in the Julian Alps and cragged on the nearby cliffs, they drifted apart. Different objectives. Different priorities. They both returned to Patagonia for climbs on Cerro Torre but with different partners. Still, Irena Jeglič, when asked who Janez's most important climbing partner was, answered without hesitation: Silvo Karo. Silvo would not be Janez's last climbing partner, however. That position was reserved for another young alpinist from nearby Kamnik. His name was Tomaž Humar.

FIFTEEN

Flying Solo

He stood, wild-eyed, on the streets of Podujevo, Kosovo, dumped there by a Yugoslav National Army Jeep. Tomaž Humar looked more like a beggar than a soldier. His uniform was tattered and filthy, and he smelled like a latrine. In his hand was a spent Kalashnikov. He had neither ammunition nor food.

Frightened and vulnerable, he waited while a group of Albanians approached him. What was he doing there? Where was he going? When they learned he was from a distant northern place called Slovenia, one of the Albanians mentioned that his brother worked in a munitions factory near Kamnik. Tomaž knew the factory; it was just two kilometres from his home. In an instant the pair made a human connection, despite their differences in ideology and religion, and the propaganda that their respective leaders were feeding them. Tomaž boarded the express train that rumbled into the station from Greece and almost immediately fell into a deep sleep of exhaustion and relief as he headed north.

◆ ◆ ◆

Tomaž had been out for a run near the Yugoslavian army base where he was doing his mandatory training, when he learned from his fellow soldiers that they were scheduled to leave the next day on a secret mission. Only 20 years old, he was soon in Kosovo, serving shoulder to shoulder with Serbian soldiers, guarding Albanians who were ostensibly trying to create an independent Kosovo.

Tomaž never believed that the Albanian threat was real, but the cruelty and atrocities were certainly real, and Tomaž saw his share of them while in Kosovo. Mass rapes, sterilization programs, murders and torture. "I discovered the bottom of humanity," he said. All for a cause he didn't believe in and a war he detested.

The war that brought Tomaž to Kosovo in 1988 was an unnecessary conflict created by greed, ambition and intolerance. The covert action in which Tomaž participated was the direct result of incidents that had taken place a few years earlier in the central stronghold of Belgrade. By the mid-1980s Serbian nationalism was being kindled by a group called the Committee of Serbians and Montenegrins. They told stories of torture, intolerance and rape in the Kosovo area – crimes against Serbs who lived there. Crimes committed by Albanians. A well-publicized memorandum issued in 1986 by the highly respected Serbian Academy of Sciences and Arts alleged that Serbs faced potential genocide from marauding Kosovo Albanians. The document threw Serbs into an enraged frenzy.

Slobodan Milošević, Serbia's president, responded by sending the Yugoslav National Army to crack down on ethnic Albanians in Kosovo. A covert action led by Colonel Aleksandar Vasiljevič, it was initially unnoticed by the other Yugoslavian states.

When he arrived back in Slovenia, Tomaž was a changed man. Weighing only 63 kilograms, his body was as starved as his soul. Moody, angry and aggressive, he escaped to the mountains, sleeping in caves. His broad open smile was rarely seen. He became suspicious of his friends. Affected by the violence of war, his most frequent companions were anxiety, despair and fear. His family members were patient in their attempt to bring him back into the fold, giving him what he needed – food – and what he rejected – love.

♦ ♦ ♦

The Humars were a hard-working, religious family who lived a frugal existence in the postwar socialist state. Tomaž, who was born on February 18, 1969, was unaware that his father Max's outrage at the madness of the war in Yugoslavia had once prompted him to escape across the mountains into Austria. Once there, he regretted his impetuous decision and turned himself in to the authorities, who sent him back. Max stifled his restless desires and worked first as a shoemaker and then as a builder. He married Tomaž's mother, Rosalija, in 1968, and within a year, Tomaž was born. From outward appearances he was a well-behaved little boy and a model student. But something was brewing inside their fair-haired son. "I was already strange as a child...I was born on the carnival day," he said. Two more sons and the family was complete.

. Tomaž worked with his father on construction jobs from the age of 6 and showed talent as a builder. But then he discovered the excitement of climbing. His first experiments took place in the basement, where he hoisted himself from beam to beam in monkey-like acrobatics that filled his mother with dread and his father with irritation. A waste of time! It wasn't long before he was out on the local rock crags, showing off his first climbing harness: a discarded Fiat seatbelt.

Tomaž's relationship with his father deteriorated, and they argued more than they talked. When he joined the local Kamnik mountain club in 1987, he discovered a camaraderie that enveloped him like a warm blanket. What a relief from the constant chores and bickering at home. The club offered friendship, equipment and mentorship, including a more experienced climber who took Tomaž on – Bojan Pollak, the same man who so irritated Marko Prezelj with his strict, archaic rules. But the seeds of independence were already sown in Tomaž's character, and eventually he broke free of the Alpine Association's web of control, and support.

When Tomaž returned from Kosovo, his relationship with the club became strained. He climbed constantly, for it provided him relief from the demons of war that terrorized his sleepless nights. Tone Škarja recalled that some club members became jealous and tried to push him aside as he climbed increasingly difficult routes, often alone. Solo climbing was taboo within the club, and Tomaž was duly reprimanded by the leaders. He ignored them, soloing routes that many referred to as "sick," they were so dangerous. He relied on the rock to bring stability to his life, which teetered on the edge of insanity.

Nejc articulated that feeling in *Pot*:

I admire people
Whose life is a peaceful plain.
Vast fertile fields of wheat,
Only now and then waving lightly in the wind...
For my own life is like a wild river
Rushing madly against the primordial rock
Of utter despair!
But long days on my fingertips
Teach me how to live with my feet on the ground.
When I become a true master of dancing on vertical walls
I will also know
How to walk on firm ground.[168]

Tomaž's best friend at the time, Danilo Golob, supported and encouraged him. As Tomaž spent more time with Danilo, he was horrified to discover that he was falling in love with Danilo's girl-friend, Sergeja. The feeling was mutual and obvious to everyone except Danilo. Then, one fateful January day in 1989, Danilo was killed while ice climbing near Grintovec.

Sergeja leaned on Danilo's circle of climbing friends for support, and the simmering attraction between her and Tomaž blossomed into an intense love affair. A few months later they married. Shortly after, their first child, Urša, was born. Tomaž was 22 and Sergeja only 20. Now they were a family. According to Tomaž, "My concept of marriage was for life." Although still a climber, he was practical enough to accept his priorities. "The Himalayas were out of the question. I had responsibilities. I had to fill the car with gas – feed the family."

And for a while he did just that, working long hours at his elec-tronics job to pay the bills. Despite the financial strain, their relationship was full of love and happiness. "What we had between us, no atomic bomb could destroy," Tomaž later recalled. "We loved each other. We were a cell."

Three years later, as their finances improved, Tomaž's climbing dreams resurfaced. Work began to get in the way and, to the horror of his family, he quit his well-paying job. Even his boss tried to dissuade him from making this rash decision. What was the rush to go climbing? He could do that later, when his family responsibilities had eased. When he was 50. Tomaž laughed in his face: "At 50 your life is over! At 50 there is nothing more to do – just go to a spa or something."

◆ ◆ ◆

Tomaž's first big climbing break came in 1994 when he was invited to 6770-metre Ganesh V, at the far eastern end of the enormous Ganesh massif on the border between Nepal and Tibet. The icing on the cake was the leader of the expedition: Stane Belak (Šrauf), Tomaž's hero. "For me it was like climbing with a god," Tomaž said. But it was actually Tone Škarja who had orchestrated the invitation. Although Tomaž didn't know it, Ganesh V was a performance test, as Tone was considering him for Annapurna the following year. Tomaž's attention was on Šrauf, however, the man so deeply respected for his boldness, so loved for his outrageously gruff exterior and his wonderfully soft interior. Among the Eastern European climbing stars in the Himalaya at the time, Šrauf was one of the best.

Tomaž was keen to prove himself to Šrauf, yet he wasn't the only one on trial. Šrauf had fallen on the North Face of Triglav two years before and was still recovering from a crushed ankle. He had hoped to be on Dhaulagiri's South Face in 1994, but he wasn't sufficiently strong. Some Slovenian climbers had written him off. Finished. Old generation. Šrauf felt nowhere near finished; Ganesh would be a nice little warm-up for his future endeavours. He referred to the climb as a "ski hill" and the team as a combination of "old ones," veteran high-altitude alpinists, and "pups," novices. Tomaž was one of the latter.

Šrauf stormed his way up the mountain and the pups followed. When the weather turned bad, he raved and swore, ranting that he was being screwed twice over: once for his injury and now on Ganesh. When he broke a tooth on a prune pit – the climber's wonder food, in his opinion – he swore some more. The pups listened with respect, and then ate more prunes. After a couple of false starts, the team of Šrauf, Gregor Kresal and Tomaž was climbing above Camp II when Šrauf fell into a crevasse. Then Gregor injured his ribs. Šrauf announced it was time to descend, but he hadn't counted on the upstart in the group, Tomaž, who had no intention of quitting. Šrauf ordered him down. Tomaž said, "No." Now in a rage, Šrauf screamed, "I cannot leave you here!"

"You can scream all fucking day. I want just one chance," Tomaž yelled back.[169]

After a full day of arguing, Šrauf agreed to give it one more try.

They reached the summit together on November 13, 1994. Fifty-four-year-old Šrauf and his protegé, the 25-year-old Tomaž. Tomaž was overcome with happiness, and even Šrauf was pretty pleased. It was a triumph for both of them, for completely different reasons. But as they celebrated, the sun slid below the horizon and they knew they had to go down.

Theirs was a typical high-altitude night descent. The ropes froze. Their hands froze. They couldn't see. Finally the young pup collapsed on the snow. Šrauf cajoled and implored, but Tomaž wouldn't budge. He had nothing left – a classic case of a climber using all the energy to get to the summit. He hadn't accounted for what he would need to get down. He was too green to know that the real crux of a climb is descending. When they finally reached base camp, Tomaž realized that he had extended himself much too far and that if it hadn't been for Šrauf, he most certainly would have died up there. He vowed to learn from the experience, should he ever have another chance.

He didn't have long to wait, for he was about to play a role in Tone Škarja's dream of placing Yugoslavian climbers on all 14 of the eight-thousand-metre peaks. The eight-thousander on deck for 1995 was Annapurna. The tenth-highest mountain in the world, this Nepalese giant is also considered one of the most dangerous. Škarja's 1995 team was a big one, with stars like Viki Grošelj and Stipe Božić, Mexican climber Carlos Carsolio and skiing sensations Davo and Andrej Karničar. In fact, the plan was for the Karničar brothers to ski from the summit. Tomaž would be there in support: to carry loads, break trail and help set up the camps.

Viki was curious about this youngster Šrauf had taken under his wing. At first he seemed quiet, even shy. But once he found his confidence, the real Tomaž emerged: a younger replica of Šrauf. He talked and gesticulated like a wild man, enthusiastic and loud. Stipe enjoyed Tomaž's wild ways: "I thought that since he was born near the Kamnik Alps he was a little crazy from all of the wind, that he had a kind of madness." Stipe could see, even after this first encounter, that Tomaž was not destined for a normal life.

Tomaž followed Tone's orders, climbed up and down with loads of food and equipment, set up tents and waited his turn. He knew he wasn't the first string, but he felt sure he would summit. Finally he was in a good position, at Camp III at 6600 metres, together with three team members and the Sherpas. He was stunned when the order arrived from base camp. All but Tomaž were to go up; there weren't enough supplies for him. The next afternoon a bitter and frustrated Tomaž arrived at base camp, where Tone greeted him.

"Tomaž, great to see you. What a fantastic job you have done in breaking trail and helping to set up the camps. Here, take some tea."

Tomaž threw the cup on the ground. "Why did you order me to descend when I was climbing so strongly?" [170]

Tone dismissed the insubordinate behaviour as that of a spoiled brat; he didn't waste too much time because he had bigger concerns. He had climbers high on the mountain. When the Karničar brothers descended from the summit on skis, the expedition was deemed a complete success. It was time to go home.

Not so fast. Tomaž didn't fully understand the concept of "team success" in the high mountains, where, once one or more climbers make the top, the expedition is considered a success. Placing additional climbers on the summit is optional and certainly not mandatory. Tomaž was one of those *additional* climbers. Against Tone's orders, he went back up and repeatedly disobeyed Tone's demands to descend. Finally, Tomaž turned off his radio and summited alone. Once again he had pushed himself, probably further than he should have. Tomaž survived the climb, however, and when he arrived back at base camp, Tone tried to be civil. He even congratulated Tomaž, but he added that this kind of behaviour would bear consequences.

Tone had a point: as leader of the expedition, he was in charge. His decision should have been final. That's the way expeditions worked. Certainly there was room for discussion, as had happened with Franček Knez near the end of the Everest 1979 expedition. Franček had asked Tone for permission to go off and do a solo climb, and Tone had agreed. But Tomaž hadn't asked for permission. That was unacceptable.

Tomaž had acted rashly, yet his motivations were not much different from those of many others in his generation. He was simply more vocal than most. The young climbers coming up through the ranks were not as interested in group objectives as their elders had been. Of course they loved their country and were proud of its achievements in the Himalaya, but their personal climbing ambitions came first. Tomaž was neither the first nor the last young climber to push back against the socialist ideal.

◆ ◆ ◆

Tomaž returned to Slovenia, full of confidence about his climbing but overwhelmed with family responsibilities. Sergeja was pregnant again. He became reacquainted with the small pleasures and routines of home, and he painted towers and steeples to pay the bills. When he wasn't working, he climbed with Šrauf, who was now a close friend.

Two days before Christmas of 1995, Šrauf and Tomaž were working together on Šrauf's house, which he was building with help from his climbing friends. Šrauf was in a shaky frame of mind, struggling with his climbing and his increasingly complex and troubled personal life, as well as the aging process. He offered Tomaž a lift home and asked if he wanted to go climbing the next day. Tomaž was tempted, but he declined because he wanted to spend Christmas Eve with his family. Their conversation ended when Šrauf announced that he would ask Jasna Boratanič to go, a young woman whom most assumed was his love interest. They shook hands and Šrauf drove off.

The next day, Šrauf and Jasna were killed in an avalanche on the North Face of Mala Mojstrovka in the Julian Alps. After six months of searching, their bodies were finally discovered when the sun melted the tons of avalanche debris heaped on top of them. His death shocked the climbing community as none had since Nejc Zaplotnik's. How could Šrauf have died? He was indestructible, in that final blaze of strength and power. He was a legend. He was a careful climber, a skilled climber, a strategic climber. After shock came anger. The avalanche hazard had been obscenely high, and Šrauf, of all people, should have known better. It was unthinkable. Inexcusable.

The funeral was a huge affair, with Slovenian president Milan Kučan and hundreds of climbers filing into the Catholic church. Tomaž, like so many others in the tight-knit community, was crushed by his grief.

But what about Šrauf's family? How would they manage now that he was no longer there? There had never been enough hours in the day for Šrauf. He was bursting with plans, always rushing. Every day was too short. Every week was a blur. "On Monday he was tired from being in the mountains, on Tuesday he had a mountain association meeting, on Wednesday it was a mountain club board meeting, on Thursday it was a mountain club meeting, on Friday he was on his way to the mountains, on the weekend he was in the mountains, and on Monday he was tired from the mountains," his wife, Jožica, laughed, years later. "He was either planning an expedition, going on an expedition or writing a report about an expedition." All of that, plus raising a family, building a house, guiding, instructing climbing and skiing, working on the rescue team, and on and on. Things had been about to change, she explained. He was finished with climbing expeditions and was only going to lead trekking groups and work as a mountain guide part-time from home. Life promised to calm down, become saner, safer. But it hadn't. Only 49 at the time, Jožica was left with a half-finished house, one child still in school and the added shock of two recently deceased parents. She felt responsible for the entire world.

Although he grieved the loss of his friend and mentor, Tomaž was already planning his next trip to the Himalaya. A few months later, in 1996, he and Vanja Furlan climbed a difficult new route on the Northwest Face of 6812-metre Ama Dablam, an elegant and slender peak not far from Everest. Their climb won them the prestigious Piolet d'Or, but tragically, Vanja wasn't there to accept it. Three months after the expedition, he fell to his death in the Julian Alps. The prize catapulted Tomaž into alpine prominence, yet there was a cost. "Ama Dablam gave me the chance to become a Himalayan climber, but the cost was my family. That was the deal. I didn't know it at the time." Sergeja delivered their second child, Tomaž Junior, while he was on Ama Dablam. The delivery was difficult. Alone during that traumatic period, she never completely forgave Tomaž for abandoning her.

◆ ◆ ◆

The 1990s were cruel to Slovenian alpinists: Nejc, Šrauf and Vanja all died. And by the time of Vanja's death in 1996, the carnage was far from over.

Born in 1958, Slavko Svetičič was a serious-looking man with a mop of brown hair and a narrow face anchored by a meandering nose and softened by a gentle smile. He moved with a kind of negligent grace, like a dancer. There was something about him that was dismissive of both himself and the world around him. His introverted manner belied his hard-ass performances in the mountains, particularly as a solo climber. He was also famous for his ability to party hard until the early-morning hours and then proceed directly to a route. His list of ascents is mind-boggling: more than 1200 climbs, of which 460 were first ascents. Slavko pushed to the top edge of his technical limit, even when soloing. His winter repeat of the *Direttissima* route on the Eiger, along with many other solo ascents in the Alps, the Andes, the Julian Alps and New Zealand, and most notably, his solo attempts of the South and West faces of Annapurna, earned him tremendous respect from his peers.

Despite the war in Slovenia and other parts of Yugoslavia, Slavko set off for Annapurna in 1991. Darko Berljak was supposed to lead this expedition of two climbers, but the spread of armed conflict throughout Croatia prevented him from participating, so Slavko went alone. He solo climbed a new route on the 2600-metre West Face of Annapurna in late October, reaching a point less than three hundred metres away from moderate terrain to the summit. Hurricane winds and freezing fingers forced him to traverse to the North Face, where he descended via the normal route, reaching base camp on November 3. His staff, who thought he had died on the mountain, had already packed up and left. Slavko walked out alone.

Two years later, he was back with Franček and Marija Knez, hoping to complete the route that French superstars Pierre Béghin and Jean-Christophe Lafaille had tried on the South Face. When Franček became ill, Slavko decided to try it alone. He began climbing on October 3, but after bivouacking at 6800 metres, he descended because of avalanche danger. On October 8 he set out again but was swept down one hundred metres by an avalanche. The route wasn't climbed until 2013, when Swiss alpinist Ueli Steck soloed it in 28 hours, setting a new standard in high-altitude climbing and finishing the job that Slavko had attempted 20 years earlier.

In 1995 Slavko set his sights on a solo ascent of the West Face of Gasherbrum IV. The fourth highest of the six-mountain Gasherbrum group, it is also the most difficult. Slavko was one of the few alpinists in the world capable of climbing it. The mountain's first ascent in 1958 by Italians Walter Bonatti and Carlo Mauri set the mountain-eering community on fire. As did the first ascent of the West Face: Austrian Robert Schauer and Polish alpinist Voytek Kurtyka climbed the Shining Wall in 1985, stunning the alpine world. After six days of demanding climbing, they became stranded near the summit in a three-day snowstorm. They were out of food, out of gas and out of time when the storm finally broke and they topped out on the ridge and began their descent. Although they didn't tag the summit, their ascent remains iconic in the history of Himalayan climbing.

But the West Face of Gasherbrum IV is an enormous piece of terrain, and Slavko was convinced there was at least one more inter-esting line up it. He had his eye on the left section of the wall and arrived in May with three other climbers, although he intended to solo climb. They set up base camp near a Korean team also intent on the face. Slavko acclimatized for two weeks before beginning his ascent on June 14.

Nejc had understood the lure of a solo climb and described the anticipation, the nervousness and the fear at the base of the Triglav wall:

This is probably going to be my hardest solo climbing test so far, and the longer the evening the more my carefree happiness disappears. I sit quietly in the corner, a pipe in my mouth, listening as a group of Bulgarians sing and play the guitar. An odd melancholy comes over me...I am waiting, expecting something great and beautiful that will lift me, but at the same time this animal fear for survival awakens in me...To me, climbing is not just sport. To me, climbing is life...Solo climbing is the highest form of alpinism. Moving on the edge between life and death shows you what it means to be truly alive.[171]

Slavko made good progress up the wall, maintaining regular radio contact with base. The Koreans watched him with their spotting scope. He bivouacked at 6300 metres on June 16, and the next day, at 7100 metres, he radioed in to report that the most difficult climbing was behind him. He only had to find a way onto the steep snowfield that led to the summit ridge.

Just as it had for Robert Schauer and Voytek Kurtyka ten years before, however, the weather changed. A nasty storm blew in and obliterated the face. Yet even though he could no longer be seen, Slavko maintained radio contact. Then something went quietly wrong. On June 20 base radioed Slavko with a strongly worded request to come down. There was no reply. For the next three days there was no sign of Slavko, and the storm continued to rage. The Koreans tried on June 23 to reach him by radio, but silence reigned on the face.

On June 25 a helicopter sponsored by the Korean Broadcasting Station flew into base, hoping to search the face for Slavko. Heavy winds forced it back. It returned the following day but could fly only as high as six thousand metres, sweeping back and forth across the face, looking for some sign of life. They saw nothing. After ten days of waiting for a miracle, the two teams held a memorial service for Slavko at base camp.

For two years there was no news about Slavko, about his location, about what might have happened. His death remained a mystery. In 1998, however, another Korean team arrived at the West Face. On their way down from the summit, they found Slavko's body at 7100 metres, resting below a couloir. Yu Hak-jae recalled that Slavko was lying down, facing the mountain, next to his backpack and a 30-metre, seven-millimetre rope. His harness was not attached to the fixed line, but Yu speculated that Slavko might have been preparing to descend, because the rope was secured to the wall and appeared ready to be used. His clothing and body were intact. No signs of a violent fall. It was as if he had lain down to rest and never woken up.

The carnage continued when two more Slovenian climbers, Bojan Počkar and Žiga Petrič, were killed on Kabru, a mountain in eastern Nepal. Several of the best Slovenian alpinists were gone within a year.

SIXTEEN

War and Suffering

While Slovenian alpinists were dying in the mountains, a tragedy on a much grander scale was being realized in the nightmare that engulfed the entire Yugoslavian nation. Although Slovenia (with Slobodan Milošević's tacit approval) had extracted itself from the chaos with a tidy ten-day war in 1991, other Yugoslavian states weren't so lucky.

Croatia, Slovenia's closest neighbour, is a borderland country, wedged between central Europe and the Balkans, between the Mediterranean and the continent. A long curving arc, Croatia's exposed and vulnerable frontiers were invaded by Serbs in 1991. Croatia craved independence, but Serbia was determined to regain Croatian territory that had formerly been occupied by Serbs. Soldiers roamed the hills in camouflage fatigues, carrying automatic rifles, knives and grenades. Croatian climber and journalist Stipe Božić was there.

Formerly a pacifist, Stipe was transformed by the conflict. "I was in some kind of euphoria about the war – I thought I could change everything." Since Stipe knew the mountainous border regions well, he guided Croatian soldiers who fought face to face with the Yugoslav National Army, now controlled by the mad psychiatrist from Sarajevo, Radovan Karadžić. At one point, Stipe even met and interviewed Ratko Mladić, the Serb military leader who was eventually accused of war crimes, genocide and crimes against humanity.

In the winter of 1991, high on the harsh and snowy mountainous frontier, Stipe tried to enter a hut that was booby-trapped. The mine exploded, injuring both Stipe and his partner and alerting the surrounding Serb troops, who began firing on them. Although wounded by shrapnel, the two were rescued by their own soldiers.

Back in Split, Stipe tended to his injuries, even while the city was being routinely bombed. He and his family huddled in their apartment, dreading the inevitable explosions. Viki telephoned him and urged him to relocate his entire family to Slovenia, which was by now safe and independent. Stipe refused. "I told him that if we leave Split, we have given up." After all, Split was his home. But the next summer, Viki invited Stipe to join an expedition to the South Face of Annapurna. "After thinking a lot, it was my ticket to get out of the war," he said. "Annapurna was safer than war."

Indeed, the war had become increasingly vicious. Even discounting Milošević's plan to absorb large portions of Croatia into Greater Serbia, it was easy for Serbs to hate the Croatians. Memories of the Second World War were still fresh, memories of when Croatia's Ustaše regime – the pro-Nazi movement that Hitler had orchestrated – earned international notoriety for slaughtering tens of thousands of people, including Jews, Gypsies and Serbs. Many were killed in the Jasenovac detention centre, not far from Zagreb. The Ustaše had surpassed their teachers in the finer techniques of torture and murder, and Serbs had not forgotten. Forty years later, after thousands more deaths and thousands more missing persons, the United Nations finally brokered a truce. But not before the interior of Croatia was left a charred wasteland and a third of the country was under occupation.

Ethnic cleansing takes time, and eventually, even though Serbia and Croatia were at each other's throats, they discovered something in common: their interests in Bosnia. When Serbia attacked the Bosnian town of Bijeljina on April 1, 1992, it was the beginning of the war in that country. For the next two years, the mountainous nation was systematically and brutally destroyed. The most famous of four concentration camps – Omarska, in northern Bosnia – was soon "processing" unwanted Bosnians and Croatians. The prisoners wore greasy rags infested with lice. Barefoot and sunken-cheeked, they appeared ghostlike. Their faces were ashen, and their emaciated hands were limp, like their spirits. The guards at Omarska were mostly young men from surrounding villages, but on weekends the specialists would arrive. These men were adept at breaking arms and legs, smashing skulls and tearing out organs. Although the number of fatalities could not surpass that of Nazi Germany, the cruelty was greater. Once the torture door had been opened, an entirely new world revealed itself: a world of sadistic pleasure. How the perpetrators ever imagined that the rest of the world would not discover their crimes is a mystery. As Rezak Hukanović wrote in *The Tenth Circle of Hell*: "They can't eliminate us all...Wherever wolves feast, they leave a bloody trail."[172]

Croatians were soon killing Bosnian Muslims, as well. By the summer of 1992, to be Muslim in Banja Luka, Bosnia's largest Serb-controlled city, was as dangerous as being a Jew in Berlin 50 years earlier. Any Muslim who could leave Bosnia did so, signing over all property and possessions to the Serbs. They took only their academic diplomas, in the hope of finding meaningful employment wherever in the world they might land. As the war dragged on, the West's arms embargo to Bosnia prolonged Bosnians' misery and ensured their complete inability to defend themselves. United Nations troops arrived to create and defend "safe areas" in the country that were the most profoundly dangerous places on Earth. But when a Serbian mortar shell landed in a Sarajevo marketplace in the summer of 1994, television footage finally precipitated enough international outrage that a large allied air attack slowed the slaughter.

The wars in Yugoslavia were not the fault of the international community. Foreign powers aggravated the situation with their lack of understanding and reluctance to intervene, but the impetus to implode came from within Yugoslavia, not from ordinary citizens, but from a group of men who had everything to gain from the country being ripped apart and divided up like the spoils of a kill. Yugoslavia did not die a natural death. It was deliberate, systematic and heartless.

Slovenia emerged relatively unscathed, and those Slovenians lucky enough to have avoided fighting in the dirty wars, or at least to have survived them, enjoyed the freedom to work, own property, vote, pay taxes and travel. And of course, to climb. Many chose to ignore the bloodshed and concentrate on just that.

◆ ◆ ◆

During and after the Yugoslavian wars, Janez Jeglič and Tomaž Humar were in their physical prime. Although they weren't close friends, they teamed up in 1997 to try a new route on the South Face of Nuptse W2, 7742 metres high. Two kilometres away, a 20-person Slovenian team was on Everest, so they joked they would even have neighbours from home.

Irena Jeglič was accustomed to Janez being away on expeditions. That was his life when he wasn't teaching soldiers to climb. They rarely discussed his climbs when he was home, but he wrote her long, newsy letters whenever he was away. Irena loved those letters. She knew that he was thinking of her, and the letters gave her an understanding of his mountain life. But she wasn't naive. She knew the letters were no guarantee that everything was going well or would end well. They were simply letters from the man who loved her. She hoped that his Nuptse trip would be much like the other trips: a climb he had been dreaming about for some time. Another challenge for Janez.

The Nuptse team consisted of Janez, Tomaž, six more Slovenians and Carlos Carsolio, the Mexican high-altitude climber. They acclimatized on nearby peaks, but when it came time for Nuptse, only three climbers remained interested and healthy: Tomaž, Janez and Marjan Kovač. Then, while they waited seven long days for a storm to blow itself out, Marjan became ill. Now it was only Tomaž and Janez.

Although Irena didn't receive any letters from Nuptse, she spoke with Janez on the satellite phone from base camp. She remembered the call well. It was unpleasant. They had agreed in advance that on a certain date he would come home, regardless of whether the route had been climbed or not. It was true that the weather had been bad and he was delayed, but he had promised. And now he was reneging on his promise. He wanted to stay, and she wanted him home. They argued. He stayed. She was angry and disappointed but said only, "Be careful, Janez."

The weather cleared on October 25, and two days later Janez and Tomaž stepped onto the face. They left the rope behind; soloing would be faster, therefore safer. They took only a five-millimetre Kevlar static line in case of emergency and threaded their way through a complex network of crevasses near the bottom of the face to a steep ice couloir, which they called the Orient Express. They flew up it, stopping only to glance at the teetering seracs above them, threatening them every moment. At 5900 metres they found a safe spot for their first bivouac. All the frenetic activity stopped and darkness slipped over the mountain.

That night, a depressingly dense fog crept in. They managed just four hours of climbing the next day, gaining four hundred metres of elevation amid the murk and mist. It was like climbing blindfolded. Their second bivouac was crammed into an overhanging crevasse at 6300 metres. The next day was not much better, with missiles of rock and ice hurtling past them on a regular basis. Although they couldn't see them coming, they could hear them – a horrible whining sound that instilled utter terror.

The next bivouac was both uncomfortable and unsafe. Carved out of a sheer, icy slope, the cramped ledge lay directly in the path of falling debris. But because their hands had begun to freeze, they were forced to stop and secure their little tent to the wall with ice screws. The wind howled all night, drifting snow onto their miserable abode. Their heads began to throb, for they were slowly being suffocated by the snow. When they realized what was happening, they dug out from the drifts and remained awake the rest of the night, propping up the tent with their bodies.

The following day they rested, eating and drinking and psyching themselves up for the next thousand metres of climbing. That night Janez confided to Tomaž: "If we climb this, we'll be happy the rest of our lives, and if we don't, we'll make half of Slovenia happy!"[173] His observation was probably accurate. Such is the world of alpinism, a competitive sphere that is rarely acknowledged as such.

The two began climbing at 4:00 am on October 31. The shrieking wind added to the discomfort of the −30°C temperature. At around seven thousand metres they refuelled with some tea and chocolate. At 11:30 am they radioed Marjan at base camp that they were above the difficulties and were at approximately 7500 metres. Marjan warned them of what he could see: a sinister-looking lenticular cloud streaming over the summit of Everest. They decided to continue climbing until 2:00 pm and then turn around, regardless of where they were. The two o'clock rule – it seemed a safe bet.

Still climbing solo, they waved their ice axes to each other periodically, Janez out front. At 1:00 pm Tomaž looked up to see Janez waving with even more vigour. He must be on the summit. Tomaž waved back, relieved that the end was near. Fifteen minutes later he arrived at the summit ridge and was assaulted by a blast of wind. He could see Janez's footprints leading toward Peak W1, a subpeak of Nuptse. Tomaž began to follow them but was confused. Were they not on the correct summit? Why continue on? Wouldn't it be safer to go down rather than wander around up here in this gale? As he flailed about on the ridge, he looked down again. There were no more footprints. He backtracked, looking for two sets of tracks. But there were only his. Janez's footprints had ended. He returned to the last footprint, and there on the snow, was the radio that Janez had been carrying. It was in the open position, ready for transmission. Janez had simply vanished.

Tomaž thought for a moment that he could see Janez on the ridge. Then he fell over, tossed down by the strong wind. He screamed Janez's name. Howling, again and again, but no answer. He grabbed the radio and called Marjan.

"Base, come in, base...Marjan, what's happened? Marjan!"

"What's the matter, Tomi, where are you?"

"Johan! Johan's gone!" (Johan was Janez's nickname.)

"What do you mean, gone? Where did he go?"

Tomaž lost track of time as he lay on the ridge, next to Janez's footprints, willing them to be filled by his friend and grappling with the realization that they wouldn't be. Fighting the fear of his situation: alone at the top of a 2500-metre wall, in a storm. Marjan called him, urging him to focus, to start down. It was 3:00 pm, and he had to begin descending or he would never reach the bivouac. Tomaž agreed and started down.

At first things went well. When he left the exposed ridge the wind velocity dropped, and he down-climbed quickly through the thickening gloom. Then he lost his goggles. By the time he reached 7100 metres, it was completely dark. His headlamp died. He inched down the slope, trying to remember the route, feeling his way. He would occasionally rest on his axes, only to be woken from an exhausted slumber by the sound of Marjan's voice urging him down.

Always down. Two things kept Tomaž alive that night: Marjan's voice and his own determination not to die standing still.

Marjan began playing music over the radio to keep Tomaž awake. Around midnight Tomaž thought he saw the tiny tent. But he couldn't be sure, as the moonless night was inky black. At that moment his concentration lapsed and he fell, careening down the icy slope. A mound of debris at the bottom stopped him short, and just nearby was the tent. He crawled over, unzipped the door and collapsed inside.

Almost immediately he began to hallucinate. "I distinctly saw seven people in the tent with me," he recalled. When he regained consciousness, he called Marjan and tried to start the stove. Since his headlamp was dead, he lit a candle. The stove wouldn't co-operate, so, frustrated, he fell back and drifted off again. Then the tent exploded in a fiery inferno. Tomaž had neglected to turn off the stove valve, and it had leaked fuel into the tent. That, combined with the open flame of the candle, had done the trick. He tossed the stove out the door, but the tent was in tatters. He collapsed onto his scorched sleeping bag and passed out once again. Snow sifted in, and his mind wandered into dangerous terrain. A white tunnel, with Sergeja beckoning him. Then his children, Urša and Tomi, and finally his parents. Family, warmth and love. His seven friends returned. The bearded man on his right encouraged him, "Don't worry, we'll take care of you." Tomaž decided not to enter the tunnel but to simply rest in the remains of his tent until he had the energy to continue.

At 11:00 am the following day, he woke to frantic radio calls from Marjan. An hour later he crawled out of the tent and headed down through the Orient Express. When he was almost at the bottom, a deafening roar overwhelmed him. He didn't need to look up to know what was coming. He slammed his body against the wall, securing both axes as well as he could, and waited. He was an easy target in this funnel and would surely be spit out the bottom. The roar intensified and chunks of ice ricocheted off the sides of the couloir and him, but when it ended he was still there, hanging off his axes.

By the end of the afternoon Tomaž had reached the edge of the crevasse field, drifting in and out of consciousness whenever he stopped moving. Marjan arrived at midnight to help him limp down to base camp on frostbitten feet.

♦ ♦ ♦

Back in Slovenia, Irena Jeglič was pregnant with her third child. She returned home from an outing with a friend and was surprised to see her entire extended family gathered in the living room. They sat silently, terror and dread in their eyes.

"What happened?" Irena asked. "Is anything wrong with Janez?"

Their gaze remained fixed on their hands.

"What is going on?" she pressed. Then finally, "Janez, is he dead?"

They nodded.

She refused to accept the news. Deeply religious, she suggested praying. Later, when the news flooded the media, Irena continued to pray, willing the story to be untrue. She knew the facts; they had found his radio on the summit ridge, but that didn't prove he was dead. She remembered her last conversation with Janez. It had been a difficult call, he wanting to stay, she wanting him to come home. Why hadn't she pushed harder and persuaded him to come home?

Janez had been popular with the climbing community and was one of the safest and most reliable of them all. He had enjoyed many close friendships, more than Tomaž. Although both were praised for their incredible climb, many blamed Tomaž for the accident. He struggled with the guilt that all survivors face, and with questions he knew he could not answer. Why does one person survive and another not? Who gets to decide? He wondered if they had ignored some subtle signs. Had they pushed each other too hard? There was no peace in his life. He eventually felt that the wrong man had returned from Nuptse.

When Tomaž visited Irena, he learned that she needed a death certificate in order to receive the pension she was owed – the pension that all Slovenian climbers' widows received from the state. She desperately needed the money: two small children and a third on the way. Since there was no real proof of his death, Tomaž had to confirm it before a civil court. The certificate was issued, and the financial strain eased. Friends called. Climbers came by. Irena was completely drained. Although tempted to blame someone for Janez's death, she knew that her pain would not ease by pointing a finger. Unlike many, she never blamed Tomaž.

Emotionally and physically destroyed, Tomaž began experiencing short-term memory loss from his time on the mountain. He crawled into a shell and shunned contact with all but his family. Sergeja, his wife, recalled that difficult time: "He was consumed by his pain and didn't know how to deal with it. It was like living with someone in a coma. For the first time in my life, I doubted my ability to endure it." Despite her strength, Sergeja had less time and energy for his problems. As he had become more of an absentee husband, she and the children had moved steadily away from him, and now, there was little to talk about. Tomaž was left alone with his grief.

As was Irena. She thought of their lost future. They had talked a lot about his career – where it was leading, how dangerous it was, and how they could manage it. He had nearly finished his international guide's training and had built a house for their growing family. It was a home full of photographs and books and the warm smell of baking. Janez had been ready for a change.

Years before, Nejc had felt the same:

> I am no longer drawn to the highest peaks. I no longer possess the terrible driving force that, until now, has never allowed me to ask myself, why all this? I don't know. Perhaps Everest was my swan song…Perhaps I really was prepared to give too much…I don't know how to dream and yearn anymore. Maybe the dreams that came true in the mountains as well as in the lowlands awoke a vision of a peaceful and quiet life, a vision, however, that was soon shattered…I no longer know anything, anything at all. I am only aware of the fact of my existence, my increasingly real, painful and lonely existence. The people dearest to me have grown so distant from me.[174]

♦ ♦ ♦

Sixteen years after Janez's death, Irena sat with her daughter Mirjam at her dining-room table in the house that Janez built, cradling a steaming cup of coffee in her hands. "He was a grateful man," she said, smiling. "He was easy to live with, not a difficult person. He ate everything I cooked for him," she laughed. Then with a serious tone, "He was trustworthy and he loved God." It was important to Irena that people understood how spiritual he was. "When Janez was away on expeditions, we prayed at the same time each day." Prayer was one more thing that kept them close, even when they were half a world apart.

Mirjam watched protectively as her beautiful mother with her easy smile and sad-looking eyes told her stories. Then she struggled to articulate her own memories of her father, unsure if they were real or merely imaginary pictures. One image had her standing between her father and the door – preventing him from leaving. Another, staring up at the sky, watching the big silver bird lift off from the nearby airport, her father on board.

Irena listened to Mirjam's stories and then added how grateful she was to Janez, and to God, that she had been able to live with him. Their marriage had been good. Too short, but good. All those dreams. All that love. So much sadness. And yet those eyes, both mother's and daughter's, even though brimming with tears, spoke of respect for the man who had left them, and bravery for the life they created after he disappeared.

SEVENTEEN

Dhaulagiri Real-Time

T wo years had passed since Tomaž's tragic climb on Nuptse with Janez Jeglič. Janez's death had revealed the extent of the Slovenian alpine community's distrust of Tomaž. Not everyone thought ill of him, yet he was definitely not "one of the boys." He was too brash, a self-promoter and definitely not a "purist." But he was still an alpinist. And a very good one. Pulling himself up out of the despair he felt after Janez's death, Tomaž began training and preparing for the climb of his life in the spring of 1999. It was a climb that would forever connect him to Šrauf.

Dhaulagiri had haunted Šrauf for years. Its cracks and ledges and falling rock kept luring him back, up the South Face and to one side or the other until his life ended. And it was Šrauf, above all others, who inspired Tomaž Humar. Everything about Šrauf resonated with Tomaž: his language, his character, his passion and his choice of mountains. The South Face: so steep. So committing. Although Šrauf had climbed the South Face, the summit had eluded him.

Tomaž fancied himself a kind of modern-day Šrauf. From their first climb together on Ganesh V, he strove to be like him, sometimes even surpassing the original. He took "Šraufisms" to a new level. High Definition and Surround Sound. So it shouldn't have been a surprise when Tomaž decided to tackle Dhaulagiri's South Face in 1999. Šrauf's project. Except that Tomaž would take it one step further: straight up the middle, alone. A line up the South Face of Dhaulagiri that was as straight as possible. An arrow from the base to the summit. This was a climb where speed would be his friend, and speed is best achieved when climbing alone.

Tomaž was fully versed in astrology and other spiritual ways, so he consulted with the higher forces when choosing the right moment for his climb. But as engaged as he was with astrology, he also relied on past alpine experience to inform his decision making. Then it came to him: October 25, the night of the full moon. It would provide good visibility for night climbing and cold temperatures – a safety margin on this face, notorious for its rock and icefall.

Like Šrauf, Tomaž knew that this climb was a one-way ticket. At some point the only way down would be up and over the other side. Unlike Šrauf, he broadcast the fact widely. He announced that he would have but a 20 per cent chance of success. Success meant survival. He may have been stating the obvious, but his melodramatic pronouncement irritated many.

Assembling a team was challenging, since few relished the prospect of an 80 per cent failure rate. Viki Grošelj was among those who said no. But Stipe Božić not only said yes, he agreed to film the climb. This would solve any Tomo Česen-like problems, should there be questions about his claims. Tomaž invited his doctor, Anda Perdan, and an unlikely bunch of climbers, all close friends. Friends were important to Tomaž. Although his energy seemed limitless, much of it came from those friends who encouraged him, or simply liked him. For Dhaulagiri, Tomaž brought six. When financial support from the Alpine Association dwindled to a trickle, Tomaž convinced Mobitel, a large telecommunications company, to finance his climb. Now he had six friends and a sponsor. He also had a vision surpassing anything that had been done to this point.

Tomaž embraced all types of media. A child of the Internet, he anticipated how plugged-in everyone was becoming. Whether it was the Internet, phones, video or audio, he understood the lure of communication – particularly real-time communication. In addition to inviting Stipe, a filmmaker with several good films under his belt, Tomaž planned for a live Internet link-up between his base camp and Slovenia. He would stay in constant touch with base camp, and they would communicate with the world out there. Reality television.

The team went first to the north side of the mountain so that Tomaž could acclimatize on the normal route. Bad news confronted them at every turn. The weather forecast was poor. Conditions on the mountain were dangerous. Every team on the mountain – the Mexicans, the Swiss, the Japanese and others – retreated, one by one. They were horrified by Tomaž's plan to try the South Face alone.

In addition to being dangerous, this was an incredibly complicated climb, even in good conditions. After acclimatizing, Tomaž and Stipe flew by helicopter to the south side of the mountain. The rest of the team headed over French Pass into the Kali Gandaki valley, where they positioned themselves with supplies to support Tomaž's descent. Everyone needed to be in constant radio contact.

Back on the south side, Tomaž and Stipe stared at the brooding wall, memorizing its features, tracking the movements of ice and rockfall, trying to predict when each would take place. Tomaž packed sparingly for this lonely adventure: food, a stove, fuel, pitons, carabiners, a sleeping bag, one 50-metre, five-millimetre rope, a few slings, and one of his son's baby shoes, his good-luck talisman. He and Stipe disagreed about which day to begin; Tomaž was convinced that the full moon was his friend. Stipe recalled those days. "I was very confident of his abilities to climb it but I was worried about the conditions on the mountain...I felt helpless. It was nerve-racking."[175]

Tomaž began climbing at 5:00 pm on October 25. Almost at that very moment a massive avalanche came crashing down the central couloir. Nothing had changed from Šrauf's time: the South Face was still a pile of unconsolidated rock, ice and snow. When the roar subsided, Tomaž carried on, climbing until he reached a ledge late that night. A troublesome ledge, as it turned out. He tried getting off it all night without success. At 5:00 am he radioed Stipe to say that he was stuck. And with the dawn, the situation would only worsen as the mountain began to disgorge debris. Tomaž tried to leave at 5:00 pm but was soon awash in flowing water and soft, mushy snow. He tried again at 7:00 pm. Same thing. Finally, at 10:00 pm, he made a bit of progress. One day lost.

The next morning he rope-soloed, hauling his 30-kilogram pack – tedious, dangerous work, particularly as the day warmed up. Almost smothered by sliding slush, he fluctuated between sheer terror and inspired confidence. From where did this calmness come? From his belief in his power to communicate directly with the mountain. A connection that provided him wisdom, comfort and support.

But he didn't limit his conversations to Dhaulagiri. He and Stipe radioed back and forth: Tomaž reporting on his progress, and Stipe reading him messages from supporters all over the world. Another example of a two-way communication that provided comfort and support. Human contact – something that Tomaž, although he was alone on the South Face of Dhaulagiri, craved. Even Stipe, who was initially skeptical of the Internet experiment, now saw its merit. "In this case it was helpful, since Tomaž knew he was being followed," Stipe said. "It gave him a voice and he felt responsible to all these people. He needed to come back alive."[176]

Despite all the love, life on the wall was bad and getting worse. Tons of snow sloughed off around Tomaž as he hung from his belay anchor during the night. Then a brief lull in avalanche activity gave him a chance – perhaps his only chance – to mince across a 25-metre-long ice traverse. It would be impossible for him to protect himself; he would need to solo this ballet, with a thousand metres of exposure beneath the tips of his crampons. The smell of death burned his nostrils as he cramponed diagonally across. The act was dizzying and completely irreversible. In mere minutes it was done. A few moments later an avalanche scoured his tiny point marks in the ice. Had the mountain told him the exact moment to cross? He was sure it had.

By October 29 he was high enough that conditions began to improve. Colder now, the ice, snow and rock were more firmly attached to each other, making it easier for Tomaž to stay attached, as well. But he was starting to show wear and tear: small injuries, hunger, an infected tooth and fatigue. Still, this was not the time or place to slow down. Every daylight hour counted now that the mountain had stabilized, and he made good progress up mixed terrain. He calculated the difficulty level as M7+, 5.9.[177]

Then history began to repeat itself. Although Tomaž was closer to the centre of the wall than Šrauf had been in 1981, he ran up against a similar impasse. By the end of the day on the 30th, Tomaž could no longer continue directly up the face. What to do? Left to the Polish ridge, or right to the Japanese? What had Šrauf done? He went right, and so did Tomaž. Slovenian climbers scoffed at his exit from the face, so close to Šrauf's. What was the difference? they asked. What made Tomaž's climb so special? It was basically a repeat of his mentor's.

He slept on the ridge that night, relieved and confident of the summit. Again, just like Šrauf. But the ridge exposed him to the full fury of the wind, so strong that it threatened to hurl him over the edge. With fresh memories of Janez being blown off Nuptse, Tomaž now diverged his Dhaulagiri story from Šrauf's. He concluded that he would have to traverse back onto the South Face. It's hard to imagine how depressing this decision was, after the initial relief of having survived the face. But back he went, dry-tooling on loose, steep rock above 7700 metres. Frostbite began to creep into his extremities, and at 7900 metres he was forced to stop. An open bivouac with no stove or tent. His eighth day on the face.

That night Tomaž felt near death. His exhaustion and the altitude and his injuries had accumulated to the point where there was little power left. But he had perfected a technique that might just save him. In a systematic and conscious manner, he lowered his pulse and concentrated his blood circulation to his core and his head. He focused on two things: his breathing and his heartbeat. Employing this advanced form of meditation, he could ignore his injuries, his pain, his thirst and his hunger. He explained the technique: "You live through a computer reset; nothing is important, only yourself…In those moments it is as loud as it gets, it starts to scream…the noise of silence…you do not see and you do not hear anything, you are absent, you do not exist. The wall has its soul. And you have to sneak under its skin, become one with her. Only when you are one with her, when you *are* her; only then you receive. In those times I climb and I am climbed. I caress the rock and get warm from the wall."[178]

Even though Nejc knew that mountains were inanimate, he also understood the climber's desire to create an emotional or spiritual connection:

> The mountain itself has no thoughts of its own – it is indifferent to what it looks like. Together with the night, the stars, the moon, the sky, the rock walls around it and the green valleys below it, the mountain forms a perfect whole that is disturbed only by man. His

longing drives him to try to bring the rock wall to life and force it to serve him, to offer up its cracks and ledges and allow him to reach the summit. He loves the mountain for serving as a stepping stone in his ambitious life. But if it rejects him with an overhang, a smooth slab or a snowstorm, or if it hits him with falling rock, he begins to hate it and runs away. And then he sees himself as a hero for persevering in this inhuman environment – and surviving.[179]

After living through the night at 7900 metres, Tomaž returned to the ridge. Like Šrauf, he knew that continuing up to the summit would mean death. His descent was not nearly as cruel as Šrauf's had been, however, for he was met by teammates who helped him off the mountain.

Upon his return to Slovenia, life would never be the same. Reinhold Messner was waiting at the airport to congratulate him, announcing that Tomaž's climb "marked a new watershed in contemporary extreme mountaineering."[180] But it wasn't only Messner's blessing that catapulted Tomaž into the media stratosphere. Endorsements from other high-altitude climbers and from Elizabeth Hawley (the official Kathmandu "gatekeeper" of all Himalayan ascents), and the unprecedented number of followers on his website, all added to his fame. And although he hadn't summited, the boldness of his climb on such a severe and dangerous route – alone – signalled something special.

But the climbing world is an insular one, closely monitored, severely judged and extremely competitive. Some alpinists were aghast at his blatant self-promotion. The real-time coverage of his climb was distasteful. Marija Štremfelj said, "He broke the unwritten rule in climbing…that climbers should do things without publicity."[181] Others felt he overdramatized his time on the face with all the rockfall, injuries and suffering. Slovenian alpinists pointed to Šrauf's climb in 1981, insisting that this was the *real* first ascent of the South Face of Dhaulagiri. Tomaž's climb was a copycat climb. They questioned why Messner had shown up to celebrate Tomaž's Dhaulagiri ascent when he had completely ignored Šrauf's. Some suggested that Messner had been a rival of Šrauf's; now that his climbing career was over, he could hitch his wagon to the current star: Tomaž.

In a piece for *Outside* magazine, American alpinist Mark Twight stated that Tomaž had expanded the psychological capacity of climbing – a great evolutionary step. Others challenged his grades, doubting the difficulty level that Tomaž claimed. The flurry of disapproval whirled and swirled, but all of it in somewhat of a void, since nobody had actually been there. Perhaps the most concise and accurate assessment came from Silvo Karo, who thought it was an excellent climb, but one Tomaž didn't finish.

Bojan Pollak, one of the elders of Slovenian alpinism, watched the goings-on and concluded that it was the usual bickering, fuelled by envy. But it may have been more than envy. The contrast between Tomaž and many other Slovenian climbers was dramatic. Tomaž – when he chose to be – was a showman. He courted publicity. He understood its power and what it could do for his career, particularly as a sponsored climber, still a relatively new concept in Slovenia. On the other hand, many of his critics were less motivated by publicity and more driven by the need to remain within the protective fold of the Alpine Association, their primary funder. Many Slovenian climbers who were active at this time were partially funded by the state, either directly through the Alpine Association or through their work with the police or army. The benevolent arm of the socialist government was their friend. But like Tomo Česen before him, Tomaž had found a different way. His way was sponsorship, which required profile and self-promotion. He was an entrepreneur. Neither strategy was bad; they were simply different.

Despite the furor within the climbing community, Tomaž's profile had far surpassed that of other climbers: he was a national hero. Slovenian citizens had followed him up the wall, and now they wanted to honour him. His life was a whirlwind of press conferences, lectures, travel, parties and attention. "Let's have another drink," he would say. "It's liquid oxygen, you know." His smiling, boyish face was everywhere, his story on everyone's lips. It brought pleasure and pride to ordinary citizens. "Welcome home!" they called, when seeing him on the street or in the grocery store. They wined and dined him. Someone always picked up the tab. The president of Slovenia befriended him and gave him the Honorary Emblem of Freedom, the country's highest honour.

Although Tomaž was a naturally sociable person, he began to lose perspective on his priorities. And eventually he lost control. Sergeja described it: "Our marriage became madness."[182]

Along with the adulation came pressure. Like his climb, his fame was a one-way ticket; there was no turning back to a normal, quiet, private life or to normal, quiet, private climbs. The alpinist he had once been vanished. His Dhaulagiri ascent was the most futuristic climb ever, but it implied bigger and better, more outrageous performances in the future – not just for Tomaž, but for other high-altitude climbers, particularly in Slovenia. Years later, Marko Prezelj reflected, "I think Tomaž Humar created another cathartic moment of alpinism because he inflated a balloon that couldn't survive…One generation was almost lost because they couldn't follow him."

◆ ◆ ◆

Tomaž's balloon burst in late October 2000 when he fell from the floor joists into the basement of his unfinished house. After years of climbing dangerous Himalayan walls, surviving lonely bivouacs, avalanches, rockfall and injury, it appeared that a home construction project would take down one of Slovenia's finest alpinists. His first feeling after regaining consciousness was relief. He could finally stop running, talking, negotiating, arguing and socializing. Like Nejc, years before, he could stop being a stranger to his children. In fact, he nearly stopped living. It would be years before the pride of Slovenia would touch another Himalayan wall. But in those years of recovery, he rediscovered himself with the help of *Pot*.

> I was surprised at not having to hurry, by how pleasant and easy it was to walk slowly. I was surprised by the absence of restlessness that precedes exposure to risks, the absence of the need to keep constant track of time. I noticed that the path was soft and the shadows cool and the raspberries sweet and the stream cold. And wonder of wonders, the birds were singing! They took their time and spent most of their day singing, flitting from branch to branch. I didn't have to talk to anyone about where I nailed in a piton, what handhold I did or didn't use, what this or another route looked like, or how much time a certain climb took me. We only talked about

the things that we all observed, and that I noticed when my children showed them to me...they slowly awoke in me a man who walks a path, not just a path going toward a mountain hut but rather an allegory of an eternal path, a path to some yet unknown hut, to some yet unknown home, a path leading to my inner self and, through this inner self, back to the people...I realized it was not I who conceived my children. My children conceived me. I realized that they brought a value to my life that I either didn't recognize or refused to acknowledge before. The path will remain as it is in its countless forms. It will not make the incline less steep. It will not make the summits any lower. It will not build bridges across ravines. It will wind on as before, only the images alongside the path are becoming fuller and clearer. My children turned the path back to me. They brought me joy at the little things. They gave me back the sight and hearing that were weakened by the din of the race.[183]

EIGHTEEN

Canadian Adventure

Marko Prezelj hacked at the frozen rubble with his axe, trying to excavate a narrow bivy ledge on which to spend the night. Steve House, his partner, estimated that it was, at best, three butt-cheeks wide. Not great, but good enough. They laid a foam sleeping pad on the ledge and prepared for the night. Steve was focused on dry socks, which would keep his feet warm on this sub-zero Canadian night in April 2004. He unlaced his boot. For a fleeting moment he wondered if he should clip it to the anchor. It would be easy to do so since he had already attached a thin piece of cord to the back of the boot for that very purpose. Instead, he placed the boot in a safe position between him and the wall.

Marko was preoccupied with assembling the stove.

Steve replaced his sweat-soaked socks with dry ones from his pack. He wiggled his toes, revelling in the warmth. He loosened the laces of his inner boot and slid it over his cozy, dry foot. He reached behind to retrieve the outer boot, threading his finger through the thin loop of cord. He slipped his toe into the outer boot and pulled. Suddenly it went slack. "The boot stutters and floats quietly in my headlamp for a moment before it plunges into the dark, and is gone. Silence. All I see is the weak cast of light illuminating the space in front of me where moments ago my boot was. It's gone."[184]

High on the North Face of North Twin in the Canadian Rockies, there was no way to retrieve the boot. They had nowhere near enough gear to retrace their steps down the face. Besides, where would the boot have landed? It could be anywhere. The seriousness of the situation settled in. No boot = no crampon. No crampon = no climbing. No boot = no skiing. They were more than 30 kilometres from the closest road, separated by one icecap, several glaciers and too many precipitous rock walls to count.

Marko Prezelj, one of Slovenia's star climbers, and Steve House, an equally famous American climber from a small town in northern Washington State, who, some say, looks like a farm boy, may have seemed unlikely rope mates. But their trajectories were destined to cross. And here on Alberta's North Twin, they threatened to remain.

Steve first came to Yugoslavia in 1988 as an exchange student. He travelled light: three pairs of jeans, seven T-shirts, a few under-garments and four super-sized jars of peanut butter. High school in Maribor, Slovenia's second-largest city, didn't interest him much, but when he went to the local mountaineering club, his spirits soared. "I have found a new school: one whose language I readily understand. The school of Slovenian alpinism."[185]

Marko first met Steve while climbing in Alaska. They shared a lot of things, including the Slovenian language, which Steve learned when he was studying in Maribor. But their inspired partnership had more to do with their similar spirits, described by Marko: "You appreciate being in the mountains and sharing the moments, having fun, challenging yourself, testing your limits." And although they were not exclusive partners over the years, together they became a formidable force in the climbing world.

When Steve invited Marko to climb with him in the Canadian Rockies in early April 2004, Marko didn't hesitate. He was already scheduled to deliver a lecture in the United States, so he planned his trip to allow some time in Canada. They would stay at the home of a local climber, Barry Blanchard, in Canmore, Alberta.

Steve said to Marko, "I have a good idea."

"What is your idea?" asked Marko.

"North Twin."

Barry watched the two prepare for the climb, particularly amused by Marko, whom he compared to a well-dressed Formula One driver, with his strong, square face and precisely trimmed widow's peak. They discussed the weather forecast, which looked good: five yellow orbs lined up in a row on the Weather Network website. Steve thought the climb would take three to four days, which was a bit tight for Marko, since he was supposed to be speaking in Boulder, Colorado, five days later. Steve reassured him that if they climbed the route, Mark Twight, the lecture organizer, would forgive him for being late. It was only then that Marko began to suspect how important the climb was to Steve. How interesting and significant this ascent might be. For Marko, it was a mystery. He knew nothing about the mountain. He didn't know its history. He didn't know its reputation. He didn't even know what it looked like. In retrospect, he wondered if Steve had North Twin specifically in mind all along. Marko finally took a look at a photograph of the mountain on Barry's wall and remarked in his trademark straight-to-the-point style, "Looks good. Where is it?"

Several climbers had written about the alluring peak. Henry L. Abrons described North Twin in the *American Alpine Journal* back in 1966: "In one of the more remote valleys of the sub-arctic rain forest called the Canadian Rockies there is a mountain wall which acts like a strong drug on the mind of the observer. So dark, sheer, and gloomy is the North Face of North Twin, like a bad dream, I shall say very little about it."[186] Ten years later, American climber Chris Jones stated that the mountain probably had some meaning for a future generation, but he wasn't sure exactly what.

At 3731 metres, North Twin is one of a pair of peaks that form a massif at the northeast corner of the Columbia Icefield in Alberta. Much more important than its height is its dark, forbidding pyramidal north wall: only the upper section sees any sunlight at all, and that is just one hour of weak, early-morning rays. Its reputation is fierce, although not well-known in European climbing circles. The mountain was first climbed in 1974 by American climbing legends George Lowe and Chris Jones, and climbing historians later evaluated their ascent as the most difficult alpine route in the world up to that point. It was 11 years before the second ascent, this time by an even more demanding line. South African climber David Cheesmond and Canadian Barry Blanchard opened a route on the great north pillar surging straight up the centre of the wall. Now 30 years had passed since the first ascent and 19 since the second. No wonder Steve House was nervous.

They packed their gear and enough fuel and food for four days. They drove west to Lake Louise, then up the Icefields Parkway to the Sunwapta River. Leaving the car, they walked across the river flats, waded the river, and scrambled up the narrow gorge leading toward Woolley Shoulder, a high feature on Mount Woolley that would give them access to the remote Habel Creek valley.

The pair had established a brusque communication style that suited their no-nonsense characters. Marko's voice was strong, and his command of the English language was sufficient to express whatever it was he needed to say but was bereft of inane niceties. He and Steve could joke with each other, even roughly, without fear of insult. They trusted each other's skills and judgment, so any route-finding disagreements could be solved by honest discussion. They had endured some difficult days in the mountains together. "Marko and I have a kind of pact, born of a shared distaste for posing and respect for the nobility of mountains," Steve said. "When we decide to go climbing, we go climbing. We grow serious; we don't laugh much once we start. We break when we have to, not when we want to. We go to work, and we work until we get the job done or until we are forced to accept failure."

Marko refused to allow family concerns to interfere with his focus on the job at hand. When asked about that tricky balancing act, he replied, "We are not talking about climbing. We are talking about life. This is how you gain confidence with your family...They know I'm not an idiot who says I have just a 20 per cent chance to come back. This puts a huge pressure on the family. I don't even say that I *will* come back. If you need to say it, it's already over the edge." For Marko, family is family and climbing is climbing.

Marko detected a different vibe about Steve on their approach to North Twin. A slight tension. When they reached the top of Woolley Shoulder, Marko had his first look at the north side of the mountain. He wasn't disappointed. "Now we are going into what I really like," he said. They skied down the other side of the shoulder, their heavy climbing packs throwing them around like drunken puppets. Heavy as they were, the packs held only the bare necessities: one sleeping bag between them, a couple of thin foam pads to insulate them, a tarp, stove and fuel, energy bars, one chocolate bar, a few freeze-dried meals and a bit of instant coffee. That, and extra clothing. This was definitely not luxury camping.

They stashed their skis, to be retrieved after the climb, and soloed up the first snow slopes to a bivy site. This was the life: two friends climbing on a stupendous face in a remote location. They agreed that the next day would be a big one. Better get up at 6:00 am to get an early start. Marko set the alarm and they settled in for the night.

They woke up at 8:00, two hours later than planned. Steve was angry and started shouting at Marko.

Marko downplayed the outburst. "Come on, it's just a climb," he insisted.

But Steve was stressed and convinced that the sleep-in had compromised their climb.

Again, Marko responded with calmness. "It's not too late. Hey, slow down." Years later, he thought back to that morning. "There was a moment...But I didn't realize yet why." Later he speculated that Steve's nerves were stretched taut as a bow, thanks to the mountain's ominous reputation and his keen desire to climb it.

After a quick breakfast, they headed up. Fine dry-tooling cracks; snow-covered aprons of ice; deep, dark chimneys; and amazing exposure: lots of variety and plenty of problem-solving. Their climbing commands ricocheted off the wall, the only sounds other than shards of ice clattering down from their axes. The ascent was going well, and they joked around at the belay stances, the morning's tension gone. After a full day of climbing, their second bivouac was uneventful.

The next morning Marko led out first, Steve following with the haul pack. Switching leads as they went, they danced up delicate, snow-covered holds and cracks that seemed to get smaller the higher they climbed. As the thin winter light faded into twilight, they were forced to stop on that tiny, uncomfortable ledge for their third bivouac. Marko was excited as he assembled the stove for the evening meal of freeze-dried potatoes, and he kept glancing up, certain that he could see the exit line leading off the face. It looked good.

Then Steve dropped the boot. He let loose a howl of horror, then a series of curses. "Fuck! Fuck! Fuck! Fuck!" Nothing changed. The boot was still gone. He looked over at Marko, dreading his reaction. Marko sat in silence, staring at Steve.

Finally, Marko asked in a flat, almost uninterested voice, "What happened?"

Steve held up the broken piece of cord. There was nothing more to say.

Marko's mind was racing. "I realized then we were in trouble," he recalled of that moment. "Steve's eyes were big and now he was serious with his swearing. Looking down, I saw how far we had come. Without a boot we couldn't go down." As Marko continued cooking, he tried to calm down, to think clearly and analytically. There must be a solution. But the facts were not encouraging: winter conditions and sub-zero temperatures; just 12 ounces of fuel, enough to produce eight litres of liquid; three ounces of dried potatoes, half a stick of butter, six energy gels, four energy bars and a bit of coffee. No radio and no phone. And they wouldn't be considered overdue by Parks Canada's rescue service for another three days.

The only solution was up.

There wasn't much talk after the boot incident, but the dynamics of the climb – and the partnership for the duration of the climb – shifted. Marko felt the pressure most because he had just become the leader of a rescue mission. Steve's entire focus was now on following as efficiently as possible. The complex psychology of a successful climbing partnership is based on trust, and on this point Steve and Marko proved they were in perfect sync. "I'm not really keen on judging climbs, but just from a pure adventure point of view I can say that this was one of the biggest adventures in my life," Marko later said. "All this: how isolated we were, what had happened there, all this adventure and isolation was getting into my mind. I started to feel smaller and smaller." The climb had started so innocently for Marko. He hadn't known anything about the history of the place, and for him it was simply a joyful game – another climb with Steve. He had been relaxed about it, unlike Steve, who had been dwelling on the mountain's history: the unsuccessful attempts, the difficulties, the remoteness. He felt angst from the first step.

By morning it was snowing heavily. Steve taped three plastic bags and one giant zip-lock bag over his inner boot. This would have to do for the remaining exit pitches on the face and for the long, tedious trek across the Columbia Icefield and down the Athabasca Glacier, now the only possible way out. He had no idea if the makeshift covering would survive the abrasion or be even remotely waterproof.

Marko led all day with a tireless rhythm that devoured the vertical terrain. After 14 pitches of climbing, they topped out onto the icefield and began plodding across it, Steve out front with the GPS, trying to navigate in whiteout conditions. One foot was cramponed, and the other still only clad by his inner-boot and plastic bags. After hours of slogging, they felt their way down through the three giant steps of the Athabasca Glacier, where it tumbles down between Snow Dome and Mount Andromeda. Near the bottom they spied a group of ski-mountaineers heading up. Steve later recorded the humorous exchange in his book *Beyond the Mountain*.

"Where are you coming from?" The tone sounds somewhat incredulous . . .

"North Twin," Marko says, and keeps walking.

"Where?"

"North Twin." Now Marko sounds annoyed with this interruption.

"Where are your skis?"

"We left them there...We climbed the North Face." Marko still hasn't stopped walking and is past them, stepping into their ski track. They crane their heads around to watch him go as I approach.

Feeling the need to fill in some of the details, I slow my pace. "We climbed the North Face of North Twin and had to descend across the icefield. We've been out five days," I say..."We haven't eaten all day and want to get to the road before dark."

They say nothing in reply, and huddle into themselves, so I resume full walking speed. Then one of them says loudly, "North Face of North Twin?" He pauses, and then swivels towards me. "Who are you guys?"

"Nobody," I say. "Just two guys."[187]

The two guys had pulled it off. Steve knew what they had done, and soon everyone did. Marko understood its significance only later, which made it even more precious. "For me, it was one of the purest joys of completing it, without any knowledge of what anybody else would think about it," he said. "I was just happy. It was a joyful climb in terms of technical difficulties, close to the limit, good problem-solving, friendship was good." Like Franček Knez on Trango Tower, he felt it was a climb "very well done."

◆ ◆ ◆

The next few years could be described as Marko's "American phase." He and Steve forged a 16-pitch new route on the West Face of 5719-metre Cayesh in Peru's Cordillera Blanca. He teamed up with two other Americans, Stephen Koch and Dean Potter, for two impressive routes on Patagonian monoliths Cerro Torre and Cerro Standhardt. Then he was back with Steve and Vince Anderson in 2007 for the first ascent of 6858-metre K7 West, a stunning achievement on this Karakoram gem. A short film about the climb, called *Ice, Anarchy and the Pursuit of Madness*, began its credits with the basic information: "2 sleeping bags, 3 guys, 4 days, 5 screws, 6 nuts, K7." A series of gullies filled with rotten ice; soaring granite walls; a spectacularly fluted, corniced ridge; loose, unconsolidated snow; a false summit to test their wills; and steep climbing from the very first metre provided Marko with exactly what he craved. The following year, 2008, the trio was again in the Himalaya, trying for the unclimbed West Face of 8485-metre Makalu. Despite being unsuccessful, Marko and Steve completed a new route on the unclimbed West Face of 7678-metre Kangchungtse. They tried the West Face of Makalu several more times in the ensuing years without reaching the summit, but they always returned intact.

Although Marko grazed far beyond Slovenia's borders for his partners, it was Steve House who appeared most often at the other end of his rope. They shared slightly different values but a similar spirit, and they had implicit trust in each other's decisions in the mountains. Steve explained that level of trust: "If I'm nearing the end of a pitch, Marko will sometimes break down his anchor and start climbing before I have him on belay. This is generally unacceptable behaviour, breaking many of the norms of roped climbing. However, he knows I'm going to get an anchor in soon and he is so confident he can move safely upward that he will risk both our lives. And he's right to do so. I not only trust him to not fall off and potentially kill me, but believe that his decision actually adds to our overall safety by speeding us along on our climb."

But Marko, not one to be pigeonholed, refused to single out one partner in his career. "Every person was part of the picture," he said. "Some are small pieces, but if you take them out, there would be a missing part. I don't want to bring attention to one small or big piece. It's a picture that continues to evolve."

Marko expects a lot from his partners, including a limited amount of talking, particularly when it gets serious. "If you open the discussion about tricky issues, it's opening the discussion to go down," he flatly stated. "If you can't change it, you leave it. Keep your mouth shut and just deal with it."

Both Marko and Steve evolved into roles as climbing mentors in their home countries. They still climb together, but their life rhythms began to differ, with new family responsibilities and changing life partners and employment. Their attitude about media also diverged, Marko becoming increasingly private, almost secretive, about his climbs. "I feel like I don't want to share my climbs with the general public so much as I did when I was younger," he explained. "I try to be more private. Steve is opposite. I know he is on Facebook and Twitter and everything." Marko expressed frustration, even anger, at the cyber-world. His comments were reminiscent of passages in *Pot,*where Nejc struggled to understand his own feelings of withdrawal:

> It was late fall and I came across a chamois in the wall. When the chamois grow old they retreat to precipitous walls and slowly pass away...Why did I begin to retreat from people long before my hair turned grey?...
>
> The larches are shedding their needles. Snow lies on the ledges and the rock is cold but I would so much like to linger just a little while longer...to take my time for a slow descent to the valley...to convince myself that there is no need to hurry. In fifty years, no one will know about this poor confused nobody who searched for himself and for the world. So why hurry? Why keep trying? Just to feel satisfied with myself, to be able to shake my own hand on the summit...to return to the valley grinning and full of strength, to be able to live and smile in company when I feel like screaming and forcibly opening the eyes of people who wander blindly through the human anthill of city streets.

What did this year of alpinism bring me? Peak-bagging, not unlike some people's collecting of stamps or matchboxes. It was beautiful and it was difficult. I can say both. But in what way was it beautiful? What was beautiful? Why was it beautiful? This I don't know because I didn't have time to look. And where was it difficult? Why was it difficult? I don't know that either because I have forgotten already. But now, in this very moment, I will sit down on this sunlit peak...I will wait for friends still climbing on a neighbouring route. Just to be able to smile at someone and see them smile cheerfully in return and give me new faith in life.[188]

NINETEEN

Death in the Mountains

The race across the mountain continued, but the mountains still glowed when it was their time to glow. They still cried when it was time for rain. And they still told you stories, if you only knew how to listen to them. But I was no longer one of those who knew how to listen…who knew how to laugh and cry with them…I was an athlete…I was an alpinist. I spoke of walls and overhangs. I ran and trained and counted my ascents. I fell prey to the folly of categorization, adding up points, comparing myself to others and making myself poorer and poorer. I was turning into a shallow and stupid craftsman. All I saw were numbers, summit heights, sizes of walls, estimations of difficulty. I only saw Roman and Arabic numerals, commas and plus and minus signs. My hands and legs were strong and unstoppable but my head became empty and my heart no longer beat faster because it was being overwhelmed by beauty – only because of physical effort. My path was rapidly turning downhill while the curve of my success continued to rise. One climb became indistinguishable from another. I functioned like a well-oiled machine that will continue to run on empty if no one stops it. And thus the wheels of my machine kept turning without purpose, faster and faster, until my children reminded me that the birds in the forest were still singing.

—Nejc Zaplotnik, *Pot*[189]

After Tomaž Humar's fall into his unfinished basement in 2000, his career as an alpinist appeared over. Confined to his wheelchair (which he baptized his "red Ferrari") and the living-room couch, Tomaž had plenty of time to reflect. He returned to his favourite, dog-eared volume of *Pot* countless times, and although it didn't solve his problems, Nejc's writing brought him comfort.

But it wasn't all about lying around and reading *Pot*, as Tomaž wasn't quite ready to give up his passion. He travelled to Germany for complicated surgery on his leg and heel, and he endured months of physiotherapy. He graduated from his wheelchair to a bike. Then to lurching along with crutches. And finally he began climbing again, dancing up the razor-sharp limestone cliffs, then stumbling his way back down the trail. Like Nejc, he functioned better on vertical ground than on horizontal surfaces.

From *Pot*: "All I do is put on a helmet, attach a few slings and pitons to my harness and I'm already completely relaxed by the first contact with the wall. I feel like I'm dancing a gentle waltz, just me and the girl, without onlookers, far away from the crowd on an overcrowded dance floor. There is music but I don't know where it's coming from."[190]

Tomaž's heart wasn't on rock walls, however; it was in the high mountains. In 2002 he joined a Russian team on Shishapangma, where his steel-reinforced and slightly shorter leg seemed to work just fine. In quick succession, he climbed a new route on the South Face of Argentina's Aconcagua, highest mountain in South America, tried to solo a new route on Jannu's East Face and climbed a partial new route on the Northeast Face of Cholatse, both in Nepal. Friends noticed a shift in style. Dhaulagiri had been a public climb from start to finish. His post-accident climbs seemed more private. As he pointed out, "I decide when to have media. I'm the switcher guy."

Tomaž had a big project in mind and, at least initially, planned to turn the switch to the off position. But life sometimes gets in the way of plans. His marriage fell apart. Then his sponsor pulled out. So Tomaž defaulted to a proven formula: partner with the media. With newspaper and television sponsors, he would be able to pay the bills and continue with his dream of a new route, solo, on the Rupal Face of Nanga Parbat, a 4500-metre wall of rock and ice on Pakistan's second-highest mountain.

He arrived at the mountain in July 2005 and acclimatized in wet, stormy weather on the Messner route. As the storms intensified, he waited at base, worried and impatient. His daily media reports contained nothing of interest, just more bad weather. His anxiety intensified with the knowledge that a permit had been issued to another team for the same face that summer; Marko Prezelj's frequent climbing partners, Steve House and Vince Anderson, would be arriving any day now.

Finally, a three-day window of "less bad" weather was forecast. But the mountain was draped in snow. Tons and tons of unstable snow. It would take several days of sun to slough off. However, Tomaž didn't have the time or patience to wait any longer, so he started up. He made good progress for two days but was stopped at around 6350 metres on a steep, icy cone blanketed in a thick slab of unconsolidated snow. Then the weather closed in. He dug into a slot on a slight arête and hunkered down to wait out the storm. Day after day of snow and rain and continuous avalanches followed. He couldn't move up. He couldn't move sideways. And he certainly couldn't move down. After four days in his ice coffin, out of food and fuel, he was forced to do the unthinkable – call for a rescue.

Any serious alpinist will admit that calling for a rescue is difficult, even shameful. Many have done it and owe their lives to their rescuers. But it's a last resort. Asking for a rescue at over six thousand metres on the Rupal Face of Nanga Parbat, with the entire world monitoring his website, was beyond difficult. Climbers around the world scoffed at Tomaž and this "circus" that he was ringleading, apparently for the benefit of the mass media.

The rescue was epic. Coordinated from Slovenia by Tomaž's old friend Viki Grošelj, the six-day effort involved rescue specialists from Switzerland and Pakistan and the presidents of both Slovenia and Pakistan. After a couple of false starts and increasing pressure from President Musharraf to get the job done, two Pakistani helicopter pilots, Rashid Ullah Baig and Khalid Amir Rana, managed to execute the highest high-angle technical rescue ever attempted.

They performed the impossible and were hailed as heroes for their daring achievement. Tomaž, on the other hand, was vilified by climbing journalists and his peers. He had broken the alpine code of honour. Dying would have been the honourable thing to do. Slovenian citizens reacted differently, having followed his plight every day on the evening news. When he was plucked from the Rupal Face, they rejoiced. Many Slovenians urged him to run for president.

A few weeks after the rescue, Steve House and Vince Anderson climbed a new route on the Rupal Face in impeccable style. When Steve came to Slovenia shortly after the climb, he was hounded by reporters and eventually agreed to do an interview. Tomaž retreated, shunning the media and ignoring the naysayers. He was a wounded animal. His humiliation was complete. Once again, he leaned on *Pot*:

> People grew more and more afraid of me. They were upset and confused when near me because they didn't know how to pigeonhole me, which niche to place me in, under which heading or subheading to describe me. I no longer belonged anywhere, and I was becoming more and more alone. Some people began to follow me; others began to avoid me. But those who stood by me, content to see the reflection of their souls in my eyes, were very few…I want nothing so much as to pack up my pack, hoist it onto my shoulder and return home – to the place where I feel warm and pleasant. Nevertheless, I refuse to do so, if only to remain true to myself and my journey.[191]

Although Tomaž tried to remain true to his journey, it turned out to be tragically short. His life returned to a semblance of normalcy, but under the surface he was deeply troubled. His marriage was over. He was like a blazing comet that had simply burned out. He had lost the respect of his peers and had lost faith in them. He became increasingly suspicious. "These people are trying to eat my soul," he said. His distrust of climbers, his doctors and finally even his closest friends approached paranoia. Stipe recounted with sadness that, in those last years, Tomaž was very alone. "I think maybe I was his last friend," he said.

As Nejc wrote in *Pot*:

> I no longer trusted climbing partners, nor did I trust myself. Nothing went well for me any longer. I lost that fierce passion in my heart to climb. The rocks seemed distant and forbidding. I forced myself. I climbed a few good routes but with difficulty and without grace or

enthusiasm…Today I realize what it was. Fear. Fear of death. Fear of blood…An odd melancholy overwhelmed me…my life was running through my hands like sand flowing through an hourglass. All the precious time, all the vital force flowing down through the narrow neck, down to be lost in the sand…I had been desperately in love and was exhausted with the fear of never being able to live with the woman I loved. I hid behind humour that grew increasingly more sarcastic. I was burning in a strange fire, not in the warmth- and light-giving flame, but in the destructive flames of arson. I tried to extinguish it with alcohol, but it was like a dousing in petrol. The mountains no longer glowed. They didn't give me power and energy. They became dark, like the storm that was brewing wildly within me.[192]

Tomaž continued to climb, but with the media switch positioned firmly to off.

In late October 2007, he soloed a South Face route on Annapurna I East, reaching its summit. There were other climbs and summits, unreported and unheralded. He was preparing for something big, something that would assure his place in history. Part of his preparation was the South Face of 7227-metre Langtang Lirung in northern Nepal in early November 2009.

Somewhere on the face, however, something went wrong. He made a couple of satellite calls, first to his girlfriend to say goodbye, then to his Nepalese cook at base camp. "I am near the end," he said. A rescue effort was launched by Swiss rescue ace Bruno Jelk, but his broken and lifeless body wasn't found until five days after the first call.

This complex, driven and conflicted man had lashed out when, years earlier, he was asked if he was courting death. "You know how I love my children," he had yelled. "I want to be a grandfather." Everyone had wanted that to be true, particularly his family. But like others before him – Nejc, Šrauf, Janez and Slavko – Tomaž had walked too close to the edge. And finally, he crossed it.

◆ ◆ ◆

Tomaž was one of that small group of climbers who preferred to climb alone. They valued the safety margin of speed gained from climbing solo. Tomo Česen was aghast at the number of weeks Yugoslavian climbers were exposed to extreme danger on the South Face of Lhotse in 1981. As well as speed, Tomo believed that his extreme focus was best achieved alone. "I know that if your concentration is very high you can take more out of your body...And I'm sure that nearly everyone can do much more than they think they can do." He referenced Messner on Nanga Parbat and Ueli Steck on Annapurna as examples of what the human body could do. "But you have to be forced," he explained. "And then you will realize that you can do much more." Preparation and training were key to Tomo's performances. Although he insisted that a few of his contemporaries climbed better than he did, he was privileged in the prime of his career to have full support from his sports club. He was a professional climber. He trained every day, all day. And in the end, few could match him.

Both Tomo Česen and Slavko Svetičič were primarily soloists. There are parallels between them, but their approach was fundamentally different. Tomo used a rational, systematically planned, and sportsmanlike approach to his climbs, while Slavko was much more impulsive. His inspiration often motivated him to solo climb above his normal abilities, whereas Tomo soloed well below his top grade.

Although Tomaž was also a soloing specialist, he believed he could communicate with the mountains on which he climbed, creating a kind of make-believe partnership. This belief surely helped him on the South Face of Dhaulagiri, on his descent of Nuptse and on his solo climb of Bobaye in 1996. But it couldn't have brought him much comfort on the south wall of Langtang Lirung. On that day, he was fundamentally, and finally, alone.

As Swiss superstar (and solo climber) Ueli Steck said, "If you do not stop this kind of solo climbing...it will kill you. No question."[193] In the case of Slavko Svetičič, as with Tomaž, Ueli couldn't have been more correct. Of Slavko's 1200 climbs, many were solo: hard routes in the French Alps, even harder routes in the Julian Alps, aid routes, free routes, winter routes. He soloed routes in South America and in New Zealand, then went back to the Dolomites for his hardest solos yet. Slavko climbed fast. But on Gasherbrum IV, even his speed couldn't save him.

The premature death of an alpinist is never easy to accept, despite logic dictating that it shouldn't be surprising, that it should even be predictable. With climbers whose lives are so meteoric, so intense, so dangerously lived, it is hard to reconcile their capacity for risk with their reflections on aging. As Rebecca West wrote in her 1941 book about her Yugoslavian travels, *Black Lamb and Grey Falcon*, "Only part of us is sane: only part of us loves pleasure and the longer day of happiness, wants to live to our nineties and die in peace, in a house that we built, that shall shelter those who come after us. The other half of us is nearly mad. It prefers the disagreeable to the agreeable, loves pain and its darker night despair, and wants to die in a catastrophe that will set back life to its beginnings and leave nothing of our house save its blackened foundation."[194]

Death on a mountain – alone – is a horrible thing. Unimaginable loneliness and despair. But the death of a partner can be even worse. Stipe had remained loyal to Tomaž right to the end. Perhaps because of his own exposure to tragedy in the mountains: Ang Phu in 1979 on Everest, again on Everest in 1989, and most profoundly for Stipe, in 1993 on K2. While still in Camp IV, after having summited the mountain, Stipe noticed that his suffering tent mate, Boštjan Kekec, looked strangely old and was foaming at the lips. "I thought, oh, my God, maybe altitude sickness," Stipe said. He tried to rouse Boštjan and help him descend, but he didn't respond, drifting in and out of consciousness. All through the night, Stipe and two others tried to revive Boštjan and prepare him for descent the next day.

In the morning they pulled him out of the tent, wrapped him in a sleeping bag and attached him to the rope. They dragged him three hundred metres but couldn't manage one metre more. Stipe called base camp, asking for advice. Base camp responded that Stipe would know what to do. "But I didn't know what to do," Stipe insisted. "I had to decide – will we stay with him and die with him, or will we leave him and he will die and we will live?" Then began the most difficult internal debate of Stipe's life. He gave himself until 1:00 that afternoon to make a decision.

At 1:00 pm they began to descend. Boštjan was still motionless on the slope. "But when I turned back it seemed to me that he was moving a bit. I was in a terrible state," Stipe said. They turned around and tried again to move Boštjan, struggling for an hour with little progress. Then they looked closely at Boštjan; he was dead. "With that, he saved our lives," Stipe stated in a flat, emotionless voice, his eyes dark with the memory.

Boštjan became K2's 29th victim and another in the long list of Slovenian climbers who remain in the mountains forever. Climbers who lost sight of the fact that climbing is essentially an earthbound activity. Climbers who flew too high. As French alpinist Lionel Terray once wrote: "Living in the courts of the sky I forgot I was of the earth."[195]

TWENTY

Legacy

The history of Himalayan climbing is like a grand world tour. The Austrians led in the 1950s, with five eight-thousand-metre first ascents: Nanga Parbat, Cho Oyu, Gasherbrum II, Broad Peak and Dhaulagiri. The Japanese swarmed the Himalaya in the 1960s and 1970s, and a new approach appeared with the British: difficult faces and ridges. The Poles ruled in the 1980s, with new routes, winter ascents and daring alpine-style ascents. The Russians moved in next, with exceedingly demanding climbs. And Yugoslavia was there, too, raising the level of difficulty even higher.

What made the Yugoslavian and Slovenian ascents so special was that, although they missed out on the classical era of Himalayan climbs, the first ascents of the eight-thousanders, they made up for it on the great walls and ridges in the 1970s and 1980s. These were their golden years. Their achievements ranked at the top of elite Himalayan climbs: Makalu South Face, Everest West Ridge, Cho Oyu North Face, Kangchenjunga South Pillar, Jannu North Face, Melungtse, Ama Dablam Northwest Face, Nuptse West Face, West Face of Bhagirathi III, Shishapangma Southwest Face, Api Southeast Face, Bobaye Northwest Face, Nampa South Face, Gyachung Kang North Face and Dhaulagiri South Face. Reinhold Messner, in his book *The Big Walls*, singled them out: "To be sure, modern mountaineering is a British, and also a Central European, invention...Finally, it was Slovenian climbers who then took the whole thing one step further."[196]

The first climbs that alerted the international alpine world to Yugoslavian alpinists were the 1972 and 1975 Makalu South Face expeditions. That they came so close in 1972, as complete unknowns, spoke of their strong skills, their dogged determination and the inspired leadership of Aleš Kunaver. That they would succeed in 1975 was almost a foregone conclusion. Like Chris Bonington's Everest Southwest Face team, they had put in their time on the route. Ultimately, it was Šrauf and that unsung hero, Marjan Manfreda, who finished the job: Šrauf, with his staggering ambition and strength, and Marjan, with his profound determination and generosity. Marjan's oxygen-free ascent, completed with severely frostbitten feet, remains a point of honour in Slovenian climbing history.

The Yugoslavians' return to the Himalaya in 1979 to tackle the yet-unclimbed direct West Ridge of Everest was inspired and forward-thinking. Once again they had no intention of failing. Yet despite their research and preparation and mechanical support, they didn't know what to expect on the upper part of the mountain. Tom Hornbein and Willi Unsoeld had taken a good look at it in 1963 but had wisely traversed left and up the Hornbein Couloir. Again, it was left to that quiet man from Bohinjska Bela, Marjan Manfreda, to find the key to the ridge. And again he suffered for his efforts, losing several fingers, as well as sacrificing his chance for the summit. Nejc and Andrej finished the job, with more technical climbing and devious route-finding, all above eight thousand metres. The Everest West Ridge Direct climb was hailed by Messner as the most difficult route on Everest; however, outside Slovenia, it remains somewhat unheralded.

Šrauf's Dhaulagiri obsession made its South Face almost a Slovenian face. His 1981 route was a landmark, even if it didn't quite reach the top. Tomaž Humar's solo ascent in 1999 secured it as a Slovenian face. The fact that neither reached the summit confirmed the serious nature of that piece of vertical ground.

A similar story emerged on Lhotse's South Face. The 1981 attempt was far ahead of its time and came so near to success. What an effort. What a sacrifice. What a shame. Think of all the climbers whose lives might have been saved if they had succeeded. Instead, many more died seeking that prize, the first ascent of Lhotse's South Face. And how differently might Tomo Česen's life have turned out, had he not claimed it? He might have continued on with his Himalayan career, instead of stepping back after the Lhotse debacle.

Andrej Štremfelj and Marko Prezelj's new route on the South Summit of Kangchenjunga set a new standard, for which they won the inaugural Piolet d'Or. In fact, Slovenian climbers came to dominate the Piolet d'Or: many have been shortlisted for the prestigious prize, and several have won.

But not all of the great Slovenian climbs won prizes. Although it predated the Piolet, Janez Jeglič and Silvo Karo's Bhagirathi III ascent in 1990 garnered little attention in Slovenia, despite its difficulty and the fine style in which they did it. Perhaps this was because Tomo's Lhotse claim dominated conversations in climbing circles that year. The first ascent of Melungtse by Marko and Andrej was well received, yet it didn't win them any golden ice axes, either. Many agree that Tomaž and Janez's Nuptse climb was possibly the best climb of their too-short lives; however, it also won no prizes. Even more were shocked when Tomaž's Dhaulagiri solo didn't garner a Piolet nod. Marko's K7 West climb with his American partners, Steve House and Vince Anderson, was a technically brilliant achievement, but it didn't win the golden ice axe. Defining success and choosing winners in the mountains is a tricky task, one that is ultimately subjective, even for a Piolet jury.

Defining the golden age of Slovenian climbing is also a difficult job. Younger climbers point to the mid-1970s and early 1980s. The older generation of alpinists, who were the architects of those earlier ascents, refer instead to the late 1980s and early 1990s. Most agree that the generation of climbers in the 1980s were unmatched. Their physical abilities, psychological focus, motivation and training, combined with a relatively easy economic reality – thanks to socialism – produced a cadre of superstars. Franček Knez led the pack, but he wasn't alone. Silvo Karo, Janez Jeglič, Pavel Podgornik, Tomo Česen and Slavko Svetičič, are names that resounded around the world of elite mountaineers, from the Slovenian alpine faces to Patagonia and the Himalaya. Together with slightly older and extremely experienced expedition climbers like Andrej Štremfelj, Šrauf, Marjan Manfreda, Viki Grošelj, Filip Bence, Croatian Stipe Božić and several

others, Slovenian alpinists were considered the best in the world. The
cost, as is the case for most golden eras of climbing – British, Polish
and Russian – was tragically high. In his editorial comments for the
1997 *American Alpine Journal*, an edition dominated by Slovenian
reports, Christian Beckwith wrote:

> Unfortunately, their stunning successes – perhaps the most signifi-
> cant of the decade – have arrived hand-in-hand with high losses.
> Since the beginning of 1995, six of their finest alpinists have died in
> the mountains: Slavko Svetičič, killed while attempting a solo ascent
> of Gasherbrum IV; Stane Belak [Šrauf] and Jasna Bratanic [sic], killed
> in an avalanche in the Julian Alps; Vanja Furlan (whose article on
> the first ascent of Ama Dablam's Northwest Face, perhaps the most
> impressive climb of the year, begins this volume), killed on a moderate
> route on the North Face of Velika Mojstrovka in his home mountains;
> Bojan Pockar [sic] and Ziga Petric [sic], who died while acclimatizing
> for an attempt on the unclimbed East Face of Jannu East.[197]

Christian added that, unlike the 1996 saga on Everest, "which did
nothing to push the physical or mental evolution of climbing, the
Slovenian climbing achievements are firmly rooted in the heart of
significant climbing."[198] True enough, although it probably did not
give much comfort to the surviving families and friends of those who
lost their lives gunning for the greatest alpine prizes, or to the next
generation of alpinists, for whom it was now unavoidably clear just
how dangerous alpine-style climbing on the highest summits was.
The golden age brought standards so high that the next generation
would need to be creative in order to push them higher. And, as Nejc
understood years before, they would need to accept even higher levels
of risk:

> I want the summit more and more badly. It's everything I am still
> living for...You read obituaries about how greedy for fame alpinists
> are. They are written by journalists in warm offices and by people
> who never take off their house slippers. It isn't because of glory. Ever
> since the world has been standing, they die because of an arduous
> desire to discover hidden forces inside them that will transport them
> above the boundaries that trap them in a quiet domestic life...This

desire keeps pushing you to experience danger and overcome it with your own mind and your own hands. In that moment, with your head held high, you dare to look danger in the face.[199]

Where are the survivors of that golden age of alpinism? Some have taken on public personae, working with media to tell their alpine stories. Stipe can't walk down a street in Split without a dozen strangers approaching him, asking for his autograph or simply greeting him with a broad smile. Stipe is their Himalayan hero. Viki is also a public figure, immediately recognizable in Slovenia as an author and television personality. Both men have shared their mountain experiences with others through photography, writing, lectures and films.

Franček Knez, on the contrary, has become even more reclusive in recent years. He lives with his family and still possesses neither a car nor a driver's licence. Even after over five thousand climbs, more than eight hundred of them first ascents, and surviving a broken back, he continues to put up new routes in secret places. He has never sought media attention and refuses to promote himself. Instead, this quiet, modest man, dubbed the guru of modern climbing in Slovenia, has held a regular factory job while carrying out his unbelievable array of climbs. How did he get to those thousands of climbs? Hitchhiking or taking buses. When his memoir, *Ožarjeni Kamen*, was launched at the mountain film festival in Ljubljana a few years back, hundreds showed up to see him. The only one missing was Franček. He is currently working on another book; it has little to do with climbing but rather centres on his unique approach to life. And when he's not climbing or writing, he carves exquisite sculptures in wood.

Franček's frequent partner, Silvo Karo, still climbs, most often on the cliffs of Osp, where he operates a climbing hostel. In his spare time he directs an internationally acclaimed mountain film festival. Silvo has countless stories to tell about his almost two thousand climbs, his 170 first ascents and his 24 expeditions. He insists that he's writing his memoir. We are waiting.

Marjan Manfreda has no interest in publicity. He lives in Bohinjska Bela, his idyllic home village perched on a hillside at the base of a limestone playground. He hasn't moved far from his youth:

his home is adjacent to the one in which he grew up, and his mother still lives next door. He married twice, but neither marriage lasted, in large part due to his climbing obsession, he freely admits. He became a mountain guide, more for personal than professional reasons. For Marjan, climbing has always represented pure happiness. It is the complete package that attracts him: time spent in nature, the physicality of climbing, and performing to his absolute limit. He never aspired to be a support climber. He was focused on top performance and summits.

Which is what makes his Everest experience so cruel.

In 2005 he returned to Nepal with a group of Slovenian climbers. First, he soloed Ama Dablam on a beautiful, calm day. "It was one of my most beautiful pleasures in the Himalaya," he recalled. But Ama Dablam was just a distraction. After the climb he walked to Kala Patthar at the base of Everest. "I went alone, just to have a look at the mountain that had defeated me and that had been obsessing me all those years," he said. "It was foggy…A little before sunset the fog lifted momentarily, and for a few moments, there it was in all its splendour. It was a meditative moment for me and I finally found my peace with Everest after 26 years." He became that place and it became him.

As Marjan sat there, a young man arrived and began playing the didgeridoo. "The sound and that view will always remain with me as a moment of peace."

Nejc understood that state of grace and wrote in *Pot*: "If I were a poet I would be struck speechless upon entering this unearthly landscape. I would lay myself down in the shadow of the blossoming snow-white rhododendron and remain silent forever. Such beauty makes poetry, however lofty, seem ridiculously inadequate. Words fade into emptiness…You can't even attempt to express it, because you have become completely aware that true beauty can only be given and felt. It cannot be described."[200]

Although the beauty and grandeur of the Himalaya are but a distant memory for Marjan, he still needs adrenalin. He is lean, muscled and intense. He climbs, often solo, and rides his motorcycle with a vengeance. To satisfy his creative side, he has taken up woodcarving. He also wrote a book, *Ledono Sonce*, which he admits was ridiculously hard to do. A grandfather five times over, he lives alone. "I like to be alone," he says, lounging in a hammock on his wooden deck overlooking the valley. "I am not lonely," he clarified. "I am alone." He speaks with the voice of someone who knows what he has done and who is at peace with himself.

Tone Škarja, leader of so many expeditions, is retired from his duties with the Alpine Association but still appears at the office from time to time and remains interested in the younger climbers. He goes to the mountains whenever he can, but he enjoys a more relaxed pace than he once did.

Tomo Česen didn't lose touch with climbing, either, despite his exit from the Himalayan scene. In 1995 he began coaching competitive sport climbers and organizing international climbing competitions. Many of Slovenia's finest sport climbers count him as their coach, including Martina Čufar, who was World Champion in 2001. He next took over as president of the Technical Commission for the Alpine Association. His work is now connected with the world of professional guiding and has given him an entirely new perspective on the mountains. "Climbing isn't the only important thing – even for the climbers. When you are totally in it, maybe yes, but...twenty years later you see differently and more objectively...When I look back now I see that sometimes I did really crazy things, dangerous things that were not fair toward the family." He admitted to a certain level of self-absorption. "Climbers are kind of egoists," he said, adding the simple fact: "You have a family – if you are not an egoist you will stay with them." Tomo still lives in the same house where he has lived since the age of 7, together with his wife and mother.

Andrej and Marija Štremfelj couldn't possibly stuff one more activity into their life. Their home overflows with children and grandchildren; the climbing cave downstairs is full of neighbourhood kids; the kitchen table is surrounded by people and conversation; the garden is buzzing with bees, tended by Andrej's father; and patrolling the entire affair is their large German shepherd. The energy that Andrej remembered from Nejc seems to have been absorbed by osmosis into Andrej's super-active body. Despite several serious injuries, Andrej continues to climb. Despite a full-time teaching job, plus guiding throughout the Alps, often with his wife, Marija, Andrej continues to climb. Despite caring for their children and grandchildren, all of whom live nearby, Andrej continues to climb. Despite giving lectures and acting as a jury member for the Piolet d'Or and being active in his church, Andrej continues to climb. If there is one hour left in the day – a possibility for one more route – Andrej will climb. He loves climbing. He is a passionate advocate for the sport, and his face lights up at the mere possibility of going climbing.

He must have read Nejc's words about stuffing life to the brim:

> And this is how alpinism became my life. It doesn't lead anywhere but back to the beginning, and I have learned that a moment, once experienced, becomes history, shuttered and locked, because in front of me there is a bright new shiny little pebble...But I regret every moment that was unproductive or empty. I am used to training like a madman, climbing, running from one end to the other, ironing, washing laundry, washing my dishes, cooking, telling fairy tales, teaching and learning, reading, writing all night long. I know that after a few hours of sleep I can open my eyes and continue the endless work. Even so, I'm sorry for every empty minute...And at the end, I turn a page and, together with Edith Piaf, sing *"Je ne regrette rien."* That was my anthem.[201]

There are times when Andrej misses those intense Himalayan climbs where he laid everything on the line. "I miss that deeper sea of emotions," he reflected. "After some years away, the infinity of the Himalaya seems frighteningly sweet, the charm of the thin air almost dangerous, reminding me of the lure of that narrow border between life and death." But Andrej is also a practical man whose final thoughts are more spiritual. "I'm happy to have survived and to have a chance to think about another Himalaya and behind the sea: and which shall only come...once."[202]

A positive man, his only pessimism is about politics. Andrej is convinced that little has changed in the corridors of power, despite Slovenia's democratic status. He avers that the wrappings of power may change, the names of the parties may change, but the people in power keep getting recycled. Tomo Česen agrees. "I remember when we became independent, I was quite optimistic. But now after 20 years I can say that it's total shit." He added, "I see that all the governments – right, left or in the middle – take care of power for themselves. It doesn't matter who is on top at any given moment."

After years of employment by the army, Marko Prezelj is now a freelancer. He lives with his wife and two sons in a sleek modern house he designed, perched on a terrace overlooking the Mengeško Polje – the fields around Mengeš. Marko runs, cycles, rock climbs, ice climbs and whatever else is required to stay in top shape, as he now climbs with the young guns of the Slovenian alpine scene. The leadership torch once carried by Aleš Kunaver and Tone Škarja has been passed on again – this time to Marko. Adopting a leadership style that differs from that of his predecessors, he advises the young alpinists about equipment, training and objective danger, and about how to organize expeditions and navigate the labyrinthine channels of mountaineering bureaucracy.

Marko's work is cut out for him, because the young Slovenian climbers are some of the finest alpinists on the planet. Marko's reputation as a hard man has not faded. Nor have his standards. "It's not easy to live up to my standards," he admits. "I'm the first one to look down on my own work. 'Perfectionist' is also a label that people give me. 'Elitist' is next, and 'intolerant' is the last one. I am all three," he says, laughing. But he appears to have softened his contempt for the Piolet d'Or; in the spring of 2015 he returned to Chamonix with two young Slovenian climbers, Aleš Česen and Luka Lindič, to accept the prize for the third time.

As passionate as he is about alpinism, there is something that tops this obsession. When Marko begins talking about Tim, his firstborn and a natural scientist, and Bor, his second son and a musician, his smile grows so wide his face splits in two.

◆ ◆ ◆

What of the families of those men and women who reached too high, for challenge, for inspiration, for greatness? Whose ambitions outstripped their capabilities? Who were struck down in their prime? Who never grew old and wrinkled and fat?

Dušica Kunaver is a loving caretaker of her husband's memory and the entire generation of climbers that he led. She understands their place in history and is determined to nurture their legacy so that the world will not forget. Vlasta Kunaver, their daughter and a fine alpinist and paraglider, celebrated that first expedition to Trisul back in 1960 by flying off the summit in 1987. Vlasta has nothing but respect for her father and for the climbers who frequented their home, but she cautioned against placing halos on their heads. "They were climbers, not saints," she said with a knowing smile.

Jožica Belak, Šrauf's widow, is the picture of quiet strength. A compact, straight-shooting woman, Jožica inherited an unfinished house, young children, money issues and emotional turmoil when her husband was killed in the avalanche beneath Mala Mojstrovka. She had been his climbing partner and life partner, and then he was gone. She gathered support from the climbing community, their mutual friends and the government, which provided her with a pension. She never remarried, and she dwells not on the past but rather on her children and her garden. Life goes on for Jožica.

For Irena Jeglič, life continues as well, albeit in a different manner. She remarried, rebuilt and refocused. Her children, the church and a non-climbing husband became her life, and although Janez remains an important chapter, he was exactly that. She remains close to the climbing community, but she has moved beyond it.

Sergeja Humar was no longer married to Tomaž when he died on Langtang Lirung in 2009. But she is the mother of their children and so remains tied to his memory. "Urša and Tomaž are grown up now. They are wonderful and smart kids," she says, adding, "Tomaž would be proud." She eventually moved back to the family home where she and Tomaž had created a space for their family in the country, near the Kamnik mountains they loved.

When Nejc Zaplotnik died in 1983, smothered by an avalanche on Manaslu, his wife, Mojca, was just 29 years old, with three young boys, Nejc, Luka and Jaka. Only 10 years old at the time, Luka retains sharp memories of those years: the barrels of equipment, the house full of climbers, and his father telling stories. "I remember my mom and dad spending hours and hours in the evening talking to each other," he recalled. "They would close the glass doors, and we could see them talking together and smoking, the smoke swirling around them so that we could hardly see them. He always smoked." In contrast to Šrauf's more chaotic existence, Luka remembers an orderly home life, punctuated with barrels. The barrels represented expeditions, and expeditioning is what his father did. Luka saw it as normal.

When the news first came back from Manaslu, the family was ripped apart by grief and stress. But life soon assumed a familiar pattern for Luka, because even when he was alive, Nejc had been absent for at least a few months each year. "I think that very soon it began to be normal to be without a father," he admitted.

Then the second tragedy hit.

"Actually when we look back, the signs were there for a long time but we didn't see them," Luka explained, speaking of his brother Jaka. "He was more philosophical, like my father. And he was smart. But it was as if he was absent, lazy, sitting beside you but being somewhere else. After we found out, he was sent to the hospital for two weeks...but after he left the hospital, I think he stopped taking his medication. And he shouldn't have." Jaka had been diagnosed with schizophrenia. He hated his medication; it made him lethargic. Yet when he refused to take the pills, he heard voices and experienced terrifying hallucinations. "Then he jumped off the bridge," Luka said, looking up with pain in his eyes. Jaka Zaplotnik died on February 6, 2006. First Nejc, and then Jaka. "My mother is very strong, but I would say that she barely made it," Luka said. "In a year she was ten years older."

It's impossible to ignore the similarities between Jaka and some of Nejc's writing in his unfinished book *Peter Simsen* (the surname is the Slovenian word for "meaninglessness" spelled backward). This poetic, impassioned piece of writing, which he was working on at Manaslu base camp, is more than a simple linear narrative; it's a self-portrait, as well as a personal manifesto. The main character, alternately a teacher and a student, is clearly Nejc's alter ego and even looks like him, with a large-boned, wide face and a toothy smile. He is a traveller without a cause, a person who feels called by an inner voice that occasionally turns into a scream.

Mojca is content with her new life, but she never forgets those difficult early years after Nejc's death and his gift that helped ease the way. He had dedicated *Pot* to her: "Dedicated to my best friend in the world, my wife Mojca." "It was always reprinted when we most needed the money," Mojca smiled. "In this way Nejc still lives...This small little booklet...is still living. People read it, and this is the most important thing. It is written exactly as we have in fact lived."

From *Pot*:

> I no longer felt like an alpinist when I was among alpinists, although I still adored the walls and the abysses and still prepared my body and mind for extreme effort. Climbing in itself was no longer important; once a wall was behind me . . . all that was left was the satisfaction and joy at remaining young and open-minded, at growing younger still, at becoming a child. At remaining trusting, although I had been robbed countless times. At still believing, although I had been lied to a thousand times. I forgot to count the hours and the metres and the points. I even forgot to count the days and the years. Time disappeared.[203]

The modern Slovenian climber has plenty to ponder. Some of it is baggage, some of it legacy, and much of it expectation. "Our climbing community knows everything about each other," says Tomo Česen. "And we know things that nobody knows and we know things that we don't want to talk about." The community is a microcosm of the larger Slovenian population, mired in history, some of it violent and sad. The weight of that legacy is serious: Slovenia vies for the top suicide rate in Europe. Political infighting permeates not only alpinism but all aspects of Slovenian public life, from academia to the economy and the arts.

Even though the mountains symbolize the very essence of Slovenians, they are not powerful enough to truly unite. The country is dominated by steep mountains and narrow valleys. Deep feelings of loyalty to valley, church, clan and village persist. Such loyalties sometimes preclude open-mindedness and co-operation, acceptance of "other" ways of operating. There is an insular feeling among the climbing community that is surprising, considering its visionary beginnings and stellar performances. When alpinists are confronted with the fact that most outsiders know little about Slovenian climbing history, the response is often: "Who cares! It's their problem." When faced with the prospect of their story being told, many climbers react with distrust, bringing up old grudges in the hope of avenging them. They suspect both the lies of the famous and the excuses of the undiscovered. Most of all, they doubt the memories of the survivors: memories that are embellished, adjusted and edited.

Contemporary Slovenian climbers still receive some government support, although nothing like in the old days. The point system also continues to exist, allowing top climbers to be paid to climb and teach with the army and police. But young alpinists have challenges their predecessors were only starting to face. The extreme difficulties of modern climbing objectives in the great ranges require them to train like athletes. Training takes time, self-discipline, coaching, mental preparation, dietary considerations and science. The world is different now from how it was when Nejc began climbing:

> When Tone and I climbed [Čop's Pillar] we had no equipment, just a few carabiners, some pegs and some additional ropes that we used to make aiders...My shoes were so torn that in the scree under Luknja, the sand was passing in and out around the sole...Only two nails held the sole to the shoe but we didn't care. We never felt the lack of equipment. As long as we could climb we were happy...We were filled with enthusiasm. We were thrilled with life, and the strength that was hiding within us...Sure, sometimes at the top of the face we had cramps in our hands, but so what? In a few days they would be rested and then we could do another route. How wonderful to be young and not be hindered on your path by these petty obstacles that, for an older person, seem insurmountable. And how much more wonderful if you can stay like that for your entire life?[204]

Despite these challenges, Slovenian alpinists today profit from an outstanding climbing heritage. The legacy and standards of Aleš Kunaver's generation are inspirational. They sprang from both team effort and individual performance.

Nejc inspired not only with his climbs but also by nudging climbers to recognize the deeper meaning of their own experiences in the mountains, something they found difficult to articulate. In a way, he did it for them.

Šrauf's strong personality made him a role model, a teacher and a generator of ideas. He was a natural leader, and his restless spirit and stubbornness shattered the limits of possibility. His ambition was balanced by his desire to share his success with the people around him. Above all, Šrauf was a generous person. As Marko reflected, "To all of us who had the good fortune to play a role in one of his 'dramas,' he left a small bit of himself and his limitless energy. And how *great* were these days of living with him we cannot tell."[205]

Although Everest in 1979 was a huge team effort that functioned almost like an army offensive, success at the end depended on two individuals heading into the unknown. When Andrej and Nejc climbed past the last fixed line placed by Marjan, they put everything on the line for their team: their knowledge, their experience and their lives. "An individual without support from his team was worth nothing back then, just as an expedition without the work of its individuals could not reach its goal," Andrej recalled. "It was our way in those times. For me, Everest represented the best of that solidarity."[206]

That solidarity eventually ended. The ten-year period following Slovenian independence and the seismic shift in Slovenian alpinism was, with a few exceptions, thin on success. Some blamed Tomo and the Lhotse scandal; others blamed it on Tomaž's overt, public style. The reasons are probably less dramatic and impossible to pin on just two individuals. The economic reality of independence meant much less financial support for climbers. "We were in a kind of shock," Silvo said of that time. "We had more freedom, but much more responsibility than we were used to." Along with that freedom came growing personal ambition. "The best climbers outshone their clubs," Andrej explained. "It was like one man – one band," Silvo added. The power and influence of the Alpine Association waned as the internal arguments festered and individuals went their own way.

That may be changing. Young Slovenian climbers are rebuilding their community, guided by a few from the golden age who provide a knowledge bridge. These youngsters are talented. Their challenge will be to absorb the wisdom of their elders, yet discard the baggage. But they are also part of a larger community, a global community of high-altitude performers who are bound together by their love of soaring mountains, difficult objectives, similar values – and the Internet.

Like Aleš and Marjan and the others who braved the South Face of Makalu when no one else on Earth could imagine it, the next wave of Slovenian climbers have new boundaries to shatter. Like those early alpine warriors, today's climbers can create masterpieces of their lives. Like Nejc, they can discover the wonder of wild places, feel the power of sheer rock walls and shimmering blue ice, surrender to the seduction of climbing up toward the sky, embrace the wildness within themselves, and treasure the gift of friendship in the mountains:

> How beautiful the world is when you have had to make a real effort to experience this beauty. Alpinism is like art. You put all your strength, your entire soul into your work. You forget everything. You only live for that metre ahead of you, and when you stand, exhausted, on the top of a snowy mountain and bask in the warmth of the sun, you feel beauty within you that cannot be described. You feel the world. You feel the earth, the sun, the wind; everything breathes with you and intoxicates you. The friend with you keeps silent. Only his eyes glow above his sunken cheeks. And without asking him, you know that he has exactly the same experience. That he is living life itself.[207]

Like Nejc, they must be prepared for the loneliness of the alpinist's way. "I am sentenced to freedom, so free that, among the crowd of people who love me, as well as those who don't care for me, I continue to be alone. Alone with my wishes, dreams, desires; alone on my endless path."[208] And like Nejc, they must be prepared to live, like cranes in a storm. "The terrifying will to live, like life itself, without questions and without answers."[209]

ACKNOWLEDGEMENTS

The seeds of this book were planted seven years ago when I was in Slovenia doing research on the biography of Tomaž Humar. As I listened to Slovenian climbers, I became increasingly amazed at the depth and richness of their community. And I was equally astonished at how few of these stories and alpinists were known outside Slovenia. Of course, there were the international stars like Tomo Česen, Marko Prezelj, Silvo Karo and Andrej Štremfelj, well-respected climbers who had profiles outside their country. But there were so many others with remarkable climbs and inspiring lives who were virtual unknowns.

Apart from extensive interviews and email conversations with the climbers and their families, one of the greatest resources for my research was the body of climbing literature published in Slovenian and Serbo-Croatian. I am hopeless in both languages. Thanks to Jona Senk and Eva Antonijevic for translation assistance early in the project, and to the tireless efforts of Mimi Marinsek, who spent the better part of a summer with me on Skype, translating aloud to me hour after hour. I could not have written this book without Mimi.

But face-to-face conversations are critical, and I thank everyone who took time from their busy lives to talk to me: sometimes on a hike; often while climbing; hundreds of hours at kitchen tables, occasionally with a glass of wine. Many thanks to Jožica Belak, Stipe Božić, Tomo Česen, Tina Di Batista, Urban Golob, Viki Grošelj, Sergeja Humar, Irena Jeglič, Mirjam Jeglič, Silvo Karo, Franček Knez, Dušica Kunaver, Vlasta Kunaver, Marjan Manfreda, Zdenka Mihelič, Marko Prezelj, Tone Škarja, Ines Skok, Janez Skok, Andrej Štremfelj, Marija Štremfelj and Luka Zaplotnik. Many others provided quotes and opinions on this period of history, for which I am grateful: Barry Blanchard, Carlos Carsolio, Rolando Garibotti, Steve House, Rodolphe Popier and Steve Swenson.

Thanks to the Alpine Association of Slovenia and Zdenka Mihelič for their great co-operation and assistance, and for allowing me to reference their official catalogue of important Slovenian climbs. I was helped enormously by The Himalayan Database: The Expedition Archives of Elizabeth Hawley; and 8000ers.com, Eberhard Jurgalski's brainchild and labour of love. Thanks, as well, to Lindsay Griffin for scouring the manuscript for errors. But probably the greatest thanks for his meticulous research goes to Bob A. Schelfhout Aubertijn, whose knowledge of Himalayan climbing history and passion for detail is second to none.

Many wonderful photos were put at my disposal. Special thanks go to Dušica Kunaver, who provided digital images of hundreds of important historical photos. Many more were generous, as well: Jožica Belak and the Belak collection, Stipe Božić, Urban Golob, Viki Grošelj, Tomaž Humar Junior, Irena Jeglič, Silvo Karo, Tone Škarja, Janez Skok, Raphael Slawinski, Andrej Štremfelj, and Luka Zaplotnik and the Zaplotnik collection. Thanks to you all.

I appreciate all the feedback I received on this manuscript, both officially and unofficially. Early critical reads came from Karolina Born, Cécile Lafleur, Voytek Kurtyka and Bob A. Schelfhout Aubertijn. I was fortunate to have access to the great editing skills of Marni Jackson and Jennifer Glossop. And to Don Gorman and his team at Rocky Mountain Books – Chyla Cardinal, Frances Hunter, Meaghan Craven, Rick Wood and Joe Wilderson – thank you so much for believing in and supporting this project.

I would be remiss if I did not clarify that this is not a definitive history of Yugoslavian or Slovenian climbing. That story is much bigger than the 90,000 words allowed in this volume. Many significant ascents and important Slovenian, Croatian and Bosnian alpinists are not included. I apologize to any who might feel ignored and thank you all for allowing me into your world and sharing your stories.

Thank you to my husband, Alan, who patiently stood by while I disappeared into the world of expeditions, Slovenian mountain myths and Balkan wars.

And finally, thank you, Nejc Zaplotnik, for your inspiring words, which were my partner and guide on this journey.

NOTES

INTRODUCTION

1 Nejc Zaplotnik, *Pot*, trans. Mimi Marinsek (Ljubljana, Slovenia: Libricon, 2009). Author's Note: All quotations from Slovenian and Croatian publications are referenced, but because the English versions presented here are oral translations (performed by Mimi Marinsek on Skype) and have not been published, I do not provide page references.

2 Ibid.

3 Ibid.

ONE: *DARE TO DREAM*

4 Nejc Zaplotnik, *Pot*, trans. Mimi Marinsek (Ljubljana, Slovenia: Libricon, 2009).

5 Ibid.

6 Aleš Kunaver and Friends, *Trisul: Varuh Boginje*, trans. Mimi Marinsek (Ljubljana, Slovenia: Dušica Kunaver, 2006).

7 Ibid.

TWO: *TRIGLAV IN WINTER*

8 Stane Belak, *Veliki dnevi*, trans. Mimi Marinsek (Ljubljana, Slovenia: SIDARTA, 1997).

9 Ibid.

10 Ibid.

THREE: *A LESSON IN PATIENCE*

11 Nejc Zaplotnik, *Pot*, trans. Mimi Marinsek (Ljubljana, Slovenia: Libricon, 2009).

12 Urban Golob and Peter Mikša, *Zgodovina Slovenskega Alpinisma*, trans. Mimi Marinsek (Ljubljana, Slovenia: FRIKO, 2013).

13 Aleš Kunaver and Friends, *Makalu*, trans. Mimi Marinsek (Ljubljana, Slovenia: Dušica Kunaver, 2006).

14 Ibid.

15 Ibid.

16 Ibid.

17 Ibid.

18 Zaplotnik, *Pot*.

19 Ibid.

20 Ibid.

21 Ibid.

22 Ibid.

23 Ibid.

24 Ibid.

25 Ibid.

26 Ibid.

27 Ibid.

28 Ibid.

29 Ibid.

30 Ibid.

31 Ibid.

32 Ibid.

33 Ibid.

34 Ibid.

FOUR: *FRIENDS LIKE THESE*

35 Aleš Kunaver and Friends, *Makalu*, trans. Mimi Marinsek (Ljubljana, Slovenia: Dušica Kunaver, 2006).

36 Ibid.

37 Ibid.

38 Ibid.

39 Stane Belak, *Veliki dnevi*, trans. Mimi Marinsek (Ljubljana, Slovenia: SIDARTA, 1997).

40 Ibid.

41 Kunaver and Friends, *Makalu*.

42 Belak, *Veliki dnevi*.

43 Kunaver and Friends, *Makalu*.

44 Ibid.

45 Ibid.

46 Belak, *Veliki dnevi*.

47 Ibid.

48 Kunaver and Friends, *Makalu*.

49 Ibid.

50 Ibid.

51 Ibid.

52 Dušica Kunaver, *Aleš Kunaver*, trans. Mimi Marinsek (Maribor, Slovenia: Založba Obzorja Maribor, 1988).

53 Nejc Zaplotnik, *Pot*, trans. Mimi Marinsek (Ljubljana, Slovenia: Libricon, 2009).

FIVE: *THE FIRST CASUALTY*

54 Nejc Zaplotnik, *Pot*, trans. Mimi Marinsek (Ljubljana, Slovenia: Libricon, 2009).

55 Ibid.

56 Ibid.

57 Ibid.

58 Ibid.

59 Ibid.

60 Ibid.

61 Ibid.

62 Ibid.

63 Ibid.

SIX: *EVEREST WEST RIDGE*

64 Nejc Zaplotnik, *Pot*, trans. Mimi Marinsek (Ljubljana, Slovenia: Libricon, 2009).

65 Tone Škarja, *Po Svoji Sledi*, trans. Mimi Marinsek (Ljubljana, Slovenia: Planinska zveza Slovenije, 2011).

66 Zaplotnik, *Pot*.

67 Ibid.

68 Ibid.

69 Ibid.

70 Ibid.

71 The UIAA grading system was originally intended to begin at I (easiest) and finish at VI (hardest), and for many years VI was the grade that described the most difficult routes. Eventually a + was added to VI to differentiate the level of difficulty, but improvements in climbing standards have now led to the system being open-ended.

72 Zaplotnik, *Pot*.

73 Ibid.

74 Ibid.

75 The unreferenced dialogue between Andrej and Nejc in this chapter comes from my interview with Andrej Štremfelj.

76 Zaplotnik, *Pot*.

77 Ibid.

78 Ibid.

79 I queried Andrej several times about the level of difficulty in the chimney and the rock

steps along the ridge; the answers kept getting easier: "Maybe French 6a...I'm sure it wasn't harder than 5c."

80 Zaplotnik, *Pot*.

81 Ibid.

82 Stane Belak, *Veliki dnevi*, trans. Mimi Marinsek (Ljubljana, Slovenia: SIDARTA, 1997).

83 Zaplotnik, *Pot*.

84 Belak, *Veliki dnevi*.

85 Ibid.

86 Franček Knez, *Ožarjeni Kamen*, trans. Mimi Marinsek (Ljubljana, Slovenia: Založba Sanje d.o.o., 2009).

87 Ibid.

88 Škarja, *Po Svoji Sledi*.

89 Zaplotnik, *Pot*.

90 Laura Silber and Allan Little, *The Death of Yugoslavia* (London: Penguin Books, 1995).

SEVEN: *THE GREATEST PRIZE*

91 Franček Knez, *Ožarjeni Kamen*, trans. Mimi Marinsek (Ljubljana, Slovenia: Založba Sanje d.o.o., 2009).

92 Ibid.

93 Ibid.

94 Aleš Kunaver and Friends, *Lhotse: Južna Stena*, trans. Mimi Marinsek (Ljubljana, Slovenia: Dušica Kunaver, 2008.

95 Ibid.

96 Ibid.

97 Ibid.

98 Ibid.

99 Ibid.

100 Ibid.

101 Ibid.

102 Ibid.

103 Ibid.

104 Knez, *Ožarjeni Kamen*.

105 Kunaver and Friends, *Lhotse*.

106 Ibid.

107 Ibid.

108 Knez, *Ožarjeni Kamen*.

109 Kunaver and Friends, *Lhotse*.

110 Knez, *Ožarjeni Kamen*.

111 Kunaver and Friends, *Lhotse*.

EIGHT: *DHAULAGIRI OBSESSION*

112 Nejc Zaplotnik, *Pot*, trans. Mimi Marinsek (Ljubljana, Slovenia: Libricon, 2009).

113 Stane Belak, *Veliki dnevi*, trans. Mimi Marinsek (Ljubljana, Slovenia: SIDARTA, 1997).

114 Ibid.

115 Ibid.

116 Ibid.

117 Zaplotnik, *Pot*.

NINE: *FALLEN STARS*

118 Nejc Zaplotnik, *Pot*, trans. Mimi Marinsek (Ljubljana, Slovenia: Libricon, 2009).

119 Ibid.

120 Viki Grošelj, *Velikani Himalaje*, trans. Mimi Marinsek (Ljubljana, Slovenia: Planinska zveza Sloveniji, 2013).

121 Dušica Kunaver, *Aleš Kunaver*,

trans. Mimi Marinsek (Maribor, Slovenia: Založba Obzorja Maribor, 1988).

122 Grošelj, *Velikani Himalaje.*

123 Nejc Zaplotnik, *Pot,*

124 Dušica Kunaver, *Aleš Kunaver.*

TEN: *THE LONER*

125 Nicholas O'Connell, *Beyond Risk* (Seattle: The Mountaineers, 1993), 289.

126 Ibid., 290.

127 Franček Knez, *Ožarjeni Kamen,* trans. Mimi Marinsek (Ljubljana, Slovenia: Založba Sanje d.o.o., 2009),

128 Viki Grošelj, *Velikani Himalaje,* trans. Mimi Marinsek (Ljubljana, Slovenia: Planinska zveza Sloveniji, 2013).

ELEVEN: *NEXT WAVE*

129 Nejc Zaplotnik, *Pot,* trans. Mimi Marinsek (Ljubljana, Slovenia: Libricon, 2009).

130 Ibid.

131 Quoted in John Corsellis and Marcus Ferrar, *Slovenia 1945: Memories of Death and Survival after World War II* (London: I.B. Tauris, 2010). Corsellis and Ferrar note: "Quoted by Drago Jančar in *The Dark Side of the Moon,* (English version), kataložni zapis o publikaciji, Narodna in univerzitetna knjižnica, Ljubljana, 1988."

TWELVE: *SEISMIC SHIFT*

132 Mark Twight, *Kiss or Kill* (Seattle: The Mountaineers Books, 2001), 65.

133 Tomo Česen, "Kumbhakarna – My Way," *American Alpine Journal* 32, no. 64 (1990): 8.

134 Ibid., 12.

135 Ibid., 13.

136 Tomo Česen, "A Look into the Future: Lhotse's South Face," *American Alpine Journal* 33, no. 65 (1991): 8.

137 Ibid, 5.

138 Ibid.

139 The photo is included in the third photo section of this volume. *Vertical* 28 (July/August 1990): 58–65.

140 Tone Škarja, *Po Svoji Sledi,* trans. Mimi Marinsek (Ljubljana, Slovenia: Planinska zveza Slovenije, 2011).

141 Ibid.

142 Greg Child, *Postcards from the Ledge* (Seattle: The Mountaineers Books, 1998), 164.

143 Škarja, *Po Svoji Sledi.*

144 Ibid.

145 Ibid.

146 Nejc Zaplotnik, *Pot,* trans. Mimi Marinsek (Ljubljana, Slovenia: Libricon, 2009).

147 Ibid.

THIRTEEN: *A MOST BEAUTIFUL SUMMIT*

148 Marko Prezelj and Tone Škarja, "Slovene Kangchenjunga Expedition," *American Alpine Journal* 34, no.

66 (1992): 8.

149 Ibid.

150 Ibid.

151 Ibid., 7.

152 Andrej Štremfelj, "1979: Everest West Ridge Direct," *Alpinist* 27 (2009): 38.

153 Nejc Zaplotnik, *Pot*, trans. Mimi Marinsek (Ljubljana, Slovenia: Libricon, 2009).

154 Ibid.

155 See http://www.markoprezelj.com/.

156 Urban Golob and Peter Mikša, *Zgodovina Slovenskega Alpinisma* (Ljubljana, Slovenia: FRIKO, 2013).

FOURTEEN: *THREE MUSKETEERS*

157 Franček Knez, *Ožarjeni Kamen*, trans. Mimi Marinsek (Ljubljana, Slovenia: Založba Sanje d.o.o., 2009).

158 Ibid.

159 Ibid.

160 Ibid.

161 Nejc Zaplotnik, *Pot*, trans. Mimi Marinsek (Ljubljana, Slovenia: Libricon, 2009).

162 Knez, *Ožarjeni Kamen*.

163 Ibid.

164 Zaplotnik, *Pot*

165 Knez, *Ožarjeni Kamen*.

166 Silvo Karo, "Bhagirathi III," *American Alpine Journal* 33, no. 65 (1991): 45.

167 Zaplotnik, *Pot*.

FIFTEEN: *FLYING SOLO*

168 Nejc Zaplotnik, *Pot*, trans.

Mimi Marinsek (Ljubljana, Slovenia: Libricon, 2009).

169 Ibid.

170 Bernadette McDonald, *Tomaž Humar* (London: Hutchinson, 2008), 60.

171 Zaplotnik, *Pot*.

SIXTEEN: *WAR AND SUFFERING*

172 Rezak Hukanović, *The Tenth Circle of Hell* (Oslo: Sypress Forlag, 1993), 49.

173 Bernadette McDonald, *Tomaž Humar* (London: Hutchinson, 2008), 109.

174 Nejc Zaplotnik, *Pot*, trans. Mimi Marinsek (Ljubljana, Slovenia: Libricon, 2009).

SEVENTEEN: *DHAULAGIRI REAL-TIME*

175 Bernadette McDonald, *Tomaž Humar* (London: Hutchinson, 2008), 139.

176 Ibid., 149.

177 M ratings refer to mixed-ice climbing grades, with M7+ representing extreme difficulty. 5.9 is a North American rock climbing grade that is moderate at sea level but not so at this elevation.

178 McDonald, *Tomaž Humar*, 142.

179 Nejc Zaplotnik, *Pot*, trans. Mimi Marinsek (Ljubljana, Slovenia: Libricon, 2009).

180 McDonald, *Tomaž Humar*, 144.

181 Ibid., 146.

182 Ibid., 149.

183 Zaplotnik, *Pot.*

EIGHTEEN: *CANADIAN ADVENTURE*

184 Steve House, *Beyond the Mountain* (Ventura, Calif.: Patagonia Books, 2009), 200.

185 Ibid., 34.

186 Henry L. Abrons, "Northwest Ridge of North Twin," *American Alpine Journal* 15, no. 40 (1966): 30.

187 House, *Beyond the Mountain*, 207.

188 Nejc Zaplotnik, *Pot*, trans. Mimi Marinsek (Ljubljana, Slovenia: Libricon, 2009).

NINETEEN: *DEATH IN THE MOUNTAINS*

189 Nejc Zaplotnik, *Pot*, trans. Mimi Marinsek (Ljubljana, Slovenia: Libricon, 2009).

190 Ibid.

191 Ibid.

192 Ibid.

193 Freddie Wilkinson, "A Short Climb with Ueli Steck," in *Rock, Paper, Fire: The Best of Mountain and Wilderness Writing*, edited by Marni Jackson and Tony Whittome (Banff, Alta.: Banff Centre Press, 2013), 231.

194 Rebecca West, *Black Lamb and Grey Falcon* (New York: Viking, 1941), 1102.

195 Lionel Terray, *Conquistadors of the Useless* (London: Baton Wicks, 2011), 104.

TWENTY: *LEGACY*

196 Reinhold Messner, *The Big Walls* (Seattle: The Mountaineers Books, 2001), 87.

197 Christian Beckwith, "Preface," *American Alpine Journal* 39, no. 71 (1997): 3.

198 Ibid.

199 Nejc Zaplotnik, *Pot*, trans. Mimi Marinsek (Ljubljana, Slovenia: Libricon, 2009).

200 Ibid.

201 Ibid.

202 Andrej Štremfelj, "1979: Everest West Ridge Direct," *Alpinist* 27 (Summer 2009): 38.

203 Zaplotnik, *Pot.*

204 Ibid.

205 Stane Belak, *Veliki dnevi*, trans. Mimi Marinsek (Ljubljana, Slovenia: SIDARTA, 1997).

206 Štremfelj, "1979: Everest West Ridge Direct," 38.

207 Zaplotnik, *Pot.*

208 Ibid.

209 Ibid.

SELECT BIBLIOGRAPHY AND SOURCES

Much of the quoted material in this book comes from my extensive interviews with Slovenian alpinists, their families, and others. Following is a selection of the most important written sources. As noted previously, translations by Mimi Marinsek are oral translations performed during our Skype sessions.

Abrons, Henry L. "Northwest Ridge of North Twin." *American Alpine Journal* 15, no. 40 (1966).

Ajlec, Kornelija, and Peter Mikša. *Slovensko Planinstvo / Slovene Mountaineering*. Translated by Mimi Marinsek. Ljubljana, Slovenia: Planinska zveza Slovenije, 2011.

Almond, Mark. *Europe's Backyard War*. London: William Heinemann, Ltd., 1994.

Andrić, Ivo. *The Bridge on the Drina*. Chicago: University of Chicago Press, 1977.

Beckwith, Christian. "Preface." *American Alpine Journal* 39, no. 71 (1997): 3.

Belak, Stane. *Veliki dnevi*. Translated by Mimi Marinsek. Ljubljana, Slovenia: SIDARTA, 1997.

Božić, Stipe. *Put Na Vrh Svijeta*. Translated by Mimi Marinsek. Split, Croatia: Slobodna Dalmacija, 1990.

———. *Sedam Urhova*. Translated by Mimi Marinsek. Zagreb, Croatia: Profil International, 2003.

———. *Himalaja*. Translated by Mimi Marinsek. Split, Croatia: Etnografski Muzej Split, 2013.

———. *K2 Trijumf I Tragedija*. Translated by Mimi Marinsek. Zagreb, Croatia: V.B.Z. d.o.o., 2014.

Česen, Tomo. "Kumbhakarna – My Way." *American Alpine Journal* 32, no. 64 (1990).

———. "A Look into the Future: Lhotse's South Face." *American Alpine Journal* 33, no. 65 (1991).

Child, Greg. *Postcards from the Ledge*. Seattle: The Mountaineers Books, 1998.

Corsellis, John, and Marcus Ferrar. *Slovenia 1945*. London: I.B. Tauris, 2010.

Čuvalo, Ante. *Croatia and the Croatians*. Zagreb, Croatia: Northern Tribune Publishing, 1991.

Davies, Norman. *Europe: A History*. London: The Bodley Head, 2014.

Debeljak, Erica Johnson. *Forbidden Bread*. Berkeley, Cal.: North Atlantic Books, 2009.

Donia, Robert J., and John V.A. Fine Jr. *Bosnia and Hercegovina: A Tradition Betrayed*. New York: Columbia University Press, 1994.

Drakulić, Slavenka. *Café Europa: Life after Communism.* New York: W.W. Norton & Company, 1996.

Galloway, Steven. *The Cellist of Sarajevo.* Toronto: Random House, 2009.

Golob, Urban, and Peter Mikša. *Zgodovina Slovenskega Alpinisma.* Translated by Mimi Marinsek. Ljubljana, Slovenia: FRIKO, 2013.

Grošelj, Viki. *Velikani Himalaje.* Translated by Mimi Marinsek. Ljubljana, Slovenia: Planinska zveza Sloveniji, 2013.

House, Steve. *Beyond the Mountain.* Ventura, Cal.: Patagonia Books, 2009.

Hukanović, Rezak. *The Tenth Circle of Hell.* Oslo: Sypress Forlag, 1993.

Humar, Tomaž. *No Impossible Ways.* Ljubljana, Slovenia: Mobitel d.d., 2001.

Karo, Silvo. "Bhagirathi III." *American Alpine Journal* 33, no. 65 (1991).

Knez, Franček. *Ožarjeni Kamen.* Translated by Mimi Marinsek. Ljubljana, Slovenia: Založba Sanje d.o.o., 2009.

Kozinc, Željko. *Nejca Zaplotnika na Himalaja.* Translated by Mimi Marinsek. Ljubljana, Slovenia: Kmečki glas, 1998.

Kranjc, Gregor Joseph. *To Walk with the Devil.* Toronto: University of Toronto Press, 2013.

Kunaver, Aleš. *Dežela Šerp 1962.* Translated by Mimi Marinsek. Ljubljana, Slovenia: Dušica Kunaver, 2007.

Kunaver, Aleš, and Friends. *Makalu.* Translated by Mimi Marinsek. Ljubljana, Slovenia: Dušica Kunaver, 2006.

———. *Trisul – Varuh Boginje.* Translated by Mimi Marinsek. Ljubljana, Slovenia. Dušica Kunaver, 2006.

———. *Lhotse: Južna Stena.* Translated by Mimi Marinsek. Ljubljana, Slovenia: Dušica Kunaver, 2008.

Kunaver, Dušica. *Aleš Kunaver.* Translated by Mimi Marinsek. Maribor, Slovenia: Založba Obzorja Maribor, 1988.

Kunaver, Dušica, and Brigita Lipovšek. *The Lime – Slovenian Sacred Tree. Slovenia in Folk Tales* series. Ljubljana, Slovenia: Dušica Kunaver, 2012.

———. *Zlatorog.* Ljubljana, Slovenia: Dušica Kunaver, 2012.

———. *Slovenija – Dežela Legend. Slovenia in Folk Tales* series. Ljubljana, Slovenia: Dušica Kunaver, 2013.

Maas, Peter. *Love Thy Neighbor.* New York: Alfred A. Knopf, 1996.

Malcolm, Noel. *Bosnia: A Short History.* New York: New York University Press, 1994.

———. *Kosovo: A Short History.* New York: New York University Press, 1998.

328

McDonald, Bernadette. *Tomaž Humar*. London: Hutchinson, 2008.

Messner, Reinhold. *The Big Walls*. Seattle, Wash.: The Mountaineers Books, 2001.

O'Connell, Nicholas. *Beyond Risk*. Seattle, Wash.: The Mountaineers Books, 1993.

Off, Carol. *The Lion, the Fox and the Eagle*. Toronto: Vintage, 2001.

———. *The Ghosts of Medak Pocket*. Toronto: Random House, 2004.

Prezelj, Marko, and Tone Škarja. "Slovene Kangchenjunga Expedition." *American Alpine Journal* 34, no. 66 (1992).

Silber, Laura, and Allan Little. *The Death of Yugoslavia*. London: Penguin, 1995.

Škarja, Tone. *Po Svoji Sledi*. Translated by Mimi Marinsek. Ljubljana, Slovenia: Planinska zveza Slovenije, 2011.

Štremfelj, Andrej. "1979: Everest West Ridge Direct." *Alpinist* 27 (2009).

Tanner, Marcus. *Croatia: A Nation Forged in War*. New Haven and London: Yale University Press, 1997.

Terray, Lionel. *Conquistadors of the Useless*. London: Baton Wicks, 2011.

Thompson, Mark. *A Paper House*. New York: Pantheon, 1992.

Twight, Mark. *Kiss or Kill*. Seattle: The Mountaineers Books, 2001.

Ugrešić, Dubravka. *The Ministry of Pain*. New York: HarperCollins, 2006.

West, Rebecca. *Black Lamb and Grey Falcon*. New York: Viking, 1941.

Wilkinson, Freddie. "A Short Climb with Ueli Steck." In *Rock, Paper, Fire: The Best of Mountain and Wilderness Writing*, edited by Marni Jackson and Tony Whittome. Banff, Alta: Banff Centre Press, 2013.

Zaplotnik, Nejc. *Pot*. Translated by Mimi Marinsek. Ljubljana, Slovenia: Libricon, 2009.

JOURNALS AND MAGAZINES

Alpinist, volumes: 1, 5, 8, 14, 16, 19, 20, 21, 23, 27.

American Alpine Journal, years: 1972–76, 1981–87, 1989–99.

FILMS

Čopov Steber – Prvič Pozimi 1968. Aleš Kunaver.

Dežela Šerp 1962. Aleš Kunaver.

Lhotse 1981 – Južna Stena. Aleš Kunaver.

Makalu – Prvič Prvi V Himalaji. Aleš Kunaver.

Mount Everest. Viki Grošelj.

WEBSITES

http://himalaja.pzs.si/

http://www.himalayandatabase.com

http://www.8000ers.com/cms/

INDEX